W9-BAU-817

Heywood Broun

A BIOGRAPHICAL PORTRAIT

Price Studios

HEYWOOD BROUN

WITH Mount Mary College LIBRARY 40103

Heywood Broun

A BIOGRAPHICAL PORTRAIT

by DALE KRAMER

NEW YORK · 1949

CURRENT BOOKS, INC.

A. A. WYN, PUBLISHER

COPYRIGHT 1949 BY DALE KRAMER

ALL RIGHTS RESERVED

PRINTED IN THE UNITED STATES OF AMERICA
AMERICAN BOOK–STRATFORD PRESS, INC., NEW YORK

921
B79K

To Nancy

Foreword

A FOREWORD is often an apology for what you are about to read, a defense of the views expressed in the book and an explanation of just why the book was written.

Heywood never made or needed one; his writings explained themselves. Even when whimsical or mystic, they were tied tight to life. He kept a strong hold on truth as it was given him to see truth. He projected a spirit of understanding and fellowship. Reading Broun you wanted to know him; knowing Broun you wanted to read him.

Heywood was a great figure in contemporary journalism. I feel a warm glow of satisfaction when I recall that he came over to the *World* (the old *World*) to ask me for a job, saying the *World* was the kind of paper he wanted to work on. I put him on the staff and he held his job with the *World* longer than he did a job with any other paper, either before or afterward.

To feel great friendship for a man does not mean you must agree with all his opinions. Heywood had the gift of making anyone he liked feel he was his best friend. I fell in that category, although there were many things about which Heywood and I quarreled pleasantly. He was a skilled debater and never lost his temper.

Heywood died too soon, but even in the comparatively short time he was at work he brought a deep affection to those who knew him and left the world a little better than he found it.

I know of no better epitaph.

HERBERT BAYARD SWOPE

October 1949

Acknowledgments

TO MAKE special acknowledgment to all those who lent assistance to the preparation of this book would merely be to duplicate a large portion of the index. I do want to thank particularly the members of the Broun family. Mrs. Heywood Cox Broun, though climbing through the last decade toward 100—and retaining her spirit and graciousness—was of great help, especially for the early years. So were her son Irving and her daughter Virginia.

Heywood Hale Broun—"Woodie"—furnished concise eye-and-ear-witness accounts while recalling in remarkable detail things his father and mother had told him. Connie Broun was unstinting in the time and effort devoted to this biography. Her memories were of course of enormous value for the latter years and she was able to add elsewhere from recollections of things that Heywood had said.

I would like to credit the following publishers for quotations from Heywood Broun's works:

Doubleday & Company, Inc., for selections from *Pieces of Hate and Other Enthusiasms,* copyright, 1922, by George H. Doran Company; Harcourt, Brace & Company, for selections from *Seeing Things at Night,* copyright, 1921, and *It Seems to Me,* copyright, 1935; Heywood Broun Estate, for selections from *The Boy Grew Older,* copyright, 1922, by Heywood Broun, published by G. P. Putnam's Sons, and from *Sitting on the World,* copyright, 1924, by Heywood Broun, published by G. P. Putnam's Sons; Liveright Publishing Company, for selections from *Gandle Follows His Nose,* copyright, 1926, by Boni and Liveright; Charles Scribner's Sons, for selections from *Our Army at the Front,* copyright, 1918; Scripps-Howard Newspapers, for selections from the *New York Telegram* and the *New York World-Telegram;* Press Publishing Company, for selections from the *New York World; New York Herald Tribune,* for selections from the *New York Tribune.*

Contents

List of Illustrations

*The sketch of Broun on the title page was drawn
by Hendrick van Loon and appears by the
courtesy of Frank Shay.*

Heywood Broun

A BIOGRAPHICAL PORTRAIT

1

Portrait of a Celebrity at Forty

Heywood BROUN moved cautiously in the throng flowing out of the Alvin Theater. It was a cloudy night in the spring of 1928—a fateful night for Broun, although at the moment he was unaware of any portent. Those who had not seen him before whispered, "It's Heywood Broun," giving him a little room. They noticed that he really was much like a great bear and that his gait had properly been described as a shamble. Broun was glad of the slight extra space allotted him, for he suffered from a fear of crowds. He halted to light a cigarette, his mind plainly on something else. Observers could guess whether on the play—Adele and Fred Astaire in "Funny Face"—or whether he was making mental jottings for his famed column, "It Seems To Me," in the *New York Morning World*.

At the curb he glanced up the street and when a parked taxicab jerked forward his gaze went to his feet. This was nearly inevitable, for his shoulders, appearing narrow and almost frail on his great trunk, were rounded, pulling down his height from its natural six feet three and three quarters inches. He took no particular notice of his feet, but the people about him did.

They were famous feet. When Heywood Broun descended

to a below-street-level speakeasy, the guarded door was open
before he had negotiated more than a couple of steps. At the
upstairs variety, the delicate ear of the sentry easily recognized the slow approach of the massive flat feet and unhesitatingly swung wide the portals. The shoes were thirteens, and,
though of excellent make and not old, were shapeless and
broken at the backs from his custom of getting into them
from a standing position. Their lack of strings was not entirely, as many believed, due to carelessness. Sometimes the
feet required cooling and the swelling in his ankles and just
below made difficult the bringing together of the tops. His
socks were not of an equal shade of blue and sometimes the
color spread was even greater. But the story of Broun's appearance in Park Avenue's exclusive Racquet and Tennis
Club, of which he was a member, wearing one white and one
black shoe was denied by him—though not too vigorously.
He was not entirely dissatisfied with his reputation for dis-
array. His suits were always of expensive material and, at the
instigation of his father, Heywood Cox Broun, one of New
York's most fastidious dressers, he occasionally stood for fit-
tings. But a few hours of wear, owing to his bulk and his
habit of cramming his pockets fuller than Tom Sawyer ever
did, left any suit with an appearance of having been slept in.
The legend of carelessness was fostered by his own references
to his supply of suits as "the gray" and "the brown."

A small man carrying a copy of the *World* folded open to
the page opposite the editorial hurried up.

"Did you see what they did?"

But Broun did not hear, the cab having pulled up, and
the little man gave him a clap on the shoulder and disappeared into the crowd.

The cab driver made no effort to hide his contempt for
frantic signalers. He had been retained earlier. Broun

thought nothing of keeping a hack waiting for hours, or of having himself driven to his farm north of Stamford, Connecticut. He hunched into the cab and the driver watched while he turned on the seat. Drivers who knew him always consciously or unconsciously did that, waiting for the smile. Broun's smile broke slowly from a triangle whose base was his sensitive, straight mouth and whose sides were deep creases which came into his slender, almost exquisite nose just above the flair of the nostrils. His face was even more youthful than his years. He was not quite forty. Sometimes his profile under the mane of dark brown hair was compared favorably with Jack Barrymore's.

Broun's soft dark eyes were partly concealed by his broad, quizzically sloping brow. To acquaintances his eyes and the rippling vivacity of his face were prime sources of his celebrated personal charm. Anyone looking into Broun's eyes had the impression of gazing into a flattering and sympathetic mirror. His personality—strong and warm, though shy—raised a companion in his own estimation.

The cab driver was Charlie Horowitz, who drove Broun often. "Did you get there?" he asked, pulling into the traffic stream.

Broun settled back. "Just in time to see the Babe hit it." His soft voice rolled with slow, lazy clarity. "Herb Pennock had his stuff. I'm a great admirer of Herb on days like this."

"The Babe will hit 70 this year," the driver said confidently. "He looks right. So—where to? Jack and Charlie's? Tony's? We'll pick up the papers first, eh?"

Broun scratched a match. "Yes, let's get the papers." He held the cigarette in his fingers backwards, the palm of his hand out. "Maybe you better run me down to the Village to Barney Gallant's." He tossed the cigarette away after a few puffs. Though a constant smoker, he rarely burned a cigarette

3

more than a third of the way down. At the moment he was smoking a nicotineless brand because of his heart, which he insisted, against the judgment of physicians, was bad. Broun always considered the chances fairly good that he would drop dead the next moment.

When the cab pulled up to a corner newsstand, the attendant, after glancing in, whipped a morning paper off each pile, reached into his stand for a roll of afternoon papers, and handed them all through the window. He looked at Broun queerly.

"You'll win out, Mr. Broun, don't worry about that," he said.

"Thank you," Broun said absently, smiling. He heaped the papers in his lap.

The driver glanced back. "Haven't caught your column yet," he said. "Saving it for late coffee."

"You can get along without it."

The cab shooshed down empty Seventh Avenue through the garment district. Broun took his flask from his left hip pocket, its customary resting place. Heywood Broun's flask was, in a way, the symbol of the gin era and the flaunting of Prohibition. He liked his drink and it was his nature to take it in the open. Now he unscrewed the cap and took a bracer of the gin-and-bitters. Every half dozen years or so Broun got drunk, but otherwise few effects of liquor were ever visible.

He glanced at the front pages of the papers in his lap. Senator Tom Walsh of Montana had withdrawn as a candidate for the Democratic Presidential nomination. That about cinched Al Smith, though Jim Reed of Missouri was still trying. The chances of puncturing the Herbert Hoover boom for the GOP nomination looked slim. Weather: Increased cloudiness, followed by local thunderstorms.

4

The cab swung around Washington Square into West Third Street and pulled up in front of Barney Gallant's.

"Just take it easy, Charlie," Broun said, crawling out. "I think it will only be a little while and then you can take me home."

"Out to Connecticut?"

"No, up to the 85th Street house."

Little, snapping-eyed Barney Gallant escorted Broun to his usual table to the left of the entrance. The night club drew from the big-spending crowd, and its chief entertainer at the moment was fast-climbing Walter O'Keefe. Barney himself was a member of the Greenwich Village literati and made writers and artists especially welcome. Broun liked to discuss social philosophy and sometimes even personal matters with him. The eyes of half the customers were on Broun. Cosmopolites nudged uninitiated guests. Manufacturers' representatives bent confidentially to the ears of butter-and-egg men. For Heywood Broun's appearance guaranteed the night spot to be one of Manhattan's brightest.

"Well," Broun said to the waiter, "I was thinking of starting off with a Pink Lady, but maybe I'll switch to a Bacardi."

He began rumpling through the papers again, hunting for column ideas. Barney Gallant made Broun's table his headquarters, popping up and down as his duties as host required, and now and then an acquaintance inserted himself long enough to say hello. But at the moment there was no one in the place intimate enough to pull up a chair.

Broun spread out the *Morning World*, looking for an idea for his column. Despite some stringent differences with his bosses, the *World* was his favorite newspaper. He read more of the front-page headlines. The subway owners disclaimed any intention of quickly boosting the fare from a nickel to

5

seven cents. In the daily love triangle a man had been strangled with his own necktie, though whether a love nest had been involved was not clear. Bernarr McFadden's *Graphic* (newspapermen called it the *Pornographic*) would settle the point. Fascist girls in Italy had displayed athletic skills as Mussolini renewed attacks on the Vatican.

Broun leafed on. The Methodists were insisting on a dry candidate. Maybe a topic there. The item prompted him to point to his glass.

"We'll make it the Pink Lady," he told the waiter.

The Reverend John Roach Straton expected, said another story, to celebrate his tenth anniversary as pastor of the Calvary Baptist church with a sermon "Confessions of a Sensationalist." Dr. Straton announced plans for a thirty-five-story church and apartment building at 123 West 57th Street. Hellfire and brimstone preaching was paying off. Maybe a column idea there. Dr. Straton was an ancient antagonist, though the battle was on a broader scale than the usual Moderns versus Bluenoses of H. L. Mencken and other iconoclasts. Broun was a serious commentator on religion and was deeply religious by nature.

The table was small, and he folded the pages back to back as he read. The sports section had a good photo of Babe Ruth swinging, with an insert of the Philadelphia Athletics' Joe Hauser, second away from the starting line in the home-run derby (five to Ruth's six). Hype Igoe in his column "Pardon My Glove" was defending Jack Delaney against charges of having taken a dive for Jack Sharkey. Broun turned over to the editorial page. Rollin Kirby's cartoon showed a big-bellied Politics holding a squalling baby marked *7c Fare*. Up in the golden dome of the ornate red-stone *World* building on Park Row, Walter Lippmann's squad of editorial writers had run up a plan calling for two mayors—dapper, wise-cracking Jimmy

Walker to entertain, someone else to do the work. The farm bloc was advised that it courted President Calvin Coolidge's veto with the McNary-Haugen farm-relief bill. Boston had recently banned Vina Delmar's *Bad Girl*, which the editorial writers recalled in connection with New York's Padlock Law, aimed at naughtiness and nudity in the theater.

Broun swept the papers into a crumpled bundle, finished his drink, and hauled himself to his feet. He thrust out a hand to this one and that one on his way to the door.

"It's to bed for me, all right, Charlie," he said, sliding into the cab. He lit a cigarette, puffed a few times, flipped it out the window, and leaned back with the bundle of papers clutched to his stomach. The cab lashed through the quiet streets uptown, crossed west on 57th Street to Riverside Drive, and then swept along the Hudson River to 85th Street. It swung briefly to the right and halted at 333 West, the center high-stooped brownstone in a row of five, between Riverside Drive and West End Avenue. Broun climbed out, handing two limp twenty-dollar bills to the driver. He liked to get fresh new money from the bank—after inquiring courteously, since his check book was never balanced, if he had any on deposit—but he carried the bills loose in his pocket and after a while his body heat took the starch out of them.

"Does this do it, Charlie?" he asked.

"It's a lot more than enough."

"All right. Good night."

Broun had the huge icebox open and was reaching for a plate of Southern-style fried chicken when Ruth Hale called down to the kitchen: "Hello. Have you read the *World*?"

"Sure. Yankees win, Giants win, Dodgers lose." Broun set out the chicken. Mattie Wilson, the fabulous major-domo of the Broun household, always saw to it that plenty of fried chicken was ready to hand. He rummaged the shelves reading

7

can labels. He fancied himself an inventive chef and would mix anchovies and sweet corn, put ketchup in turtle soup, and had been known to poach eggs in port wine.

"I mean page opposite editorial. Your column."

Broun bit into a drumstick, still searching. "I'm saving that up for later."

"You needn't. You're fired."

Quitting the inspection of can labels, Broun picked up the plate of chicken and the bundle of papers and mounted the stairs. The main floor contained a great living room (where the celebrated Broun New Year's parties were held) and, beyond gigantic double doors, Broun's bedroom. Ruth Hale had the second floor, and the domain of ten-year-old Heywood 3d (Woodie) was on the third, when he was home from school.

"What do you mean, fired? How do you know?"

Ruth Hale followed him into the bedroom. "It's in the *World*. The phone's been ringing. Look at your column."

Broun sprawled sideways on the bed. It was a huge bed, designed by himself, with book shelves curving around the head. He could reach the books without getting up, which was helpful, for his bed was often his office. When a deadline pressed him close he went to the flat, littered desk in the corner and hammered the upright Underwood. Tumbled stacks of books and a couple of straight chairs completed the furnishings.

Ruth Hale stood watching him turn the pages. She was a small and well-constructed woman, a couple of years older than Broun. The dampness in the air had curled her light-brown hair close to her head. Her eyes attracted people, as did Broun's, but hers were gray and large and mobile. Her high-bridged nose was slightly too large and her cheekbones were high. Her speaking voice was low and musical. But her mind was polished hard and brilliant. In clashes of words with anybody, Broun was likely to yield, or seem to. Ruth Hale was apt to attack head-on and without humor, except for mordant satire. She could usually dominate the conversation of a roomful of New York's sophisticates by charm or by force. It was charged that she preferred the latter.

She was the wife of Heywood Broun by law and the holy bond of an Episcopal service. But she was not, definitely not, Mrs. Heywood Broun. The slogan of the Lucy Stone League, in the founding of which she had been prime mover, was "My name is the symbol for my identity and must not be lost." And in that she was nearly fanatical. Once she had canceled a trip to Europe because the State Department refused to issue a passport to her simply as Ruth Hale. Broun stayed home, too.

Broun turned to the *World's* famed page-opposite-editorial, or, in shop talk, Op. Ed. The usual make-up had Franklin P. Adams' column of quips and verse, "The Conning Tower," at the left-hand side of the page, set a column and a half wide. Harry Hansen's single-column "First Reader" was next to it. Broun's "It Seems To Me" customarily ran down the center, a column and a half wide. Alexander Woollcott's "The Stage," Samuel Chotzinoff's "Music," and Frank Sullivan's "Out of a Clear Sky" were fitted in, when they wrote, according to the handiest make-up.

At the top of Broun's usual space stood this notice:

The *World* has decided to dispense with the services of Heywood Broun. His disloyalty to this paper makes any further association impossible.

Broun tossed the paper aside and looked up. His slow smile stretched the triangle. "Now," he said, "that's sloppy journalism. How are people going to know whether 'dis-

9

loyalty' means that I robbed the till or sat on the publisher's hat?"

He nipped from his flask—he liked a courage shot more for the act of taking it than for the alcohol's stimulation—and then he fished into his pocket for his dollar Ingersoll watch. He tossed it on a pillow and began idly to take his pulse.

Ruth Hale sat down on the bed. Nothing infuriated her more than Broun's hypochondria, particularly his private pulse taking. She sometimes charged him, too, with laziness and lack of purpose, but when trouble was on him there was no stauncher or tenderer champion.

Broun would convince the public that the sacking lay easily on his shoulders. But he was deeply hurt—and disturbed. He was excessively humble toward his work. He often talked—humorously, but with a serious overtone—of an eternal dread of someday sitting down at his typewriter and finding that no words came. It was not a fear of slowly drying up. It was the terror that he would not be able so much as to strike the typewriter keys.

And the fear was not entirely lacking in basis. Few ever wrote so much as if opening a tap to fill a bucket from a gushing stream. He wrote as fast as he could make a typewriter go, and, though a two-finger man, he could get the machine to roar like a Model T with the cutout open. There were a few corrections with the copy pencil he always carried, but seldom any revision. Thirty minutes sufficed for his column and he could make it in less. He wrote down his feelings and his thoughts, and he was forever amazed and gratified that people were interested.

In his twenties Broun had emerged as a brilliant sports writer. From that he had stepped easily into dramatic criticism and on to being a war correspondent in France. After that had come book reviewing and the personal essays that had made him a part of the lives of tens of thousands. As far back as 1921, Alexander Woollcott had written of the "inexhaustible and immeasurable Heywood Broun," concluding, after trying him for size against G. K. Chesterton and James Barrie and A. A. Milne, that there was really no one in the world like him. "All the books and plays and people that pass through his fey mind come out recognizably colored and encrusted."

And yet someday the tap might be dry, or the flow brackish and unpalatable.

Broun and Ruth Hale talked for a long time. She undertook to write to Heywood 3d at school, advising him that money was likely to be short for a while. A Special Delivery letter came just then from the *World,* saying that payments on Broun's $25,000-a-year contract would be halted, since the publisher held that Broun had violated it.

In Heywood Broun's heart lurked that night a dread fear that his career was at an end. But there was also elation that in a major moral battle he had not flinched.

Broun slept until his usual time—noon. Then his tree-trunk legs, encased in silk pajamas—he liked the silk to be heavy and flowery—turned slowly as if powered by a winch, the feet came down, and he hoisted himself up. Ruth Hale would still be asleep. She had attacks of bronchitis that often kept her awake until very late and her day did not start until even later than his own.

Captain Flagg, a boisterous Airedale, was in the outer room, and when he heard Broun he began to assert himself. Captain Flagg's personality had made him the namesake of the celebrated character in Maxwell Anderson's and Laurence Stallings' play "What Price Glory?" The Airedale had not, however, always belonged to the officer caste. Broun

11

had picked him up as a stray. Pets of the Broun household almost always were characters. Sharing honors with Captain Flagg at the moment were a majestic land turtle and two horned toads.

Broun, thrusting his feet into slippers, suggested rather hopelessly, "Down, Flagg!" Mattie Wilson was in the kitchen when he reached the bottom of the stairs and he asked her to fix a gin-and-bitters for him. He didn't like coffee very much. Mattie had seen the *World*—she never failed to read Broun—but she waited for him to comment. A petite brown-skinned girl, she was one of the family. Almost immediately after coming North, at fourteen, from a North Carolina cotton patch, she had entered into the household as a maid's helper. Now, at twenty-three, she was practically in charge. She decided what callers might interrupt Broun, she was Ruth Hale's friend, and when young Woodie was home from school she was his companion. If there were to be twenty for dinner, or a party for fifty, a casual couple of words by mouth or note to Mattie completed the arrangements as far as Broun or Ruth Hale was concerned. She was requested only to pay help and tradesmen well—and under no circumstances to render up itemized accounts to the master or mistress of the house.

Broun took up the glass of gin she had poured out and drank half of it.

"I got fired, Mattie," he said. There was deep disappointment in his voice.

"They'll be good and sorry." She handed him a sheaf of telegrams. "The phone's been ringing like mad. You going to talk?"

"No. Ruth will when she gets up. Is it too rainy for me to paint in the back yard?"

She gave him one of the nicotineless cigarettes that she

kept handy. "It's quit raining. I'll get out your paint stuff after you eat." She began to stir up his breakfast.

Broun spent most of the afternoon painting. He had put on his painting clothes—sweat-shirt and smeared flannel trousers—but his brushes were stiff, as usual, from improper care. He supplied the lack from time to time by substituting the tip of a finger or a bit of rag. He revised his painting even less than his writing, and, if it did not come out as well, at least he was among New York's more famous primitives. The Marx Brothers had included an "early Broun" in one of their shows and Broun himself gave accounts of his sales, which went as high as seventy-five cents apiece. Some people really liked Broun's work—or liked Broun so much they couldn't separate their feelings—and his paintings hung on many walls. Arthur Brisbane had an early Broun in the foyer of his home, with a light thrown on it.

Ruth Hale came down to the small, board-walled back yard about three o'clock and joined Broun. He had opened some of the telegrams. News of his dismissal had been carried over the country by the news services. Some of the telegrams were "Go get 'em, Heywood" encouragements from friends and admirers. Several offered havens, ranging from a cabin in Maine to jobs on out-of-New York papers.

Broun asked, "Did Roy Howard call?"

Ruth Hale said that he had not called. Mattie was watching especially for that one.

Broun said gloomily, "Now that I'm fired he won't be interested."

It was Saturday, which meant a chance for solace at the week's session of "The Game"—better known in song and story as "The Thanatopsis Literary and Inside Straight Poker Club." It had been loosely founded in wartime France by Franklin P. Adams, Harold Ross, Steve Early, Alexander

Woollcott, John T. Winterich, Broun, and others who played from time to time at Nini's Restaurant in Paris. In New York they usually gathered at the Algonquin Hotel, scene also of the Algonquin Round Table, oasis of the town's wits in the era of more or less wonderful nonsense.

"Why don't you come down to the game?" Broun asked.

Ruth Hale seldom played, but she agreed to go along and kibitz.

Roy Howard did call, a little later, and Broun went to the phone. The *Telegram,* New York member of the liberal Scripps-Howard chain, was hot in pursuit of the *World.* Howard was himself whipping up the horses. He had approached Broun on previous occasions and now he repeated his offer. Other New York editors called to sound out the dispossessed columnist.

Broun was to emerge from the *World* controversy (which will be dealt with in detail in subsequent chapters) a greater figure than before. The rollicking, Falstaffian Broun remained. He was to become also a mover and a shaker and a powerful moral force in the nation.

2

Lilacs with the Golden Curls

HEYWOOD COX BROUN was thirty-eight years old, tall and dashing, with a grenadier's cascading brown mustache, when his third son was born on December 7, 1888. The Brouns lived on short, fashionable Pineapple Street in Brooklyn Heights, not far from the bay front. A listing in the Social Register was still nineteen years away, but the elder Broun's partnership in a printing and stationery business afforded a nurse for the children and servants for the large apartment, furnished in the Victorian style.

Heywood Cox Broun had come to America with his parents while in his teens: The name is Scottish—one of Sir Walter Scott's novels contains a Broun—but few ever arrived on New World shores clutching a little bit of England more tightly. The condition of the family exchequer left trade the only choice, but in other matters the old-fashioned English gentleman was to be emulated. William Makepeace Thackeray in *The Newcomes* drew a portrait of a British officer guided through life by the sentiments of duty, honor, and the correct thing. Heywood Broun was to see in Colonel Newcome his father to the life.

The young immigrant had no chance of proving his mettle on the field of battle. But he was a member of the Seventh

National Guard Regiment—which happened to be very socialite—and his bearing was military perfection. He was one of the four or five best rifle-and-pistol shots in the country.

Though too sensitive and gentle to be a ruthless baron of finance, he liked the company of the great and well placed. His company was sought after and he knew thoroughly the intimate details of New York society. He never hesitated to show his enjoyment of living. He was a connoisseur of wines, loved sports, and at whist and bridge was expert enough to compete in championship tourneys.

Thackeray was not quite able to complete the portrait in a single volume. Heywood Broun later found in his father a sizable dash of Major Pendennis. The Major, a man of great tact, spent much thought and effort on the careers of his relatives. The Broun children—a son died in childhood after which were born Irving, Heywood, and Virginia—unhesitatingly carried all problems to their father, finding in him a gentle, wise understanding.

He began at once to smooth the way for his new son by putting his name down for membership in the Racquet and Tennis Club.

Mrs. Heywood Cox Broun was tall, too, with a long, strong-featured face and flashing brown eyes. She was born Henriette Brose, daughter of a German who had become a successful broker in the United States. Henriette was a native of Brooklyn, too, but as a girl she had spent many years abroad. She spoke German and French as handily as English.

The children were conscious of their mother's powerful will. She was gracious, but also imperious, with strong views strongly expressed in regard to people, events, and matters cultural and otherwise.

It was Mrs. Broun's theory that the physical needs of the children could be cared for by servants, her own task being to provide training and instruction of a cultural nature, for their later life. The children spent much of the time with their nurse, Delia Feddis, a genial, muscular Irishwoman. There was a deep strain of romance in Delia, although even the adults were not aware of its full extent until some years later when she ran off with the French butler.

When Heywood was two the family moved to a tall, narrow brownstone house at 140 West 87th Street in Manhattan. Including the ground floor, where the kitchen was located, and the half floor at the top, the house contained five stories. The children usually ate in their own dining room in the basement, fed by Kate, the cook, and supervised by Delia. The upstairs dining room seemed a distant and glamorous region where great folks from the outside world came to sup. The children were allowed a private comfortable world in a part of the fourth floor and a playroom on the top floor. The house became in time a sort of neighborhood play headquarters. "The light pole outside Brouns'" was a common place of rendezvous. In the play section were parallel bars and other paraphernalia of sports.

No child felt unwelcome. It was not uncommon for Mrs. Broun to come home in the afternoon and find a boy, let into the house by one of the servants, playing by himself, or solemnly awaiting Heywood or Irving.

No one ever rushed to great ledgers or even baby books to record stirrings of genius in Heywood. He was large for his age and awkward. His face was soft and delicate, with liquid, trusting brown eyes, and his light, almost blond hair lent itself so readily to curls that his mother could not resist the temptation to allow them to grow long. Velvet suits and lace frills were the style. It happened that Heywood could not abide the touch of his hands against velvet, and on dress-up occasions he went about with his hands held away from his sides.

He was a sensitive, introspective child. For punishment his mother would sit him on a chair and come back to find him staring contentedly at the ceiling, daydreaming. But he could assert himself. Once his mother stood him in a corner for a fifteen-minute hitch. After serving a third of the sentence he advanced to the center of the room.

"I'm not standing in the corner," he announced.

His mother took note of the fact. The outside hallway and the corridor from the front to the rear of the home made an excellent running track of roughly twenty-eight laps to the mile. Heywood kept the pace for several laps. Then in a burst of speed his mother captured him, hauled him to the vicinity of a hairbrush, and applied it. That was the last corporal punishment. But the memory lingered. His mother continued to look on him, he thought, as a boy who could use a spanking.

In play Heywood was trusting, impetuous, and not very skillful. Bright-eyed Irving, two years older, was, on the other hand, worldly wise, aggressive, and sure of touch. When playing with toy soldiers Irving deployed his forces carefully. Heywood's strategy consisted of taking handfuls of soldiers and tossing them willy-nilly into the fray. He loved the toy soldiers and did not associate them with death. He hated and feared mutilation. Once at a lawn party he sat for a long time staring moodily at his ice-cream rabbit. At last he took up his spoon and dashed off the rabbit's head.

"There," he said. "It's dead, at least."

For a while toy soldiers were a passion, draining off every cent of his allowance. When, at seven, his mother took him abroad, the toy stores of Europe saw much of him. He

Mount Mary College
LIBRARY 40103

formed a low opinion of foreign languages. He had been slow, as a matter of fact, in picking up a suitable pronunciation of English. The clerks were often irritated by a pudgy connoisseur who, after viewing the usual stock of soldiers, demanded stubbornly, "Udder ones, udder ones!"

Otherwise he was not a troublesome traveling companion. He was capable of fishing with a bent pin for a whole day in a Venice canal, though aware that no fish lived there. He liked to sit in cathedrals and to walk through museums. His over-size did present a clothing problem. He arrived at the New York dock arrayed in a Dutch coat with big brass buttons, British short trousers, a Tyrolian cap, and other cosmopolitan odds and ends. His father took one shocked look and bundled him into a taxicab.

The long curls bothered Heywood—and caused Irving a good deal of exertion. Since he wore curls until he was ten, Irving had to be called on to deal with the older boys.

"I wish you would beat up Bill Fletcher," Heywood might say to Irving. Bill was a good friend of Irving's and a sparring partner in street fisticuffs.

Irving would go into the matter. "What did Bill do?"

"He called me Christopher Columbus." That was a nickname gathered from schoolbook photos of the great explorer wearing long hair and a velvet suit.

"That's not so bad. What else?"

"Well, he called me Lilacs and Silver Heels." The first was obscure, though connected with the curls. The second was a twist on Heywood's lack of speed afoot. Once "it," he was likely to remain so for a gruesomely long time. "Besides, he called me a sissy. I think he ought to be beat up."

Irving would set out for the corner, tax his pal Bill Fletcher or another rogue of the moment with assault upon the Broun family pride, and fight him.

Heywood appreciated Irving's loyalty, but like all little brothers he was required to play a lowly member of the ranks under the big brother's generalship. In the evening Irving might lead a scouting expedition through the butler's pantry to the cover of a screen that hid a dumb waiter in the dining room. There they would lie listening to the dinner repartee of the Gay Nineties. Sometimes, back in their own dining room, Irving would put his follower's faith to the acid test.

"Throw your plate against the wall," Irving would order.

Heywood knew that such a shenanigan would certainly bring a reprimand from Delia and perhaps worse from his mother.

Irving would persist. "I dare you!"

The plate would go against the wall.

Heywood did not altogether enjoy the boxing lessons provided by their father in the gymnasium of the Racquet Club. No doubt they were good for Irving's timing, but Heywood could not help thinking that he was filling in for a punching bag.

Heywood was also blamed for failure of the appearance of the fabulous Bouncing Brouns on the vaudeville stages of the land. Heywood Cox Broun had taken the children to see the Zouaves, a band of colorful performers accomplished in acrobatics. Irving began the training of his performers. Virginia was agile enough. Heywood was ponderous. The Zouaves had flown about the stage and in one scene had made a remarkably quick disappearance over a high wall. Irving arranged a board from which to bound onto a mattress and bed springs set between chairs. The wall consisted of a tall wooden folding bed. Heywood was distressingly slow over the wall. Irving would haul from the top while Virginia pushed from below. But Heywood hurt the act.

HEYWOOD COX BROUN

MRS. HEYWOOD COX BROUN

HEYWOOD BROUN AS A CHILD

The effort to salvage the show by bringing in Heywood Cox Broun was even more disastrous. He followed instructions to the letter and his bounce was graceful, but the springs and mattress crashed to the floor, breaking the chairs on which they had rested.

Heywood's awkwardness was no more responsible for his lack of proficiency in games than his double mental life. Physically he lived in the fleeting moment. Over the railing would come Virginia's plaintive cry, "Heywood is using my toothbrush." And the defense, "Well, she can use mine sometime." Mentally he might be living anywhere in the bounds of an imagination fired by *The Three Musketeers* and scores of other adventure stories, which he had begun to devour as soon as he learned to read. He liked to read in the bathtub, which was disastrous for books. Sometimes, finishing a story, he would get out leaving the book floating.

His imagination was also at the root of his bad bicycle riding. His mother would see him wobbling on the brink of disaster.

"Heywood, ride that bicycle right," she would call.

"Sorry," he would apologize, not straightening up. "I'm a yacht. Tacking."

The instructor hired for him gave up in discouragement, reporting that Heywood was *capable* of riding the bicycle, but just wouldn't put his mind to it. Heywood never did learn to dismount properly. It was simpler to fall off. Strangers, seeing him lie quiet, naturally concluded that he had been hurt. He would only be meditating.

In after-life he liked to report his childhood as having been somber. Even Santa Claus was a bully designed to entertain the adults. Recalling himself as a trusting child who had believed in Santa to a ripe age, he wrote at forty:

Heywood Broun

A thousand sleds could be purchased with the money I have given to psychoanalysts to bring back lost self-assertion. At times I take a stand both brave and right and when editors and idiots press me close there comes to some dark kingdom of my mind the sound of sleigh-bells worn by reindeer. The pattern reaches out like an octopus. I am the slave of Santa Claus. He who must be placated is abroad again and waiting at the chimney top.

Heywood was a boy who lived much with dragons and assorted denizens of a world not easily accessible to adults, or even masters at Red Rover and Prisoner's Base. He lived in a valley surrounded by high hills in which lived the dragons. Fortunately, they were not especially ferocious. About the worst crime one of his dragons ever committed was a night foray to nibble lettuce in a garden.

Yet the other world could be frightening. At the piano, which he played without benefit of training or ear, he would strike the keys softly and the world would seem full of beauty. White clouds rolled in the sky and gentle lights filled the heavens. Sometimes he wept. Then quickly the clouds would darken. With all his strength he would strike the keys, the bass pedal held down, as lightning ripped the skies. And then he would cower at the piano. Lightning and thunder were terrifying, for in them he saw the wrath of God.

From the very first, at Sunday-school, he had been enraptured by the stories of Jesus. He sat round-eyed, living them, and later he began to read the Bible as if it were an adventure story. As he grew older his mother reinforced the Sunday-school lessons with stern moral lectures. She had been brought up in a strict Victorian atmosphere. In her house in those days set foot neither divorced people nor any whom scandal had touched. She was a powerful lecturer and Heywood was a literal recipient. He grew up with an omni-present sense of sin. God punished. When lads sophisticated in the gutters told him dirty words and distorted facts of life, Heywood was frightened and ashamed.

But all was not somber. Heywood could handle his share of mischief.

His hypersensitivity was offset by a natural gregariousness. He perfected the defensive mechanism of poking fun at himself, approaching other boys with a shy, humorous look, ready to break into a grin if kidding began. The joking, once the curls were gone, was in good humor and did not hurt. His own banter was gentle. If his class discussed one of Aesop's fables or some other tale populated with omniscient animals, dragons, or pixies, he edited the story after school to include roles for his friends, with the moral altered to fit the current state of affairs in his circle.

He enjoyed the ride on the horse cars up Amsterdam Avenue to Horace Mann, then a private school, at 120th Street and Broadway. Generally he met Theodore Kenyon, a neighbor boy, for the journey. Heywood had a knack of getting acquainted with the drivers and he gave himself early training in the handicapping of horses. The eight-o'clock car, usually pulled by Bessie and Jessie, was sure to reach school on time. Bill and Charlie, who generally hauled the eight-thirty car, were roughly forty-five lengths better than the mares over the two-mile course. With the weather in their favor they could usually make it in time. Heywood preferred the later car. But sometimes there was a switch of steeds at the barn. Bill and Bessie didn't pull together worth a nickel. And so after school there were often lines to be written in a round, fair hand on the blackboard.

In high school—also at Horace Mann—Heywood commenced to blossom. He got the nickname Rube because of his outsize physique (6 feet 2 inches tall, 190 pounds at graduation) but his face was clean-cut and handsome. He made center on the football team and guard at basketball.

One of the favorite teachers was rosy-cheeked, bright-eyed Helen Baker, who had the gift for shaming an unprepared student while making him feel that her interest never flagged. She was a cousin of Heywood's mother. No one ever accused him of receiving special favors, but her relationship to him provided a better understanding. She taught English. As editor of the Horace Mann *Record* he won school renown.

Languages were harder. A harassed German teacher once fired an ink pot at him. He was slow in mathematics, but he liked history. One day Miss Hotchkiss, a Canadian, handed him a leaflet giving a bit of the British side of the old trouble. "After the first shock," he wrote later, "I realized that something brand-new and enormously valuable had been put into my head. For the first time in my life I conceived of any great public question as having two sides."

When the *Record* printed drawings characterizing each student, that of a large, untied shoe extended lazily under a desk was among those most easily identified. But at graduation time something happened that stayed in Heywood's mind to the most exact detail:

> When the totals of the votes were announced I was a little disappointed to find that I had not received a single vote as "the handsomest." The fact that I didn't receive any votes, either, for "the best dressed" made no difference. I wasn't running for that. But then to my great surprise there came the announcement of "the best all around." The figures were read, and they ran Heywood Broun 103 votes, Carl Fernstrom, 102.

3

The Boy Grew Older

IT IS commonly remarked that Harvard's class of 1910 was one of extraordinary brilliance, the evidence given being that in its ranks were such youths of later renown as John Reed, Walter Lippmann, Alan Seeger, Bronson Cutting, Stuart Chase, Robert Edmond Jones, and Heywood Broun. There is no record, however, that faculty members rushed into the Yard to shout huzzahs in appreciation of the riches sent to them. Neither the vastness nor the shape of the great-to-be was easily discernible.

Alan Seeger, a tall, dark youth with liquid eyes, had, it is true, the look of a poet who conceivably might write something like "I Have a Rendezvous with Death," Stuart Chase had been to Massachusetts Tech, which provided a slight ground for predicting his future grim view of the modern social scene, and Robert Edmond Jones, the famed stage designer, was already interested in the theater.

But who would have expected the football song leader and playboy, John Reed, to end a bolshevik hero in a grave under Moscow's Kremlin wall after writing a sympathetic account of the revolution? Or that rich and aristocratic Bronson Cutting after being sent to New Mexico for his health would return a crusading United States Senator?

Walter Lippmann had a smile, even if a bit cool and with-drawn, for all, and he was conceded to possess a brilliant mind crammed with information. But who was astute enough to chart his road from the presidency of the Harvard Socialist Club to eminent spokesmanship for the conservative point of view? And who was able to see the beginnings of one of America's great journalists in a youth who three times tried to make the daily *Crimson* and failed each time?

Not many Harvard men have been more prolific in celebrating the alma mater than Heywood Broun. But his nostalgia was heavily weighted with the iron of determination. He wrote from the ripe wisdom of thirty:

> The most prolific period of pessimism comes when the first attempt is made to translate dreams into reality, an attempt by a person not overskilful in either language. Often it is made at college.

The successes at Horace Mann had come, after all, with very little effort. The graciousness of the Broun home had helped to establish Heywood in his neighborhood and at school, while over the many years his classmates had come to appreciate his wit and goodheartedness. And so, without knowing exactly how or why, he had become Heywood Broun, school personage. The winning of the ballot for "best all round" may not have swelled his head, but it helped to transfer dreams into reasonable expectations.

Not being one to turn a bushel over a limelight, he would have enjoyed the role of college Big Man. But he lacked certain qualifications, especially for Harvard. Horace Mann was a long way from ranking socially with Groton and Middlesex. Compilers of the New York *Social Register* were preparing to nod austerely in the direction of the Heywood Cox Brouns. But what was that compared with the grandeur of Boston's Back Bay, or even Long Island's Oyster Bay? For a two-fisted battle for place, Heywood was also handicapped. For one thing, he was younger than the average, being only seventeen on entrance and a late developer besides. There was, in addition, his shyness, his indolence, and a tendency to be amused by the rah-rah spirit.

The role of hero on the playing field would have pleased him. But he was wanting in the tough and supple muscles of the true athlete. Nor did he have the singleness of purpose required. After getting a place on the freshman basketball squad he quickly failed in deadly application. Since shyness departed before an audience, he preferred to josh himself and the other players. Sometimes the freshmen contested the stalwarts in rural New England towns. He did his best to enhance the reputation of Harvard men for effeteness.

"Percy, old bean," he would pipe to a teammate, "would you mind hurling the jolly sphere my way?"

His athletic career was cut short by a gymnasium mechanical horse which knocked his knee out of joint and left it ailing.

None of his dreams had contained lengthy scenes in which learned men patted a lofty-browed Heywood while pressing on him tokens of scholastic victories. Even without the gregariousness which stemmed from an innate need of fairly constant companionship he could not have retreated to the quieter satisfaction of the grind. He was not a good student in the pedagogical sense. Knowledge came to him haphazardly and largely through intuition, as if acids and alkalines were soaking into a litmus mass for later chemical reaction.

And so at college he had to face reality without benefit of the traditional heavy weapons.

When Heywood came into the apartment he shared at Harvard with his brother Irving and Bill Fletcher, he was carrying a large package and looking pleased with himself. Accompanying him was tall, long-nosed Victor Schoepperle, best friend of his freshman year.

Schoepperle and Broun had met at basketball practice, though later Schoepperle had had to drop out, because in scooping a basketball off the floor he had scooped up a handful of splinters. Schoepperle came from a small Pennsylvania town; he was young for Harvard, too. For that reason the two had first been drawn to each other, and after Schoepperle's accident Heywood, lonely, had hunted him up.

Irving, slender and trim, wearing a sailor straw hat and swinging a bamboo cane, was striding up and down the room singing a current song hit—something about a lemon in the garden of love.

Irving was thinking seriously of a career on the musical-comedy stage and in anticipation he went in for amateur theatricals. Sometimes Heywood was pressed into service, since no walls had to be climbed and he had a cheerful singing voice. Irving, a junior, was catcher on the baseball team and a basketball varsity regular, besides ranking as a bit of a gay dog.

Halting the song, Irving pointed with his cane to an outfit of clothes laid neatly on his bed for donning.

"Lay off," he warned.

Heywood had a habit of borrowing Irving's clothes. To get into one of Irving's silk shirts he had to rip it up the back. Irving did not like to wear torn shirts.

"Don't worry," Heywood said. "I have something very attractive here."

He sat down, dropped the package to the floor, and tore

it open. Out of a box he hauled a dazzling pepper-and-salt suit.

"Stunning, don't you think?" he said, holding it up.

Irving winced. "Very gay." He went back to his singing.

Heywood gathered up the suit. "Just a little while, Vic, and I'll be dressed," he said.

When Heywood came back he was bright and shiny in the new suit, new black shoes, and a red-and-white polka-dot tie. His hair, though long, was brushed almost carefully.

Irving came out of a dance. "Ah!" he said. "A girl."

"Might go into Boston," Heywood said, offhand. "Show girls."

Irving resumed his dance. "Wellesley, more likely."

It was a warm spring night. Heywood and Victor took a street car to a near-by girls' college to pick up their dates. They talked of college life, of the English literature they were studying, and of the new pepper-and-salt suit. Heywood was very humorous about it. Schoepperle had early noticed that there seemed to be two Heywood Brouns. One was the Heywood doing whatever he was doing; the other Heywood watched and commented, generally ironically.

It was one of the happier, more carefree nights. They went canoeing, and there were many hours of laughter and song. Heywood's wit was too subtle, too filled with literary and allegorical allusions, for him to be a college ladies' man. But he was liked. That night he was in fine voice. Over the water in stentorian tones rang the brave and sad drinking song learned from his father.

> The mist on the glass is congealing,
>   'Tis the hurricane's icy breath
> And it shows how the warmth of friendship
>   Grows cold in the clasp of death.

Stand, stand to your glasses steady
   And drink to your comrade's eyes.
Here's a toast to the dead already
   And a cup to the next man that dies.

Cut off from the land that bore us,
   Betrayed by the land we find,
All the brightest have gone before us
   And the dullest are left behind.

Stand, stand to your glasses steady
   And drink to your sweetheart's eyes.
Here's a toast to the dead already
   And a cup to the next man that dies.

The sense of time was lost and the girls arrived late at their dormitories. The boys missed the last car home, but they didn't mind. They walked back through the soft spring night, with more talk and song.

Heywood turned gloomy when he reached the apartment. Irving had come in and was bent over his books.

"How was it?" he asked, looking around.

"Fine," Heywood said. "They were wonderful girls. But after leaving Vic I got to thinking about girls in general. You want to know something?"

"Sure." Irving turned back to his studies.

"Well, you know the lectures Mother used to give us about morals and all that. I guess they were good ones. They stuck. If the most beautiful girl in the world invited me up to her apartment, I just wouldn't be able to go. I wouldn't think it was right. I'd be ashamed."

Irving nodded. "Mother knows how to put a lecture across all right."

During his sophomore year Heywood lived in Weld Hall. His roommate was his horsecar-riding old schoolmate, Theodore Kenyon, who had delayed a year before entering college.

Before the final rooming arrangements had been made, Mrs. Broun had taken Kenyon aside. "Theodore," she had said, "are you sure that you want to room with Heywood?"

"Why of course," Kenyon had answered. "Heywood and I get along fine."

"I don't mean that. Don't you realize that Heywood will wear your clothes? You're big, but he's bigger, and your shirts and even your suits will be ruined."

Kenyon had replied bravely, "I'll keep them out of the way."

Despite Heywood's open menace to other people's clothes, no one was ever much angered by his depredations. Partly it was realization that when in a hurry he was never quite sure what he was putting on, and partly that his own possessions were always cheerfully available to others. But Kenyon was especially careful to be well ahead at packing time. Heywood's system was to throw everything in sight into his trunk and then get in and trample.

Kenyon was quick to notice the change in Heywood since the latter days at Horace Mann when he had found it easy to be tops.

But to those who knew him less intimately, Heywood now seemed almost entirely outward-going, interested mainly in card playing, baseball, and the theaters and cafés of Boston. Study got little of his attention and his gambling with class deadlines grew even more reckless than it had been in his boyhood. In French, he seemed hopeless despite the coaching of his mother during her frequent visits.

He was already a ferocious poker player. His ominous

growls were a major feature of the contests. With him the pleasures of the game were twofold. Neither had to do with the gain or loss of money. The first pleasure was the love of combat. The second pleasure was the excitement of pure chance. A successful bluff brought satisfaction, but the big glow came from drawing successfully when the odds were long.

He wanted no horseplay at cards as on the basketball floor. Once when the game was to be in Osmond Fraenkel's room he arrived to find Fraenkel and Walter Lippmann locked together and rolling on the floor. Fraenkel liked to have his room cold. The tussle had begun when Lippmann, who favored warmth, had tried to reach the grate to build a fire. Other visitors, while desiring heat, were willing that the decision be made in single combat. Broun quickly got up a movement to settle the argument by a flip of a coin.

In the baseball season the Boston teams got more of Heywood's attention than his classes. Tris Speaker had come up to the Red Sox and Heywood liked nothing better than to see the dazzling outfielder go and get a tough one. The Red Sox had the best outfield of all time—Speaker, Duffy Lewis, and Harry Hooper. The Braves got less attention except when playing the New York Giants, especially on those afternoons that Christy Mathewson pitched.

Baseball contributed indirectly, Broun claimed, to his liberalism. His economics professor had a habit of setting forth the liberal arguments during the first semester and demolishing them in the second. Heywood's attendance being the worse in the spring, the liberal notions remained.

He dipped a tentative toe into the deep purple pool of hedonism. His account of the young man facing reality continues.

Maybe he gets drunk for the first time and learns that every English author from Shakespeare to Dickens has vastly overrated it for literary effect. He follows the formula of Falstaff and instead of achieving a roaring joviality he goes to sleep.

A severe handicap was a distaste for alcohol. Liquor bottles, he thought, ought to be labeled: *Take Ten Times Every Hour until Relief Is Obtained.* His reason for occasionally dumping gin over ice cream was to improve the taste of the gin rather than the ice cream. He liked, though, to order fancy drinks from the liquor menus without inquiring the nature of the ingredients. Once during an evening's outing he chose a different drink each time. The result was two days in bed.

Heywood loved the theater as dearly as baseball and sometimes his affection extended to the actresses. The maiden who earned his greatest devotion was Marie Doro, a dainty beauty with a soft oval face, large dark eyes, and a mass of taffy hair. She played in "The Morals of Marcus" during the period of infatuation. As Carlotta, a tattered waif, she captured the sympathy of Sir Marcus (C. Aubrey Smith) and Heywood. As she became better acquainted with soap and comb, they both fell in love with her.

Many times Heywood came in and awakened Theodore Kenyon—quite accidentally, of course—and talked of Marie. Kenyon was not quite able to ascertain whether the relationship was more than that of ticket buyer and actress. In due course Marie Doro became a little bit of Marie Algarez in Broun's novel *The Boy Grew Older.*

Peter Neale [read Heywood Broun] went to the stage door and thought he had made up his mind to stop her and speak to her. He found that he hadn't. She came out slowly and when he stared at her she looked straight at him and almost smiled. He could not be quite sure of it because that was the very moment something inside rapidly wheeled him about and sent him all but running out of the alley.

Evidence of substitution was present. A French girl who worked in a delicatessen bore a strong resemblance to Marie Doro. This young lady Heywood indubitably escorted about. An incident which occurred when he took his mother to call at the corned-beef and pickle emporium seems better to fit Heywood the college Don Juan. Thoughtful of the rights of the proprietor, and nervous besides, he ordered a pound of cheese while carrying off the introduction. A few days later his mother, tracing a curious odor, dug the cheese from a pocket of his overcoat.

Heywood's first social contact with the romantic people of the stage was brought about, more likely, by his mother. For a New Year's Eve celebration Victor Schoepperle and Heywood decided to spread themselves like proper young men of the world. The place settled on was Jack's, the oyster house at 45th Street and Sixth Avenue where a celebrated flying wedge of waiters operated against undesirable patrons. There was no dearth of girls home from school. But the young men wanted to LIVE. Mrs. Broun, through friends, produced a couple of budding chorus girls who did not shy from a few cups of champagne.

Broun became a member of Delta Upsilon, which, if not at the top of the social heap, at least was a few notches from the bottom. And to partly offset failure to make the *Crimson,* he rose above the ruck in the creative-writing courses.

In English 12, "Copey" made him feel that writing was

honorable and alive. Of meager but erect body, with a large head and pinched, bespectacled New England features, Charles Townsend Copeland was a man of caustic wit. He squirmed and groaned at youthful absurdity, but a flash of penetration or good writing quickly shifted his mood to approbation.

Heywood was allowed to join the pilgrimage up the three worn, naked flights to Copey's famous quarters in Hollis Hall, either alone or to take his place with others on the floor. Winter nights were best, when a fire blazed in the fireplace and the bare branches of the elms pressed the square-paned windows. Copey sat in his big chair talking or reading.

Broun spoke his offerings with ears cocked for the groaning. Life for him, in manuscript, always wore a capital letter and stood for sham and delusion. Sometimes Copey was pushed beyond the groaning point. Once Heywood read a story in which he had afflicted his main character with stark raving lunacy. As an example of awkard contrivance, Copey had been reading a scene from Sheridan's "The Critic" wherein the author had stopped a brawl with a beefeater's insane cry, "Drop your weapons in the Queen's name."

Copey said testily, "Broun, try to solve your problems without recourse to death, madness—or any other beefeater in the Queen's name."

Taking some of the advice, Heywood appeared not long afterward with a story in which love emerged victorious over some of the toughest opposition on record. He entitled it "And the Greatest of These." In it Love, represented by a small girl named Gretchen, saves the world from the Devil. The Evil One has entered the body of her sweetheart, Hans, and is forcing him to read the terrible Devil Call—the Lord's Prayer said and spelled backwards—from a magician's leather-bound tome. Gretchen's kiss finally seals Hans' mouth before the last word can be uttered. The author, not quite able to suppress his old instincts, swept the couple out to sea.

The *Harvard Advocate* ran the story in its Spring 1909 issue. Someone made a crashing error. It was signed H. C. Brown. But the style had a natural swinging grace and clarity.

In Copeland's class Heywood vowed to write great novels. In George Pierce Baker's English 47 he decided to display the ironies of life upon the boards as well.

He was always prepared to fish a rumpled manuscript from a pocket at a moment's notice. The custom was to face the criticism of other students, compared with which the groaning of Copey was sweet applause. Fortunately, Baker or someone else usually did the reading without disclosing the author. Heywood threw the hounds off the scent by leading the attack on his own work.

For Baker he found life every bit as cynical as for Copeland. Later he felt a pang of sympathy for the man in the black-ribboned pince-nez:

> Somebody has figured out that there are 2.983 more rapes in the average English 47 play than in the usual non-collegiate specimen of commercial drama. We feel comparatively certain that there is nothing in the personality of Professor Baker to account for this or in the traditions of Harvard, either. We must admit that nowhere in the world is a woman quite so unsafe as in an English 47 play, but the faculty gives no official encouragement to this undergraduate enthusiasm for sex problems.

Broun was inclined to believe that most men suffer from unwritten plays, and he thanked Professor Baker for extracting his—or most of them—at an early age.

The aches of the *Crimson* failure were further reduced by summer jobs on New York dailies. Between his sophomore and junior years Heywood was employed by the *Morning Telegraph* (his father knew the managing editor) to gather odds and ends about the theater and sports. The paper dealt mainly in racing and vaudeville news. Between his junior and senior years he worked part of the time for the *Sun*. Once he operated in the best tradition of Richard Harding Davis.

The great capitalist E. W. Harriman was taking an unconscionably long time to die, once started. His mansion at Tuxedo Park stood atop a high, steep hill. Reporters assigned to the death watch were kept herded down below. One night Heywood, eluding the guards, circled the hill and crept and crawled through the woods to the very back door of the great house. A butler turned him around and sent him down again.

One other disaster remained in a college career in which the peaks had not been high and the valleys had been sometimes deep. When diplomas were handed out to the class of '10, none carried the name of Heywood Broun. French had been convincingly flunked. Afterwards he wrote lightly of the failure, but it was a real disappointment. In the years of fame he was to look for a message, "Heywood, come and get your degree." It never came.

4

Forging Downhill and Up

BROUN had his black felt hat slouched over one eye and was carrying his topcoat when he came into Bide Dudley's stall at the *New York Morning Telegraph*. Dudley was a few years older, but happy-go-lucky and also in love with the theater. He was writing an item about an athletic young actor named Douglas Fairbanks for his column "Smoke Wreaths."

"How about taking a walk?" Broun said.

Dudley glanced up from his typewriter. "Sure," he said.

While Dudley was putting on his coat, Broun went back into his own stall and poked through the drawers of his desk, stuffing a few odds and ends into his pockets.

They walked through the city room to go out. It was a little too early for the poker game, which usually didn't get under way until midnight. Otherwise the atmosphere had its usual intimacy. Two chorus girls sat on a desk waiting for a friend to finish an editorial. Half a dozen race-track gentlemen talked with staff members, or merely lounged around. The *Telegraph*, located at 59th Street and Eighth Avenue, in a former stable for horse-car horses, was still devoted almost exclusively to racing and vaudeville news. Broun waved to Bat Masterson, the famed old gunman who had been sheriff at Dodge City, Kansas, when Boot Hill Cemetery was being filled. Bat was sports editor of the *Telegraph*.

"Let's go over to the Eldorado," Broun suggested when they were on the street. "Elaine will dance pretty soon."

The night was chilly and he put on his coat. It was in the spring of 1912. Since finishing Harvard (except for the French) he had been working on the *Telegraph*. In the free-and-easy atmosphere he had done everything from baseball reporting to editorial writing to interviewing actresses—sometimes for the same issue. He was getting twenty-eight dollars a week, which was pretty good for a cub. But he was ambitious. Had he not had several baseball bylines? He did not quite realize that *Telegraph* newsmen were paid off partly in bylines.

Broun was thinking about money, but he made other conversation. "Will Doug Fairbanks do well in the movies?" he asked. "I think maybe he ought to stick to the stage. I don't like movies."

"He'll do all right," Dudley said.

The Eldorado was a huge dance hall not far from the *Telegraph*. They had barely checked their coats and sat down at a table when a lithe girl in a short dancing skirt and tights came up.

"Hello, Elaine," Broun said. "This is Bide Dudley. Sit down."

"I haven't time. Here." She pressed something into his hand.

"Billet-doux?" Dudley inquired. He was not an Eldorado regular.

Broun looked mysterious. "Wait."

When the dance floor had cleared, the orchestra struck up a fast number and Elaine and her male partner dashed to the center of the hall. Broun half rose to watch. After a while Elaine locked her arms around her partner's neck and he moved faster and faster until she was whirling horizontally. Broun drew back his arm and threw a shiny object. The silver dollar that Elaine had given him landed with a fine full ring and jingled richly as it bounced. In a minute a shower of silver commenced.

Broun sank back, satisfied. "It's picking the psychological moment," he said. "Many would miss it."

During the applause as the act finished, Broun leaned forward. "I didn't get the raise," he said.

"Oh!" Dudley shook his head sympathetically. "Well, next time."

Broun laughed. "I asked for two dollars a week more. The counter offer was twenty-eight dollars less. I was fired."

Being, as he said, a man of character, and living home, Broun faced the future gracefully. Moreover, he was twenty-three and, he felt, a likely heir to the mantle of the adventurous Richard Harding Davis. The only adventure which offered, however, was a trip to China—without salary—for Liebler & Co., theatrical producers, who wanted atmosphere for a play with a Chinese setting. He set off gaily, his camera at the ready. Honolulu captured his heart, though only half as much as did the Princess Nauvhinneyokalai, who came aboard there. To his mother he wrote of the princess as "the deserted bride," for the groom had departed an hour after the ceremony. However, she was on her way to join him at Manila, and Broun's heart was not accepted. He did get the princess to send a postcard to his parents.

Seasickness affected only his career as impresario. He had collected fifty dollars for a concert by a Danish singer, who fell ill. After the debarkation of the princess he was thrown back on the companionship of a Yale man and the diversion of a gambling room which the waiters had thoughtfully established.

He touched at Yokohama, visited Peking, and in Shanghai he learned the language well enough to hold up two fingers when hailing rickshaw pullers, indicating willingness to pay double for extra poundage. And so, crying "Chop chop," he would roar down Bubbling Wall Road to seek adventure at cards or in the songs of the dainty girls.

One night not long afterward, at the press club downtown on Spruce Street, he was invited into a billiards game by Fred Pitney, the star reporter for the *Tribune*. Pitney recalled Broun's magnificent if futile climb of the mountain to the back door of the Harriman mansion. He offered to speak to George Burdick, the *Tribune's* city editor, about a job.

Burdick was the author of a famous line of the newspaper trade. One night a reporter rushed in just before the deadline and sat frozen at his typewriter, the fancy lead he wanted refusing to come. Burdick padded over and self-consciously tapped him on the shoulder. "Please," he said, "just one word after another will do."

When Broun sat at the city editor's desk, telling of his struggle up the journalistic heap to twenty-eight dollars a week, Burdick became increasingly distressed. The applicant was shy, but he continued to the end of his triumphs. After a little Burdick took a pad and scribbled something on it. Then, looking out the window, he held the pad up. It read: "$25."

"Thank you," Broun said, knowing that the descent from the mountain to the valley is swift and the rise difficult. "I'll take it."

On the dignified *Tribune*, founded by Horace Greeley and owned by Whitelaw Reid, Ambassador to Great Britain, the new employee was set to covering minor cultural events along with a few general assignments. The book section not being considered very important, he carried away armloads of review copies. He could be counted on for journeys to the theater on the smallest missions. Later he was on the copy desk and within a year had graduated to rewrite.

Life in the *Tribune's* city room was less free and easy than at the *Telegraph,* naturally. But the poker game was as regular as the deadline, except for one short period after a hot-tempered Southerner pulled a knife. Not on Broun, though. His only involvement in a riot resulted from an exchange with a muscular and chauvinistic Irishman who spent much of his time deploring other nationalities and races. The Irishman began to overhear Broun defending the Irish.

"I've studied the whole question pretty thoroughly," Broun might be saying in mock earnestness to Jake Powers, another rewrite man, "and I hold that an Irishman is just as good as anyone else. Some of my best friends are Irish."

One day the Irishman, his patience gone, launched a fierce fist-swinging assault. Broun rose from his typewriter and cocked his left, which he looked on as the dynamite hand. Others managed to halt the attacker short of his mark.

The *Tribune* was pleased to be staid, if drabness was not actively sought. But a few stories demanded light treatment. These began to go to Broun. Fred Hawthorne and Ogden Reid, son of the owner, were also on rewrite. It was easy for Broun's co-workers to tell when he had something funny. Bent over the typewriter, he grinned and chuckled as his forefingers flayed the keys.

One day when Broun was passing the railed-off sports department, its editor, George Daley, called for him to come in. A tidy, determined man with a loud and firm voice, Daley

42

had been arguing for more space and manpower for his department. The sports section was a single page mostly filled with handouts, or dispatches taken from the wires.

Broun climbed over the railing and settled comfortably on the sports editor's desk. Daley pointed to a chair.

"Heywood," Daley said, "I'm going to build a team for this department, come hell or high water. You've got a light touch and that's good for sports. They've agreed to let me have two new men. I've been thinking of you and Fred Hawthorne."

Not wishing to appear overwrought by the chance to get back to baseball, Broun asked what he would have to do.

"Put on your hat tomorrow and go out and cover the Giants. I think McGraw intends to pitch Christy Mathewson. Get better acquainted with McGraw and Matty and the rest. You must have known them some when you were on the *Telegraph.* Put some color into your stuff."

Broun arrived at the Giants' clubhouse early. He knew most of the sports writers. Bozeman Bulger of the *Sun* was a special friend. The *Sun, Herald, Times,* and *Tribune* allowed no bylines (except that the *Tribune* occasionally permitted George Daley to sign "Herbert," his unused middle name). But on the other big papers a few signatures were appearing. Sports writers got more than their share, owing, some people thought, to a newly acquired gibberish for which editors wished to decline responsibility. Affable, careful Grantland Rice, up from Tennessee, liked to start off his pieces in the *Mail* with self-brewed draughts of poetry. For Hearst's *American* quiet, dandified Damon Runyon searched for the pungent phrase. Other sports bylines were Fred Ness in the *Globe,* John Wheeler in the *World,* and Sam Crane in the *Journal.*

Chunky John McGraw, with a face the color of red-hot iron topped with hair the color of the same metal grown cold and gray, was a belligerent manager on the playing field. But the atmosphere of his clubhouse was genial. He liked the reporters, talked frankly, and they in turn respected confidences without the use of any such term as off-the-record. After the game he sometimes ponied up a bottle. Then he might bait a reporter as skilfully as he did umpires—and with equal lack of animosity. If a lacerated reporter bawled a threat to force a change of Giant managers, McGraw claimed a victory.

Bozeman Bulger and Broun dropped in to McGraw's small office.

McGraw remembered Broun from his stint of two seasons before. "How's the card shark?" he asked.

Broun said he hadn't lost his touch.

"Checkers?"

"All right."

McGraw eyed him. "Boze," he said, "take him out and throw him to Matty. If he survives, he's telling the truth."

Christy Mathewson was the champion checker player of all baseball creation. When the club trained in Texas the towns for miles around sent their heroes to contest him. The slaughter was terrific.

Broun shook hands with players on the way—Fred Merkle, the man who had failed to touch second; Rube Marquard, the fabulous left-hander; Chief Meyers, the catcher; Snodgrass, and lesser lights. Christy Mathewson had finished dressing and was sitting relaxed on a bench before his locker.

"Matty," Bulger said, "I've got your checker player here."

Mathewson rose, pleasant but dignified, and extended his great right arm. The hand that wrought the fade-away gripped Broun's.

"Glad to see you back. I'll lay out the checkers."

They played three games. Broun won the second.

44

Matty clapped him on the shoulder when they had finished. "You're still a sound player," he said, taking his glove from the locker.

Broun became Mathewson's whist partner. They were invincible.

The ball games themselves were exciting enough. At the old Polo Grounds the press coop was down at the front of the grandstand amidst the crowd's roar. Other reporters affected an air of aloofness, almost boredom. Broun was often on his feet cheering.

He was convinced, however, that his heart was endangered by the crowds and excitement. One day for Eddie Brannick (later the Giants' secretary) he projected a headline on a piece of copy paper.

MATTY PITCHES NO-HITTER
AS BASEBALL WRITER DIES

Most of all, Broun liked the behind-the-scenes atmosphere. Brannick and others saw him as a young man with class, quietly feeling his way along. He rarely entered into horseplay. Others might boast of amorous conquests. Not Broun. He was a failure at dirty stories, either as teller or listener. Otherwise his full rich laugh was always ready. Usually he would be found sitting aside with a single player, or another writer. The little things which make a personality interested him, and he had a knack for drawing people out. He was learning to work beneath the surface.

The new life was leisurely. He rose late and went directly to the Polo Grounds, the *Tribune* depending on the wire services for accounts of out-of-town games.

The Broun family had moved during his absence in China

45

to an apartment at 195 Claremont Avenue (not far from the Hudson River) near 120th Street. Virginia had married and Irving had gone to Mexico to seek his fortune with the Standard Oil Company.

Heywood wrote his stories at the office or at home. Either way his evenings were relatively uncluttered by work, since he wrote as fast as he could make the typewriter go.

Down at the *Tribune* office on Nassau Street, near Park Row (New York's newspaper-publishing center in those days) George Daley's booming voice demanded bylines for his writers. They needed encouragement. Broun got a small raise, bringing the weekly total to $35, but no byline. He nevertheless went on struggling to put color into his stories. All baseball writers were busily thieving in the terminology of other occupations, usually emerging with only a word or two at a time. Broun swept up armloads.

Baseball vaudeville, which included a lot of Sarah Bernhardt and Al Jolson stuff, combined with some shivery Eva-crossing-the-ice thrills, entertained some 15,000 of the elect at the Polo Grounds yesterday afternoon, when the Giants climbed to a niche half a game behind the Phillies. The judicious interplay of multitudinous hits and vicarious errors contributed to some merry sport of a cubist and futurist nature.

In the end, though, Christy Mathewson was required to provide Homeric feats to excite his bridge partner to sufficient effort to climb among the top baseball scribes.

The Giants won the pennant, but there was a disquieting factor. In the World Series they had to face the Philadelphia Athletics. The defensive strength of Connie Mack's celebrated $100,000 infield—McInnis at first, Collins at second, Barry at short, and Baker at third—was awesome enough. But it happened that the Baker was the lank and lantern-jawed Home Run Baker, and others were not far behind in slugging prowess.

A misadventure of the night cast Broun further down. He had boarded a Seventh Avenue subway train and, eyes closed, settled comfortably for the run uptown. Shortly beyond Times Square he was disturbed by sounds unusual to the subway's roar. At the other end of the car a man held the arms of a girl while another vigorously slapped her.

Broun glanced about. Proper actors for such a scene would have included three or four strong males quick enough of foot to subdue the culprits while a slow but gallant man lumbered to the place of battle. The cast was inadequate.

He stepped forward. The code of D'Artagnan and Colonel Newcome demanded that the ruffians be given a thrashing. Besides, Broun needed to avoid appearance of cowardice, even when he alone was looking.

He said courteously, "Would you gentlemen care to step onto the platform at Columbus Circle?"

They did. And left Broun a patient for an ambulance.

He tried to ignore his bruises and talked only a little of a ticket chopper's chair and a lantern that it seemed to him the enemy had come by in the course of the struggle. More serious than the injuries, he felt, was the loss of his sailor straw hat. But not because of the hat. He had a habit of writing telephone numbers on the lining with the copy pencil he always carried. Several of the numbers were not replaceable.

On the diamond at Philadelphia the worst happened. Rube Marquard went to the mound for the Giants. Connie Mack sent out Chief Bender. The Rube stayed only a little while. Home Run Baker caught hold of one with Collins aboard to win the day. The *Tribune's* story was just another story.

And then on the second day came Mathewson. When it was

over Broun could only whisper, but there was song in his heart and his forefingers flew over the keys.

Robbed of his catcher, a wrecked machine tottering to ruin at his back and the greatest sluggers in baseball poised for the onslaught, old Chris Mathewson, master, king, emperor and ruler of all baseball pitchers at home and in the dominions beyond the seas, annihilated the attack of the Philadelphia Athletics by the might of his wizardry.

Lost to the Giants through injury were Chief Meyers, Merkle, and a couple of other regulars. The teams toiled scoreless to the last half of the ninth. And then a Mackman reached third base with none out. Almost anything meant victory for the Athletics—a long fly ball, a slow roller, even a ball hit to one side of an infielder.

It was indeed a time for heroism. Matty "stuck to the guns, his iron nerve unruffled and his matchless courage unbroken." The Athletics went down, one, two, three.

Even now Matty had not finished. When the Giants came to bat in the first half of the tenth, the time had come for him to "strike the blow and bring the first run of the game over the plate, with a clean, stout-hearted single to center."

The Giants boosted their margin to three and Matty sent Connie Mack's bullies skulking to their clubhouse.

Thousands upon thousands, friend and enemy, paid tribute to the prowess of the master who had toyed with Baker in the pinches, coddled Collins, and sent the swift McInnis hitless through the struggle.

George Daley could not give Broun a byline. But the story commanded top right front page. It sang all the way—if the trills were perhaps too many. The competition failed to match the tone. Grantland Rice's story was necessarily sketchy, since the *Mail* was an afternoon paper and he had to send it by brief takes. But for the morning *American* Damon Runyon had equal opportunity with Broun. His voice was not lyric.

> One name tells the story, and the name is Christy Mathewson. It is becoming an old tale, this tale of how the man they termed—how well they have termed!—the "Old Master" rose to a great emergency.

For the rest of the series Broun remained at his press-coop guns, but on the field the Giants faltered. The left flank crumpled under the fire of one of Connie Mack's youngsters, Bullet Joe Bush. A second onslaught by Chief Bender buckled the right. And then the Giants' center, commanded by the emperor himself, gave way. Broun's loyalty remained unimpaired. "Rising to the supreme heights of which he alone is capable, the mighty Mathewson endeavored to stem the rout, but the team behind him split apart and the triumph of the foe was complete." The Giants erred twice, indubitably. But some writers placed greater emphasis on Eddie Plank's two-hitter.

The stories raised Broun, byline or not, in the eyes of other journalists. In the press box they were praised by a homely little man whose humor sidelights for the *Mail* carried the signature Franklin P. Adams. Newspapermen and most *Mail* readers knew the name to be an extension of the initials F. P. A., which appeared under an editorial-page column headed "Always in a Good Humor." There was a touch of irony in the title, for Adams, mellow in print, already had a healthy reputation for private irascibility which often crossed the line to rudeness.

Adams was laying stones in the foundation of modern gos-

49

sip journalism with a thrice-a-week chunk of type, two to five inches deep, which he called "The Diary of a Modern Samuel Pepys." The chronicling of his lunch dates, tennis partners, hosts, hostesses, and fellow guests had been intended at the start only to fill space. Developing surprising popularity, it mirrored a section of the cultural scene. Adams moved his column over to the *Tribune* in January 1914 at the awe-inspiring salary of $25,000 a year and got George S. Kaufman, who had started contributing while still a ribbon salesman, a job filling his old space in the *Mail*.

Broun began to attract more attention around the press club and at Joel's, the unpretentious but celebrated restaurant at 41st Street and Seventh Avenue where the worlds of journalism and the theater met. Joel Rinaldo, philosopher, lay psychologist, and occasional author, personally complimented Broun on his baseball stories and predicted a journey to the top of the mountain. At Joel's, Broun met a plump reporter for the *Times* named Alexander Woollcott, a year older than himself, who was also fascinated by the theater. The Pemberton brothers, Brock and Murdock, had arrived in the big town from Emporia, Kansas, bearing letters from William Allen White. F. P. A. got Brock a job on the *Mail* and Murdock handled public relations at the Hippodrome Theater, home of the elephants, at the corner of Sixth Avenue and 43rd Street. Sometimes a band was recruited at the Hippodrome for late dancing—including the scandalous bunny hug—at near-by Henri's Restaurant.

Broun was barely aware, however, of the subsurface revolt in Greenwich Village against the mawkish, sentimental, and Puritan in American life and the arts. He was never introduced into the salon of Mabel Dodge (the extension of Greenwich Village to better-heeled Fifth Avenue), where Harvard classmates Jack Reed and Walter Lippmann shone in youthful brilliance. He missed as well the wild, vigorous talk of Big Bill Haywood and Emma Goldman and the quieter social philosophy of Lincoln Steffens and Norman Hapgood.

No one had taken him to the MacDougal Street basement —a little below Washington Square—where members of the Liberal Club dined on the cuisine of Hippolyte Havel, the owl-eyed little poet-anarchist, and talked of emancipation. He would have been shocked, anyhow, by clinical discussion of sex in mixed company. Greenwich Village was a long way from both the semi-Victorian home of his parents and the Polo Grounds.

5

A Dixie Rebel

THE editors of the *Tribune* allowed their baseball writer
to go through the 1914 spring training season unrecognized
by so much as an initial. There were big stories to cover,
which made their attitude even less generous. The Federal
League was being organized, with some big-timers, including
Joe Tinker of the Cubs' great Tinker-to-Evers-to-Chance
double-play combination, jumping to it. Many Giants were
sorely tempted by proffered bundles of money. Further excitement was caused by the Baseball Players Fraternity,
which was flexing muscles at the club owners.

Broun's stories from the spring training camps were not,
it was true, especially distinguished. He had no strong feelings about the vital issues. The Federals seemed to be little
more than a Wall Street promotion scheme and to the
Fraternity Christy Mathewson was no more than lukewarm,
saying only that, not wishing to be a "mucker," he would go
along with the decision of his fellow players. Had Matty
caught fire his bridge partner doubtless would have given
off heat.

In the *Tribune* office a few days before the season opened,
Broun jerked the last sheet of his story from his typewriter

Maurice Goldberg

RUTH HALE

BROUN WITH A GROUP OF SPORTS WRITERS. READING FROM LEFT TO
RIGHT: SID MERCER, W. G. HANNA, JEROME BEATTY, BROUN,
DAMON RUNYON, LARRY SEMON, SAM CRANE.

and reached into his breast pocket for a copy pencil. The lead had been singing in his mind for a couple of days.

Silence will grip 30,000 persons at the Polo Grounds on Tuesday as half a second comes and goes. In other cities other thousands will be held in the thrall of the same stillness. While the pitcher winds up the heart of the nation will skip a beat.

For just the barest hair's breadth of time the man in the box will seem to be at one with eternity.

Broun stepped over and tossed the copy on George Daley's desk. Daley read through the first few paragraphs.

"All right, Heywood," he said. "I'm going to the managing editor and to Ogden Reid if I have to. We might as well fight out this byline matter right now."

Broun lit a cigarette and waved it deprecatingly. "Oh, it's not really important."

When Daley had finished reading the copy and had rushed off, Broun put on his black hat and went over to the press club on Spruce Street to await the first edition. The club-rooms were in a half story at the top of an office building, reached by a flight of iron stairs from the last elevator stop. Climbing the stairs he glanced up and saw Frank Ward O'Malley, the *Sun's* famous reporter, leaning over the railing with a billiard ball in his hand.

"It's all right," O'Malley said. "Come on up."

When Broun got to the top he saw that O'Malley had a hat full of billiard balls. Broun interrogated McAllister Coleman, an old basketball player at Collegiate, rival of Horace Mann, who had been one of Broun's hecklers. Coleman was on the *Sun*. He explained that O'Malley had called up the *Times* and offered a peace conference to settle a dispute which had resulted in a club boycott by *Times* men.

53

Broun took a place in the audience and waited. When the peace delegation began to mount the stairs, O'Malley, holding his hat behind him, called down a warm greeting. And then he loosed a rain of billiard balls ahead of the innocents.

"Come on and sit down," Coleman said. "I'll sell you on Socialism." He had joined the Socialist Party a couple of years before.

"I doubt if you can swing me," Broun said. His knowledge of the subject had been limited to a few discussions with Walter Lippmann at Harvard. But he was interested, especially since his favorite playwright, George Bernard Shaw, was a Socialist. "I like the brotherhood-of-man angle," Broun went on. "If I ever get convinced that Socialism will work and really usher in brotherhood I'll probably join up. But Marx was an atheist. I'm a believer. At that, I may be some kind of a Christian Socialist."

They talked and shot pool—Broun was almost a shark—and watched an elegant entrance by Herbert Bayard Swope, the dazzling young *World* reporter who had recently come up with scoops on the murder of Herman Rosenthal, the gambler slain by hired gunmen after failing to pay off to City Detective Charles Becker. Tall and commanding, Swope appeared swinging a cane and wearing, as usual, a flower in the lapel of his exquisitely tailored suit.

Later George Daley came, looking victorious. "It's there," he said.

Broun dispensed with casualness and hurried to the *Tribune*. The pressmen, with whom he sometimes boxed, offered congratulations, and he had to wait only a little while for the first copies.

The name was not in big type like Rice's and Runyon's. But the seven-point body size was caps and black. The story seemed to read better than it had in copy.

A Dixie Rebel

Broun telephoned home, and his parents were waiting up when he arrived. The fact escaped no one that his signature was the only one in the paper spelled out. And so the promise of the old editor of the Horace Mann *Record* seemed on the way to fulfillment. And to hell with the *Harvard Crimson* and certain shortsighted executives of the *Morning Telegraph*.

And then on Sunday the byline was gone. The piece was a long one and every bit as good as the other. Broun hid his sorrow, and the next day it was back. This time brackets were around the caps. A day or so later it came out in upper and lower case. A regular byline was a new and startling thing for the *Tribune* and the editors and compositors felt entitled to experiment. On Tuesday it emerged on page one, but he had been preceded by a day to outer glory by Arthur Ruhl, a veteran of *Collier's Weekly*, whose purple tale had chronicled the execution of Gyp the Blood and Leftie Louie and Dago Frank and Whitey Lewis, the Rosenthal killers.

The spelling of Broun's name was not, he felt, exactly suitable for a byline. He remembered the *Harvard Advocate's* misadventure with his piece. Though now able to keep an eye on the compositors, he was irritated by readers who sent letters to Hayward Brown. For a while he threatened to change the spelling of his name to Broon or even Bra-woon. And Heywood he considered trading in for Campbell, his middle name.

Freedom of the byline in those days did not include, unless for adventure yarns, the use of the pronoun "I" or even "we." It did permit Broun to loosen up—occasionally, some thought, too much. He liked a play on words and especially a pun. One umpire became good copy solely because his name was Byron—soon Lord Byron to Broun. "I have not loved the world, nor the world me," he quoted the poet in starting off a story of a game in which Umpire Lord Byron had chased John McGraw to the clubhouse.

Broun's greatest asset was his ability to impart a feeling of the game's excitement. Almost effortlessly he integrated the facts with colorful allusions and the discovery was soon made that a story could stand on action and characterization by themselves. He got an early grip on a figure that was to become legendary.

> Even Branch Rickey could not save the St. Louis Browns yesterday, but he gave them a hard ride. Branch told his runners when to run; he shouted to his out-fielders where to play, and advised his pitchers where to throw, and finally, still having a few foot-pounds of unexpected energy left, he went in and took a smash at the ball himself. He even tried to coach the umpire, shouting "Inside!" and "Outside!" to guide old Tommy Connolly.

It was on a hot July day that Broun invited Alice Duer Miller and Ruth Hale into the press box. They had no particular business there. Women were generally barred, which was one more irritant for the two suffragettes. Delicate Alice Miller, who was writing features for the Sunday *Tribune,* had a passion for baseball, especially as played by the Giants. Broun was not acquainted with her companion. When the two women, looking charming in wide picture hats and carrying fans, came down to the press coop to say hello to Broun, his courtliness overwhelmed the rule and he invited them in. Alice Miller introduced her companion as a theatrical press agent, but a former reporter and drama critic.

Broun was impressed with Ruth Hale at once. Most people were, for she had a striking, high-spirited presence which, with her lively, attractive eyes and grace of body, more than compensated for lack of beauty.

That day Broun was official scorer, deciding between hits and errors (reporters pass the job around) and he was accused of several mistakes of judgment. It was not from being flustered. Afterwards he was not even sure that he had been wrong. Ruth Hale made the accusations. She questioned the thoroughness of his grounding in baseball. She had small regard for his baseball stories. Most people usually praised them. This might be the straight goods.

"Tomorrow is my day off," Broun said. "Could you elaborate?"

"That," she replied, "should not be difficult."

Their first date provided a slight basis for the legend of Broun's appearance in the Racquet Club wearing one black and one white shoe. The place of rendezvous was not the Racquet, nor was the color spread so great. The teammate of the black shoe was only brown. And the difference was of no real consequence, since their plans called for a simple walk in Central Park.

Instead of baseball they talked at first mainly of newspapers and the theater and afterward touched on other arts and proceeded to politics and relations between the sexes. Ruth Hale was abreast of the rebel movements in them all. Broun was amazed to find a young lady from the South advocating equality of the races. As usual with young people who take quickly to one another, they sketched in their backgrounds.

Ruth Hale had been born near Rogersville, a county seat in mountainous northeast Tennessee a few miles below the Virginia border. Her father, a farmer and horse raiser, had been enough of a religious rebel to be thrown out of the Presbyterian Church for refusal to believe in the virgin birth

57

of Christ and vicarious atonement for sin. Ruth adored him, but, possessed of a crusader's zeal, she had kept on selling eggs laid by her hen in order to raise funds for missionary work in China. Her father died when she was eleven and Ruth developed into something of a rebel herself, shocking the neighborhood by riding astride her pony instead of side-saddle. Her mother, Annie Riley Hale, had been and still was an unreconstructed upholder of the old Southern traditions. Of all the newfangled notions that had come along, Annie Hale had hated Women's Rights the most. And so, being wiry and tireless, she had ranged far and wide preaching that woman's place was in the home. That had meant considerable absence from home, with Ruth left in charge of her two younger brothers. Ruth had promptly become a staunch advocate of Women's Rights.

When she was thirteen and in all-out war with her environment, Ruth got herself sent to a boarding school at Roanoke, Virginia, where she became interested in painting and music. After that the farm community was impossible and she had been allowed to go to Philadelphia. There, living with some cousins, she had studied at the Academy of Fine Arts and Drexel Institute. At eighteen she had landed a job on the Washington *Star* and later, with her mother, she had founded a bureau for writing Congressional speeches. But at twenty-two she had been back in Philadelphia as drama critic for the *Ledger*. A couple of years later, in 1910, she had gone to New York as critic for *Vogue* and still later had been a reporter for the *Times*. All during her career she had met the ridicule and opposition of males and she was sick of it.

Broun's private history did not take long. He spoke a little of his ambitions to write novels and plays. But with his job as sports writer he expressed contentment. In the young

Broun, women always saw a large, unwieldy mass of talent waiting for feminine hands to shape.

"You ought to find a job writing drama," Ruth Hale suggested.

Broun shook his head. "There's more future in sports."

They were debating the point when a begging squirrel sat down before them.

"He wants some peanuts," Ruth Hale suggested, logically.

Broun was not the man to be intimidated by a squirrel. "I haven't any peanuts," he replied. "If he wants peanuts I'll give him a nickel and he can go down to the vendor and get them for himself."

The words do not at first seem to contain the essence of romance. But Ruth Hale was amused by the large young man's ability to put himself on a squirrel-to-squirrel relation with the little mendicant. She got a strong feeling that if she were to marry, this was the man she wanted.

Broun had liked Ruth Hale's fresh, confident talk. "I wonder," he asked, "if you could come over to our house for cocktails and dinner tonight."

Ruth Hale accepted.

Three events conspired to distress Broun that summer. Over two he had no control. The fist fight he might have avoided.

In early July the world had seemed stable and content. Teddy Roosevelt had announced a six weeks' rest for his voice, after which it was expected that he would erupt in the general direction of the White House, where Woodrow Wilson was behaving no more to his liking than had William Howard Taft. But Teddy's roar no longer shook the earth. The revolution in Mexico was bloody but no more so than usual. The Giants looked like repeaters, with Matty seemingly destined to win at least 25 against half a dozen losses.

Then the Archduke Francis Ferdinand fell at Sarajevo before an assassin's bullet. Within a few weeks the great armies and fleets of Europe were moving. Broun's love of military things had tarnished with his toy soldiers. He had no more expectation than anyone else that America would eventually be drawn into war. But it was part of his sensitivity that distant catastrophes affected him almost as much as those close at hand. And so as headlines grew bigger and blacker his spirits fell.

The Giants seized upon the moment to go into a slump. Broun's knowledge of the personal affairs of the players brought him, it was true, a neat little scoop. When the Stock Exchange closed to avert panic, he learned that many Giants, including Christy Mathewson, were in the market. Stalwart Matty assured the public with a statement that when the Exchange opened he planned to buy.

Germany declared war on Russia and Italy crept out of the Triple Alliance. And proving that brave words are not enough, Matty lost some of his pitching magic. John McGraw's testiness on the field increased and he drew a five-day suspension. After one of Matty's failures the Boston Braves, who had started a sensational late drive from the cellar, moved into a tie for first place.

It was at this time that Broun raised his fists in another righteous cause. One night he was with Ruth Hale in Sweeney's bar on Seventh Avenue when Sweeney, admiring Ruth Hale's dancing grace, asked her for a dance. He neglected to take up the matter with her escort. Broun advised Sweeney that such conduct was intolerable. Sweeney, paying no attention, repeated his request. Ruth Hale was far from insulted—and besides was capable of laying Sweeney low with a few well-placed words. But she looked upon the test as good for Broun. The dynamite left exploded in Sweeney's face. But it was not enough. They grappled and rolled on the floor. The rolling turned out to be wise, for a waiter rushed to the scene carrying a bottle. The fighters were separated without great damage.

As the summer waned Broun worked the war into his baseball stories ("The Giants Hear the Hun at the Door"), but they lacked his old ebulliency. He spoke of the "stumbling" Giants. And, worst of all, in the time of Matty's trouble he stood convicted of a faint heart. When stouthearted Matty threw a wrong one to Honus Wagner and the great Pittsburgh slugger rode it out of the park to win a crucial game, Broun cavalierly announced his sorrow for the champions of the year before.

In the winter the war receded in Broun's mind to some degree. He saw much of Ruth Hale, though more of intellectual companionship than romance existed between them. She communicated to him the interest in greater freedom—political, sexual, economic—for which the avant garde was agitating. He was now seen occasionally at the Liberal Club and at other Village haunts. And in the press club and the restaurants he took pleasure in the slight eminence of a by-line writer.

6

Bewitching Sprite of the Glade

THREE of the one-act plays had been completed and the scenery was being set for the fourth and last when Heywood Broun begged his mother's pardon and went backstage. It was the autumn of 1915 and, after a midsummer leap from the sports page, Broun was at the Bandbox Theatre on East 57th Street as the *Tribune's* drama critic. The journey behind the scenes was to find Lucy Huffaker, one of New York's small band of newspaperwomen, who was serving as volunteer press agent for the experimental Washington Square Players.

She was in the wings when he found her, a slight, pretty girl with prematurely gray hair. "Lucy," he said, "if I leave now I can get my review in tomorrow's paper. If I stay, it will have to be held over a day. You tell me which I should do."

She hesitated, then answered, "Oh, Heywood, why not just stay and see it through?"

The actors in the final number were her concern. Except for a few performances in the back room of a bookshop, the group had never actually played at Washington Square, but the spirit and many of the players belonged to Greenwich

Village. Among them were future stars—Katharine Cornell, Frank Conroy, Helen Westley, Roland Young—and the director, Edward Green, later achieved success on Broadway and in Hollywood. In due course the Theatre Guild was to emerge from the group. But it was the first year and amateurs were in the majority. All they could hope for was experience, a sense of breaking down barriers, and perhaps some publicity.

Broun nodded and went dutifully back to his seat. "They want me to cover it all," he told his mother. She accompanied him to most of the openings, debating their merits between the acts.

The play, entitled "The Antick" (by Percy Mackaye, a former member of Professor Baker's 47 Workshop) dealt with the blossoming of a nature from half-wintered Puritanism. The curtain rose on a New England scene. In a minute a girl skipped and danced across the stage. When Broun's account reached the *Tribune,* brittle old compositors wondered where the modern personal journalism was to end.

We regret now wasted adjectives and we pine for every superlative with which we have lightly parted. All words denoting, connoting or appertaining in any way to charm we would bestow upon Lydia Lopokova.

As Julie Bonhear, a Canuck girl, Lydia is a mite mighty in enticement. Never have we . . . But no; we'll set no time limit on our opinion, for Julie herself complains: "These Yankees, they say only that: I love you always, forever! Why not they say: I love you—all this week?"

And so, until Tuesday, October 12, we will continue to maintain that Lydia Lopokova is the most charming young person who has trod the stage in New York this season. But she did not tread. She did not even walk.

She skipped, she danced, she pranced, and, like as not, she never touched the stage. Or so it seemed.

Late next morning, when Broun wandered into the living room, still dressed in pajamas, his mother fixed him with a critical eye.

"Heywood," she said tartly, "if you want to be a reviewer, don't be so mushy. You sound like a little boy watching them dip the strawberry ice cream at a party."

Broun was unperturbed. "More like coming on a fairy dancing by a stream in the woods. Besides, I think my piece is at least sophomoric."

He went to the telephone. Lucy Huffaker was used to calls from the *Tribune's* critic. "Lucy," they usually ran, "I'm awfully sorry I lost that paper you gave me." For Broun she always made three copies. One went to the *Tribune*, the second to his home. The third was held in readiness for the call, after which she would go dashing across town.

This one was different.

"Lucy," Broun said, "do you think it would be all right if I came over to your theater? I mean, would you introduce me to Lopokova?"

The answer was favorable.

If Lydia Lopokova pasted the *Tribune* notice in her scrapbook, it was hardly with shaking fingers. For her it was no better than so-so, for at twenty-three she had already been raved about by the critics of many lands. "She is," one had written, "a winged fairy, dainty as a white violet, light as thistledown, the very embodiment of the joyous spirit of youth." The comparison to a sprite was a favorite.

She was already a major star of the Russian ballet. Daughter of a Czarist government official, she had been placed, when aged eight, in the Imperial School at Petrograd where

64

her bursting energy and tremendous love of movement had caused every act to be amusingly exaggerated. When she was seventeen Lopokova had left the school to join the original Diaghileff ballet in Paris. Two years later, in 1911, she had come to America, first dancing at the Globe Theatre in "The Echo," a musical comedy. Later she had been première danseuse of the Russian Ballet at the Winter Garden. Her purpose in joining the Washington Square Players was to gain acting experience for a Broadway production being created for her. Broun's program was audacious even for a young man who had nearly spoken to a strange actress in a stagedoor alley. He took Lucy Huffaker to dinner before going to the Bandbox.

"Lucy," he said nervously, "would you be kind enough to order dinner for me?"

"Heywood, don't be so upset. It's all I can do to order my own." She glanced through the menu.

"Well," he said, "it's not just tonight. When the waiter comes I get scared and the only thing I can think of is eggs. I get tired of eggs."

Lucy was half convinced. "All right. You can have liver and bacon."

"Thank you, Lucy. Could you change that to roast beef? Tell me about Lopokova."

"Oh, you'll like her. She has great spontaneity—lives in the moment. Everybody's crazy about her."

Broun had to wait, since Lopokova, being in the last of the plays, did not arrive until the second was nearly finished. Lucy came for him, and he went willingly though shakily.

"Did you tell her about me?" he asked.

"Oh, sure." Lucy was matter of fact. "I built you up."

They climbed backstage and Broun stopped before a wall mirror to smooth his hair. "I reserved a table at Mouquin's.

Do you think Lydia and you and Eddie Green and maybe a few others would go out with me after the show?"

Lucy patted him on the shoulder. "Ask her, Heywood. No harm in asking."

During the introduction he stood awkwardly, twisting his black hat, but his best shy smile was on his face. It was not a large dressing room and others shared it, but for the moment they were elsewhere. Lucy departed and Lopokova, anything but ill at ease, skipped about clearing a place for him to sit down. He began to relax a little.

"I knew of you," she said. "I always read your accounts of the plays."

Lopokova's Russian inflection seemed to add to her liveliness. She must have been all of five feet. She was fair-skinned, with blue eyes and a mass of dark-brown hair. Her face was a little too broad for beauty and her wide mouth turned down at the corners. But her elfin movements and gestures were as exquisite offstage as on.

Broun discovered that his request was not hard to make after all. Lopokova's was an open, easy personality; her mind was entirely without barriers. And she was pleased with this shy boy-critic who had fallen at her feet.

The late supper at Mouquin's (Broun had chosen it because of the French cuisine and Old World atmosphere) was a rapturous success. When it was over he had the promise of more suppers.

Since he did not turn handsprings at every opening night, Broun's progress in drama criticism had been as rapid as in sports writing. He had not been sure, when the job as drama critic fell open, that he wanted to tackle it as a regular thing. His mother had doubts about his grounding and he was inclined to share them. And while the *Tribune* showed more respect for the theater than most papers, owing to its former employment of William Winter, dean of critics of his day, drama ranked in many ways beneath sports.

Broun had, on the other hand, already tasted the choicer sweets of sports writing. He was New York's top baseball writer. As for backstage—who could outmatch his bridge partnership with Matty? He loved the theater as much as the diamond, and chances were good that he would enjoy its backstage even more.

Ruth Hale had pressed him to seek the drama job. Like Copeland and Baker she made the arts seem important. She also lent assurance that he was competent for the task. Alexander Woollcott had become critic for the *Times,* which was a factor, for already there was a friendly rivalry between the two men of avoirdupois.

Broun tried out and on August 18, 1915, his theatre byline appeared for the first time. The review was of Edgar Selwyn's "Rolling Stones," a comedy starring Charles Ruggles and Marie Carroll. The report was favorable.

No bright and shining armor was buckled on by Broun for his new task. He carried, however, a stave for administering an occasional slap.

We like the drama so far. In the office of the National League, just between the picture of Hans Wagner shaking hands with President Taft and the portrait of Gov. Tener, there hangs a framed motto. "Take nothing for granted in baseball," it says. This is not the motto of the theater.

The drama has succeeded in eliminating many of the uncertainties that harass baseball. Nobody can tell how a game will end until the ninth inning, but the least ex-

perienced theater-goer can predict the end of a play
pretty accurately just as soon as the hero has taken one
long lingering glance at the heroine.

He banged the rumps of the knights of contrived romance. "Whenever the long arm of coincidence intrudes in
Jules Eckert Goodman's play *Just Outside the Door,* the
author seizes it and shakes hands." George M. Cohan's farce
about Billy Sunday was pelted with a suggestion that the play
would benefit from a seasoning of the evangelist's own pungent vocabulary. In one of William S. Hart's pre-cowboy
movie melodramas the conflict was resolved, Broun noted,
by a child's falling "sick of some severe dramatic ailment."
The movies he held not far above contempt, but the major
openings received his attention. Charlie Chaplin was hailed
as an artist and Broun went so far as to interview Mary Pickford, whose smile he thought offset homeliness of features.

One slap stung enough to arouse the anger of Ethel Barrymore. After looking through the papers she remarked that
all the critics had liked her performance except one, whom
she understood to be a baseball writer. That turned the
Baseball Writers Association out en masse behind their old
comrade.

Broun kept an eye peeled for realism. When Cleves Kinkead's "Common Clay" was announced he was expectant, for
Kinkead had come out of the 47 Workshop. It turned out to
be just another maudlin piece about a poor girl seduced by
a rich young man. "Our objection," he wrote in *Collier's,*
for which editor Mark Sullivan had hired him to do a weekly
stint, "is that it is not true to life." The play turning into a
success, Broun was obliged to point out that his own views
would be the sole criterion and the public be damned. A
reasonably faint damn.

Bewitching Sprite of the Glade

Broun happily attached himself to the advanced thinkers warring on Puritanism. Or at any rate to the fringes of the attacking legions. Louis K. Anspacher's "The Unchastened Woman" was perfect for the needs of a man willing to fight but to something less than the death.

> Persons who like to see vice triumph or virtue prevail will not like it. Dr. Anspacher is one of those delightful neutrals who sets his folks on the stage and then lets them fight it out. We like it that way. It is our experience—bitter, too—that the rewards of virtue are by no means certain. Life, we find, does not deal in exact judgments.

That Broun's old friends on the *Telegraph* editorially called him the Sir Galahad of the theater was chiefly a commentary on the low estate of New York criticism under benighted newspaper publishers. But the serious people in the theater, particularly the young, recognized him at once as a force for good. His colorful style brought a sense of excitement, as it had to baseball. He was quick to lend such prestige as he could to the new and untried. "The amateur," he pointed out, "is such only until he gets a job." Except for that attitude he would not have been present at the experimental performance in which Lopokova tripped across the stage.

It was one of the after-dark sights of Manhattan—Broun, a great raccoon coat exaggerating his massiveness, ambling into Joel's with effervescent little Lopokova beside him calling up remarks. They had late supper at Joel's almost every night. New York had twice as many theaters then as now. Broun discovered, however, that failure to see all the final act was not disastrous, and if things looked complicated he

69

could depend on a telephoned report from his mother, who stayed to the end. Writing with his usual swiftness he was able to meet Lopokova soon after her performance was finished. On nights when there was no opening the scene-shifters at the Bandbox were required to spend an undue share of their time shifting Broun out of the way.

In keeping with his training, Broun had quickly introduced Lopokova to the cocktail hour and the dinner table of his parents. They had no trouble observing how badly their son was smitten. The evaluation of Lopokova's feelings was less easy. Broun himself was anything but clear.

"You know," he once confided sadly to Lucy Huffaker, "when Lydia is with me I know she's fond of me. I even think she loves me. But she lives exactly, as you said, in the moment. When we're apart I doubt that she even knows I exist."

He confided in Ruth Hale more than in anyone else. Their relationship, while close, had contained more of intellectual camaraderie than of courtship. When, in Central Park, Ruth Hale had concluded that, if she married, Broun was the man she wanted, that "if" had been very large. She was a long way from sure that she wanted to marry. And certainly not under the insulting folk customs that created the male lord and master over a wife considered barely more than a chattel.

But Ruth Hale possessed a powerful competitive instinct. She was not pleased at the sight of Broun tossing his heart into the air for Lopokova to catch. Especially since Lopokova doubtless had caught many hearts, and perhaps was accustomed to put them away lightly.

Broun had known Lopokova a little less than three months when he proposed. They were in Central Park taking Lopokova's constitutional. That was one of the daytime sights of

Manhattan, Broun and Lopokova running around the Central Park reservoir. Broun's winter track clothes included his coonskin coat. Besides, he often slowed to a walk while Lopokova, dressed warmly but for greater freedom, skipped and danced about him.

It was early January and Broun was forced to pour out his passion on the icy air. The arguments put forth were not many or involved. In five years of journalism he had made at least some progress—perhaps he would do better. At least he could support her. But she could go on with her career. He wouldn't be jealous about that.

Lopokova did not stop skipping. "And when," she asked, "would this marriage take place?"

He answered gallantly, "That would be your decision."

"All right." Lopokova rose on her toes and pirouetted. "If you want it so, we are engaged."

That night Broun introduced his fiancée to Franklin P. Adams. There was a purpose, beyond his friendship with Adams. Broun could be a subtle planter of bombs that when exploded moved things in the direction he wanted them to go.

The little bomb went off in F. P. A.'s next edition of "The Diary of a Modern Samuel Pepys."

H. Broun, the critick, I hear hath become engaged to Mistress Lydia Lopokova, the pretty play-actress and dancer. He did introduce her to me last night and she seemed a merry elf and a modest.

The blowing away of secrecy would make the engagement more secure.

There was an unplanned repercussion in the office of producer Arthur Hopkins, for whom Ruth Hale was handling press relations. A co-worker was dark-eyed little Rebecca

Drucker, receptionist and typist. She was acquainted with Broun, for he had often stood beside her desk, black fedora or straw sailor hat doffed, worried what to do with his hands and feet, while inquiring for Ruth Hale. But Ruth had always treated him banteringly and no sign of romance between them had been apparent.

Coming to F. P. A.'s item, Becky dashed into Ruth Hale's office and showed it to her.

Ruth Hale tossed the paper back. "The only thing it proves," she said, "is that Frank Adams has a big mouth that flaps in the breeze."

But there was corroboration. Across the page a news item quoted Lopokova's confirmation. Perhaps the marriage would be in the autumn, she had said. Broun had known that F. P. A.'s item would come while still in copy to the attention of the city desk and that inquiries would be made of the bride-to-be.

Lopokova had provided an extra tidbit of news. She had been invited to rejoin Diaghileff's Russian Ballet, which was at that very moment taking ship for America.

Diaghileff and his artists arrived a few days later. After a week of mad rehearsals, Lopokova scored a great personal triumph in the opening performance.

For Broun the atmosphere of the ballet was that of a distant and foreign land. And Lopokova had changed. She was, of course, intensely wrapped up in her work. Worse, in the few free moments at her disposal she seemed to prefer the company of an older acquaintance, Randolfo Barocini, Diaghileff's secretary and manager. Broun was bewildered and hurt.

The ballet company went on tour almost at once. Back in New York, it prepared to embark for Europe. Lopokova and Broun sat in Joel's while she imparted the news that he had feared. Barocini was her true love. After taking time to write a letter to his mother in appreciation of her hospitality and begging pardon for the trouble caused by the broken engagement, Lopokova got on a ship and sailed away.*

The issue of the *Tribune* that had reported Lopokova's smashing triumph in the ballet première carried Heywood Broun's byline over a sports story.

ZBYSZKO DOWNS MASKED
MARVEL IN FAST MATCH

While Lopokova's disappearance into the ballet world and her attention to Barocini had been upsetting, Broun had not bellied morosely up to bars muttering, "Make it a double Scotch," and then staggered, black hat askew, into the *Tribune* to resign his theater assignment in favor of sports. George Daley had departed and Broun had become sports editor. (The drama job had fallen to George S. Kaufman, who had moved over from the *Mail* to be Broun's assistant.) The sports editorship paid better. And a man hugging to his heart the promise of matrimony needed all the cash he could get.

The depths of Broun's lacerations were visible to all after Lopokova's departure and especially after the public announcement of her marriage a few months later. He lost weight and instead of taking one or two drinks he took three or four. Often he had been withdrawn. Now he began to brood. Death had always walked closely by his side, and now

---

* Lopokova married Barocini and continued her successes, becoming the rage of the intellectual sets in England and on the Continent. After divorcing Barocini she was married in 1925 to John Maynard Keynes (Lord Keynes of Tilton), the celebrated British economist, who died in 1946. Lady Keynes recently remarked of the romance of more than three decades ago: "Our brief acquaintance was interrupted by my rejoining the Russian Ballet and my professional career involved me in a whirl of excitement. I felt I did not want to be tied up to Heywood—so I broke it off, hurting him very much at the time, I am sorry to say."

seemed almost a friend. He wrote a playlet, "Death Says It Isn't So," and placed it among those of his works carried close to his heart.

In the playlet a hopelessly sick man lies in a darkened room. Suddenly another is present, though neither window nor door has opened. The intruder raises the shades and the flood of sunlight reveals him to be a jolly, loud-dressed fat man. Despite large hobnail boots he walks lightly and his long, tapering fingers indicate a gentle touch. He introduces himself pleasantly as Death. But having forgotten his card case he encounters skepticism. The sick man, who it happens was a former sceneshifter for the Washington Square Players, declares that from his theatrical experience he knows that Death wears a black cloak, never appears in the sunlight, and is the cruelest thing in the world. The fat man is crushed. "I'm kind," he protests. "That's my business. When things get too rotten I'm the only one that can help." In the end he convinces the sick man that comedies and exciting baseball games are the chief diversions of heaven.

Broun was dispirited also by his distaste for executive work. Allotment of assignments meant details. It was the sports editor's job to lay out his department's pages and, at the last moment, to go to the composing room and supervise the placing of the type in the forms. Broun tossed in stories and pictures much in the manner in which he had packed his trunk at college. If there was too much, he omitted whatever came last. If there was too little, he simply ordered the insertion of Christy Mathewson's photograph.

Some of the sports staffmen resented his youth and anyhow a certain number of jangles were inevitable. He irritated his old copy-desk colleague, Fred Hawthorne, by shifting him from coverage of tennis, his favorite sport. Hawthorne laid most of the blame, it was true, on F. P. A., who was a tennis enthusiast. F. P. A. was often accused of keeping fingers in pies which did not belong to him. Hawthorne thought that he wanted to control the tennis reporting and had talked Broun into making the change. Sometimes Broun's combination of personal unhappiness and job irritation caused him to boil over. Once he shocked the sports staff by publicly bawling out a subordinate who was his senior by several decades.

But most of the time he managed to be the easy-going, humorous Broun of old. His salary negotiations with W. O. McGeehan (whose later column became one of sports' best) was quickly incorporated into journalistic lore. Broun had been attracted by a *Journal* column signed RIGHT CROSS. Learning that the author was McGeehan—and that he was getting forty dollars a week—Broun sent word inquiring whether he wanted a job on the *Tribune* at higher pay. McGeehan was interested and came over.

Broun sat at George Daley's old desk inside the railing. He put his feet in his wastepaper basket and looked, as had Burdick before him, out of a distant window. The business office had suggested that he offer forty-five dollars a week and had authorized him to go, if he had to, as high as fifty dollars. He had never met McGeehan.

"Mr. McGeehan," he said, "the managing editor has empowered me to haggle with you over salary. You may have forty-five or fifty dollars a week, according to your choice. I can give you a little time to think it over."

McGeehan was a fast calculator and hesitated only a little. "Fifty dollars has a nice round ring," he said. "I believe I will choose that one."

Broun saw Ruth Hale more often after Lopokova's departure. She did not bother to suppress the desire to say "I told you so" and she teased him about being on the rebound. But she was sympathetic.

She told him to quit being a sports editor and go back to drama. Always quick to heed advice that corroborated his own way of thinking, he did.

They talked of marriage. Broun, within a stone's throw of thirty, and having lived at home longer than most men, wanted to found a family of his own. Especially he wanted a son. Wedlock to him meant having a son.

"If we ever marry," Ruth Hale would say, holding up one finger, "there will be one chance and one chance only. If it's a boy, all right." She was infuriated that a boy should be held in higher esteem than a girl.

As a gambling man Broun thought the odds were fair.

7

Honeymooning at the War

IN EARLY June of 1917 Broun was putting his affairs in
order for an extended absence from the United States. General John J. (Black Jack) Pershing was secretly crossing to
England on the liner *Baltic* and the advance echelons of the
American Expeditionary Force were preparing to embark.

Broun had been loaned for a while to George Creel's
drum-beating information committee, but now the *Tribune*
was sending him to France to report the war. In many ways
he was less than admirably suited to the task. As a hater of
firearms he had never fired a gun. The trenches seemed
hardly the place for a man with claustrophobia and if circumstances required a long march his flat feet would be an ex-
cruciating handicap. The sight of blood sickened him and he
was hypersensitive to the pain of others.

He was not seeking adventure, since few illusions about his
capacity for derring-do remained. He had two major reasons
for wanting to go. One was his instinct as a journalist. He
wanted to see the greatest upheaval of his era. The other was
that, since he believed the war to be just, his conscience demanded that he find a way to participate. The flat feet made
acceptance of him as a soldier impossible.

The largest item in preparation for departure was his

forthcoming marriage. With Ruth Hale he had hammered out a wedding bargain satisfactory to a staunch Women's Righter. It was to be an arrangement in which the partners were of precisely equal status. In France she would work on the Paris edition of the *Chicago Tribune* and after returning she would continue her career. There would be independence in private lives, too. They wouldn't have to go everywhere together, or entertain always as a team. If desired they might have separate sets of friends. Strict accountability for every movement day or night was out. Should one or the other become unhappy—or find a more suitable mate—the partnership was to be dissolved upon the asking. In short, the old-fashioned mores, especially those which stemmed from the Puritans, were to be ruthlessly trampled down.

And then after everything was settled Broun suddenly stood in grave danger of being left waiting at the altar.

The crisis arose on the eve of the wedding day—June 7— when Ruth Hale glanced through a leaflet entitled *Form of Solemnization of Matrimony,* which was handed to participants in Episcopal marriages to enable them to follow cues in the ceremony. She paced up and down the living room of the apartment on 66th Street near Fifth Avenue where she lived with her mother and her brother Richard, who was studying for a career as a singer. Her other brother, Shelton, a brilliant young lawyer, had come up from Washington, where he was serving one of the coveted year-length terms as secretary to Justice Oliver Wendell Holmes. It was a chilly, rainy night and Ruth Hale's bronchial cough was aggravated. But, hating medical advice as much as Broun loved it, she chain-smoked as she paced and read.

She announced flatly, "The marriage is off."

The passage in which the minister speaks of the marriage being performed "in the fear of God" angered her. She was vastly amused by the threat of "the dreadful day of judgment when the secrets of all heaven shall be disclosed" if any impediment to the marriage was known and not revealed. One scene called for kneeling and she tried a few ironical practice drops to the floor.

Then, pacing the room again, she intoned sonorously, "I take thee to be my wedded husband, to have and to hold from this day forward, for better for worse, for richer for poorer, in sickness and in health, to love and to cherish, till death us do part, according to God's holy ordinance, and thereto I plight thee my troth."

But the harshest words were reserved for the "obey" and "I now pronounce you man and wife" clauses.

"And why," she demanded, "can it not be 'husband and wife'? Is Broun paying four cows for me, after which I'm to labor in the fields? It's the miserable English chattel-law idea passed along through the Church of England. And what if I don't obey? Has Broun a right to take a stick to me? I would like to see that."

Shelton and Richard tried to sooth her. Annie Riley and Ruth Hale had disagreed violently on women's rights for too many years for the mother's voice to be of much assistance.

"To hell with it," Ruth Hale said. "I never approved of marriage anyhow."

She could argue brilliantly against the whole institution of marriage. In theory she believed a man and woman should be allowed to mate or unmate with no interference from organized society. But her revolt against the conventions was not quite strong enough for the turning of theory into practice in her own life. And so she was able to justify a civil ceremony. But not believing that marriages were sanctified by heaven, she saw no excuse for the clergy's hand in the proceedings.

Broun had always rather liked the pageantry of the richly-garbed Episcopalian clergy and with him its stamp of approval carried weight. In the Church-vs.-civil-ceremony debates with Ruth Hale he had nevertheless chiefly argued consideration of his family traditions.

He was caught, after all, in the crossfire of the opinions of two very strong women. Mrs. Broun was happy that he was to marry and she admired Ruth Hale. But she was determined on a church wedding. Ruth Hale's high regard for the Broun family had, in turn, been largely responsible for a negotiated agreement whereby pomp and circumstance were to be reduced. One of Ruth Hale's hatreds was the Wedding March, which she considered horrible for its music as well as for its silliness. She understood that its omission had been agreed upon. Now the official ceremony turned out to be more ostentatious than she had remembered.

In the end, though, the conciliatory arguments of her brothers prevailed.

Both Ruth Hale and Broun made their share of the arrangements haphazardly. Actress Margaret Wycherly loaned her limousine and chauffeur for a last-minute dash to the City Hall for a license. Broun called up F. P. A. and asked him to be best man. Ruth Hale said that if she had to be given away, then Shelton, the elder of her brothers, might as well attend to it.

It had been raining, but the rain had stopped when the wedding party gathered at fashionable Saint Agnes' Episcopal Church on West 92nd Street. Most of the guests were journalists, among them Alexander Woollcott, Lucy Huffaker, and the *Tribune's* current managing editor, Garet Garrett. F. P. A. had gallantly come in formal attire, but Margaret Wycherly, pressed into service at the last moment as maid of honor, was wearing street clothes.

Honeymooning at the War

Broun was nervous and Ruth Hale was grim when the time came for the procession down the aisle. The little band started bravely forward. And then from the organ crashed the strains of the Wedding March. The smile on the face of Mrs. Broun held a touch of triumph.

The ranks wavered and broke as Ruth Hale came to a dead halt.

Broun pleaded, "Oh, let it slide this time."

"I will *not* let it slide," Ruth Hale answered.

But once more she conquered her feelings. The rest of the ceremony went off without a hitch. And then in the ancient humor of wedding congratulations someone used the bride's brand-new name.

"Hello, Mrs. Heywood Broun."

Ruth Hale swung around. "I am *not* Mrs. Heywood Broun!" she flung out. "I am Ruth Hale. Don't *ever* call me Mrs. Broun!"

Next day the honeymooners were aboard a French passenger ship snaking its way carefully through the mine fields protecting New York Harbor. Their cabin was comfortable, the bar was well stocked, and Broun found poker players worthy of his mettle. But serenity did not come easily in an atmosphere which might be shattered at any second by the crash of a submarine's torpedo.

One afternoon a French sailor dashed into the saloon, shouting and pointing downward. Even those who could not understand French had no trouble gathering his meaning. Climbing into life suits they had purchased, Broun and Ruth Hale rushed to the deck and joined a group of American nurses at the rail.

The ship's guns began to crash and out on the water the submarine's periscope was plainly visible. Broun found himself as badly frightened as he had expected. The nurses were cheering with each shot, however, and he managed to emulate them. After a little the periscope disappeared.

"It is dead," said the captain.

He added that a torpedo had missed the ship by only ninety feet, which sent new shivers through the passengers. Then came the inevitable rumors of submarine packs roving the near-by seas.

When time came to sit down to his typewriter, Broun eschewed drama for the light touch. "It was distinctly a home crowd," he wrote of the cheering nurses. "Nobody cheered for the submarine." He had picked up a humorous sidelight. "W. K. Vanderbilt did not put on a life preserver, nor did he leave his deck chair. He sat up just a bit and watched the whole affair tolerantly. After all, the submarine captain was a complete stranger to him."

The dispatch did not appear in the *Tribune* until several weeks after Broun had turned it over to the censor in France. It was his first taste of censor trouble.

In Paris the honeymooners found a modern apartment near the Luxembourg Gardens. Broun's credentials were delayed a few days. They took in the sights of the city and then Ruth Hale had to go to her job and Broun prepared for his.

Having learned at press headquarters that correspondents were supposed to wear the uniform of an officer, he set out to supply the need. No regulation garb being available, his travels finally brought him to the Galéries Lafayette, where one of the clerks could speak some English. From the back of a shelf she dragged a burnt sienna tunic not unlike a smock. After only a little search she found a size 48 Sam Browne belt. Next came riding pants and puttees of a composition approximately leather. She failed to sell him spurs and in the excitement a hat was forgotten. But on the way home he remembered that the head of a soldier should be covered and he dug his black felt hat out of the paper sack containing his civilian clothes. French military police kept stopping him. One finally explained that he was suspected of being a deserter from a labor battalion. Only the warm weather prevented the M. P.s from catching him in his fur coat.

On the first of July, under a big black byline, the *Tribune's* readers learned in a general way of the whereabouts of their former baseball writer and drama critic.

A FRENCH PORT, June 28 [delayed by censor]—The dawn was gray and so was the ship, but the eye picked her out of the mist because of two broad yellow stripes which ran the whole length of her upper decks. As the ship warped into the pier the stripes of yellow became so many layers in khaki, each motionless and each gazing toward the land.

It was the historic ship *Invicta* coming into Bologne Harbor to land the first troops of the A. E. F. on French soil.

The "Sammies" (George M. Cohan's "Over There" had not yet established "Yanks" as the popular designation) had to be quickly converted into light-touch copy, since the correspondent's role, as in all wars, was to create for the members of his team a set of characteristics pleasing to the folks back home. This called for a gay and carefree Sammy—ready and able, of course, to whip a dozen of the Kaiser's bullies. Broun distilled copy from crap shooting, difficulties with the language, and the joys of the Sammies in Gay Paree.

Broun's first trip to the front was in the British sector. In the high blue sky he saw the white buds of anti-aircraft fire blossom about a German plane. And then the party of correspondents stood enthralled while beyond the blossoms two planes engaged in mortal combat. The planes went higher and higher and finally chased each other out of sight before either could make a kill. Broun was struck by the fact that a day of clear beauty is the best for bloodshed.

The American troops settled into half a dozen villages in the Vosges for training. Quarters for the correspondents were at Neufchâtel in the Hotel Providence. The loose last step on the stairs had to be looked out for and the community bath at the end of a long hall was less than adequate. But there was a dining room. The only trouble was that Adèle, who served the tables in the morning, and Henriette, who replaced her at night, spoke only French.

On his first morning in the mess, Broun ran into Wythe Williams of the *New York Times*. Williams introduced Adèle, explained the mess rules, and gave a rough outline of what could be expected in the way of food.

"You can't go out and watch the Giants play here," Williams said, "but generally you can get ham and eggs."

Broun looked nostalgic at mention of the Giants, but he pressed Williams quickly toward a table. "Good," he said. "I can order ham and eggs in French. Does it take long for them to come?"

Williams said the service was fairly rapid.

"Give me," Broun said to Adèle, "some *oofs toute suite*, please."

She stared.

"Fried *oofs*," Broun said helpfully. "I happen to be in a hurry. *Oofs, toute suite*, thank you. And some *jambon*."

Williams grasped the situation. *"Oeufs,"* he explained to Adèle, swallowing the "f" skilfully. *"Oeufs avec jambon tout de suite."*

Henceforward the *Tribune's* man was Oofs Broun to the other correspondents.

It was a frightening moment for the correspondents when word reached the hotel that General Pershing, taking the simulated officers' rank seriously, proposed to review them. By this time Broun had secured a regulation, if not well-fitting, American uniform. But he was not the man to roll his leggings in neat spirals. By nature a snacker, he always filled his pockets with cans of food, which failed to improve the outline of his figure. His can opener and a spoon were carried in the pocket of his shirt. In the army he shaved even less than as a civilian.

He arrived only in time for the final call, but he dutifully joined the glum exit to the parade ground. Floyd Gibbons of the *Chicago Tribune,* big and handsome—he had not yet lost an eye—ranged himself up front as standard bearer. Back in Milwaukee, where he had worked on a Socialist paper, and later in Chicago, Gibbons had won a reputation for Bohemian dress. But he loved the military and now he was clad in tailored whipcord. Below Gibbons military attire and bearing fell off. Broun took a place at the foot of the line.

Ramrod-backed Pershing's gimlet eye missed nothing as he passed down the line. His visage became grim and at last was granite.

Broun was standing in a manner which he confused with attention when the martinet arrived before him. Pershing took a careful look and then stepped back for an even better one. He stepped forward again.

"What happened?" he demanded, his eyes blazing. "Did you fall down?"

Being by nature courteous, Broun threw back several quick salutes. They were nothing special from the military point of view, the fingers not being extended rigidly with thumb joined. It was obvious that Black Jack Pershing had seen better. He stalked away.

Broun never became an admirer of Pershing. He took more than journalistic pleasure in being the first to print the fact that not Pershing but Paymaster Stanton had made the famous remark, "Lafayette, we are here!"

With the American troops still training, Broun had ample opportunity to go into Paris. The big gamble was on. Ruth Hale was pregnant. But she was working hard, for her paper was understaffed. Sometimes she even went up to the front.

They journeyed out of Paris to visit Alexander Woollcott, who had arrived as a member of a medical unit. Broun, learning from one of the officers that Woollcott was to be promoted to sergeant, wrote a story using the advanced rank, only to be chagrined when the promotion was held up. Woollcott wangled a furlough to Paris for the Christmas holidays. Broun and Ruth Hale had a tree for him and at their apartment he met an officer who later got him transferred to the army's *Stars and Stripes*.

Woollcott wrote to a relative about his hosts: "I wish you would get to know her. She is a most tremendously fine person, and he, of course, is a dear."

Enjoying the excitement of Paris and stirred by the war, Ruth Hale grew irritated by the allocation of biological functions whereby the female carried the heavy load of childbearing. Once she keeled over in public. The restaurant in which she was eating with Broun and Lewis Gannett, a young pacifist who had gone over as a Quaker worker, was hot and close and the food was rich. Ruth Hale went outside for air and while pacing up and down she fainted. Broun was able to administer first aid, but when a doctor came Gannett had to be pressed into service as interpreter. Ruth Hale was angered by the humiliation of lying on the pavement amidst a crowd and at the same time she was sorry for the blushing young interpreter, relaying the doctor's delicate questions. At his apartment later they gave Gannett an armload of books, including one by a Viennese doctor named Sigmund Freud, whose theories Broun had been studying.

To avoid a tangle of red tape over citizenship, it was decided that Ruth Hale would return to United States soil to bear the child. Broun, wishing to be on hand for the event, asked and received permission to return also.

Another reason for Broun's desire to get away was severe distress caused by the censorship. Final decisions rested with the French, which meant delay. Worse, the French could not judge the mood of the Sammies, the correspondents, or the American public. Certain of the rules laid down by the United States Army made simple reporting difficult. For example, no soldier training for combat could be identified. For a while only General Pershing could be mentioned by name. Heavy shackles had been forged to hold the correspondents in line. In Washington the publishers had been required to post bonds guaranteeing the good behavior of their employees. The correspondents themselves had to sign a paper pledging themselves against any attempt to evade the censorship.

Lazy reporters found the gay-and-carefree-Sammy formula pleasant enough. Actually the Sammies were not very happy. They had been quartered at first in the homes of peasants. A bad thing about that was the French idea of a proper place for the manure pile—in the front yard. But the noncommissioned men were soon shoved into the barns. Kitchens were located in cowsheds, with neither the food nor the cooks of high quality. The only bathing place would be a tiny river that barely rated the title of creek. The Sammies griped. It was true, on the other hand, that the behavior of some of the soldiers was giving Americans a reputation for bad manners.

Broun wanted to write what he saw. At first he confined his protests to a special salute when handing copy to the head censor, Major Frederick Palmer, a famous correspondent of the Russo-Japanese War and other wars. The salute consisted of a wave of his hand from the forelock, accompanied by an ironical smile. He succeeded in getting through a few lines about an order forbidding purchase of champagne by men of the lower ranks, but little else.

Then, listening to one of his favorite raconteurs, Major General Bullard, a scarred veteran of the Philippines and many other conflicts, Broun heard a story that appeared to fit the censorship problem. The hero of the tale was a sturdy, home-loving Spanish peasant known for his piety. His wife shared these virtues. One bright and sunny morning wanderlust struck the peasant while he sat at the breakfast table.

"Never having been to Seville," he announced, "today I shall go."

The good woman agreed that a day's outing would do him good. But this usually devout man had forgotten something. "You mean," she prompted, "you're going to Seville, God willing!"

"No," he answered. "I simply mean that I'm going to Seville."

The woman was not surprised when heaven quickly showed its displeasure. Her husband had barely clapped on his hat and crossed the yard when he was changed into a bullfrog. A pond being near by, he hopped into it. He was the biggest and noisiest of the frogs and his wife was soon familiar with his voice. But on the first day of the second year, coming home from a call on a neighbor, she missed the big frog's loud croaking.

Just then out of the house came her husband, pushing his hat firmly down on his head. She thought to give him a wifely kiss of welcome, but he hurried by.

"I am on my way," he said, "to Seville."

"But, husband," she cried desperately, "you mean, God willing!"

Waving a fist above his head, the peasant thundered, "I'm going either to Seville or back to the frog pond!"

Broun was inclined to the view that a serious journalist who was barred from elemental freedom was better off in the frog pond.

He wrote a series on the war as he saw it and sent off the copy, thoughtfully ignoring the censor. As it happened, the arch-Republican *Tribune* was not satisfied with the way Democrat Woodrow Wilson was running things. The stories were printed. Broun teed off on General Pershing.

Nobody will ever call him "Papa" Pershing. He is stepfather to the inefficient and even when he is pleased he says little. In the matter of giving praise the General is a homeopath.

In regard to censorship, Broun declared that "a proper and intelligent public opinion in America should not tolerate" the rules. The censors seemed "to doubt the courage of the American people." He gave the glorification of Sammy the back of his hand, concluding that while the American soldier had the makings of a good fighter he was not the miracle man of report.

He charged bluntly that American troops had been held in back-of-the-line training too long and anyhow should have trained with the British instead of with the French, because the Tommies favored offensive warfare as opposed to French defensive tactics. High officers, he maintained, had failed to keep abreast of modern warfare.

In Black Jack Pershing's headquarters subordinates muttered of disciplinary measures and prepared a statement denouncing Broun. Pershing was ready to sign when Major Palmer intervened.

"Possibly," he said to the General, "Broun did not read the pledge." He pointed out that a denunciation might be taken by the public as retaliation for the Papa Pershing article.

Pershing tossed the paper aside. "To hell with it," he said.

Broun arrived in the United States early in January of 1918. Ruth Hale had come earlier. The *Tribune* kept up its fire on the Wilson administration and Broun, though back on theater, furnished little chunks of ridicule, usually served up in boxes. The brass hats in Washington were on the alert to catch him slipping.

They did. On March 16 a story by Broun told of eighteen major generals assigned to the same ship, twelve of whom had given the sailing time in confirming their sailing orders.

The story at so late a date would have revealed nothing to the enemy. The trouble was that it was not true. Broun's source had been faulty. The War Department pounced on the bond which the *Tribune* had put up.

The affair worried Broun but little, since the political wrestling was apparent. Besides, book publishers were knocking at his door. He wrote *AEF* and a short time later *Our Army at the Front*. He enjoyed the new experience of appearing between covers and the books sold fairly well.

8

A Columnist Is Born

ONE day in the spring of 1919 Broun was dawdling about the high-ceilinged living room of his old-fashioned apartment at Seventh Avenue and 55th Street. Even the fact that Rudyard Kipling had once dwelt in the same rooms was no boon to inspiration. Neither for the moment was a small Shetland terrier named Michael, who was, as usual, angry about something.

Finally Broun sat down, rolled a sheet of copy paper into his typewriter, and hung his big forefingers over the keys. Slowness of inspiration may have been the result of fatigue. The day before he had been to the country looking at farm-houses with an eye to purchasing one.

The subject pressing at the moment was books. A few months earlier he had become literary as well as drama editor of the *Tribune*. Instead of confining his reports to the regular Saturday book department, he had received permission to run a three-times-a-week column. Broun never ostentatiously counted his "firsts" in journalism, but he later did sound a small note of pride at having fathered the daily book column. In the space, headed simply "Books," he chatted about the new offerings, including those presented in full-dress reviews in the Saturday section. Sometimes a commen-

tary ran in little pieces for weeks, with readers helping out
with letters. The innovation lightened the work and proved
more popular than the straight reviews.

Ruth Hale parted the heavy curtains at the entrance to the
long dark hallway and came into the living room. She was
dressed for the street. The hem of her gray suit skirt was six
inches from the floor, in the newest fashion. Broun noticed.

"You'll do all right," he said, "with your ankles. How's the
baby?"

"He's asleep. Remember, you're to take him for a ride in
his buggy. The nurse isn't feeling well again."

"I won't forget. But right now I've got to have an idea."

She shook her head. "I gave you half your last column.
What's in the mail?"

He shrugged toward the unopened stack and hung his fingers over the typewriter again. "I've got to have a thousand
words."

"Just fill it up. You're not so particular." Her tone was
half bantering, half serious. She charged him with laziness
and sometimes with lack of courage. But when his work was
good, she said so. He liked having a competent critic close at
hand.

She picked up the letters and commenced to rip them
open.

Broun lit a cigarette, took his usual half a dozen puffs, and
ground it out. "You think I could skip books altogether and
get away with it?"

"Why not? Here's something from Murdock Pemberton
about a luncheon next week." She tossed it toward him and
started for the door. "Do you want to go?"

Broun began to strike the keys. "Sure." His fingers were
getting the rhythm. Michael, the dog, and the house-hunting
trip to the country were being pressed into service.

It began as "a farm," but even before the catalogue arrived it was "the farm." Now we call it "our farm," although the land is still in Spain abutting on the castle. Chiefly, the place is for Michael. The back yard is much too small for him, and too formal. He regards the house with affection, no doubt, but with none of that respect which he has for the back yard.

When the thousand words were on paper he stopped.

A few days later, no objection having been filed by either editors or readers, he was tempted again. This time he was in the office upstairs from the *Tribune's* city room which had been allotted him. Across the way at the *Sun* he could see columnist Don Marquis fiddling around *his* office, trying to force himself to his typewriter. Marquis wrote animal fables. F. P. A. had his "Diary." Finley Peter Dunne had Mr. Dooley. Broun sat down and thumped the keys.

This time the subject was identified cryptically as one "H. the 3d." Discerning readers had no trouble in gathering that the small subject, just learning to say words, was the columnist's son, whose full title would likely be Heywood Broun III. The father was discussing a book which argued against baby talk in bringing up children. It was his point, backed up with examples furnished by H. the 3d, that babies themselves often insist on baby talk. Another character was identified only as R.

Off and on since the first review of Lopokova, Broun had been peeking around the type at his readers. Now he had come out for full, if brief, appearances. In the past the writers of the old-time columns even when being personal had employed a heavy overlay of cuteness. Broun's stuff came out fresh.

The *Tribune's* managing editor called Broun into his

office. "Heywood," he said, "those casual pieces of yours are better than your book reviews."

Thinking it over afterwards, Broun noticed the ambiguity of the remark. But while not exactly a compliment, it carried a certain amount of encouragement. Later he credited the somewhat vague statement with having changed his whole life. To his astonishment he found that it was possible to get paid for the simple task of writing about himself, his experiences, and his opinions.

He was fond of saying that indolence had sired Broun-the-essay-columnist. F. P. A. marked up the contributors' original copy and sent it to the typesetters. Broun copied letters sent to him in order to provide an illusion of working hard. But his output was actually terrific. Besides the book column—the title was extended to "Books and Things"—and play reviews he did a Sunday theater piece. He held himself on call (he also issued the call) for major sports events. The editor of the Sunday magazine section gave him special assignments. He directed assistants in both the theater and book departments. In addition he wrote for outside periodicals.

It was an auspicious time for a commentator on life and the arts to set up a booth in the market place. The postwar generation was beginning to stir, with the advance guard, the intellectuals, already on the way to the attack. F. Scott Fitzgerald's *This Side of Paradise,* with its first sweeping aside of the asbestos curtain to reveal flaming youth, was ready for the printer. "Right-thinking" people had only a few months of grace before Sinclair Lewis' *Main Street* would rip their protective smugness, while H. L. Mencken was practicing with his battle-ax in *Smart Set* for the day when the *American Mercury* war chariot would begin to roll. Meanwhile, Sigmund Freud's theories were being widely discussed.

No group was better equipped for glorious rebellion than the younger journalists of New York, and nowhere was the atmosphere more suitable. In the first place, with the fat rewards and standardization of Hollywood and radio in the future, the best talent had descended on New York newspapers and magazines. Many writers had had just enough association with the Bohemianism of Greenwich Village to give them a headstart in the revolt against Puritan restrictions. Nearly all had been away to the war, with a better chance than most to taste the sweet delights of uninhibited Paris.

There would never be another war, everybody knew. It was a time to be carefree, to live. Let the bluenoses try to force temperance by law and suppress books and curb plays. Iconoclasm was more fun. And so the Algonquin Round Table, or something like it, was inevitable.

The beginning of the Round Table was happenstance.

One day Murdock Pemberton and John Peter Toohey took Alexander Woollcott, back from the war to his old job as drama critic for the *Times,* to lunch. Pemberton still handled publicity for the Hippodrome. Toohey, a large, bumbling Irishman who did the same for producer George Tyler, had an anecdote about Eugene O'Neill, now risen to Broadway state, that he felt sure Woollcott would be able to use. Press agents always try to bring nuggets to trade for notices, and Woollcott was especially careful of the rate of exchange. Since the *Times* critic liked rich foods, especially pastries, they took him to the Algonquin, a small, neat hotel on 44th Street, a few doors east of Sixth Avenue, which served a deep-dish apple pie. In addition there was something of a theatrical atmosphere. Frank Case, the proprietor, a handsome, gracious host in the old tradition, once had managed the Lambs' Club, and the Barrymores and others of the stage had followed him to the Algonquin.

Case led the party to a quiet table in a corner and Toohey launched his story of O'Neill—how the playwright had once been shanghaied to sea by his father to get him out of the way until a scrape could be resolved. He was forced to proceed under difficulties. Woollcott's career as correspondent for *Stars and Stripes* had been (in the words of Samuel Hopkins Adams, his biographer) one long whoop of glory. And so he insisted on taking up most of the luncheon time regaling his hosts with tales of his adventures.

Press agents are tolerant of the ego of a man in control of space for printed words, but there is a limit. Pemberton after returning to his office found that Woollcott's self-glorification still rankled. Recalling Toohey's suggestion that the old gang, recently home from war, get together, he slid a sheet of paper into his typewriter and ran up, in the form of a press release, an invitation for a luncheon the week following. Listed were addresses on many subjects related to the war, with all the speakers Alexander Woollcott.

Broun and Ruth Hale received this invitation. So did George Kaufman in the *Times* drama department and his wife Beatrice, a tall, attractive brunette from upstate New York; Jane Grant, back on the *Times;* Brock Pemberton, learning the producing business with Arthur Hopkins; F. P. A.; and Robert Benchley, on *Vanity Fair* after having broken-in as a humorist on the *Tribune.*

Friends could be brought along. Either Woollcott or Jane Grant, or both, were bound to bring Harold Ross, who was trying to continue the *Stars and Stripes* idea with *Home Sector.* Being a city hater—and looking the part—Ross had settled in New York only because he was courting Jane

Grant. Benchley was a member of *Vanity Fair's* unholy trinity, the other members being little Dorothy Parker, recently moved over from *Vogue,* and skyscraping Robert Sherwood, on his first editorial job while recovering from war wounds. The trinity generally moved as a unit.

Toohey and Pemberton, having respectively suggested and called the lunch, felt obligated to make a few preparations. Frank Case agreed to place some tables together (the round table did not come until later). They hung up bunting and flags to fit Woollcott's mood, and Pemberton had the Hippodrome's sign painters work out a splashy number reading AWOL-COTT—a somewhat vague suggestion that Woollcott's return to the army would be appreciated.

No roll was called at that first meeting, and memories can hardly be exact for what seemed an unimportant event three decades ago. Certainly Broun and Ruth Hale attended, besides Woollcott, Toohey, and Murdock Pemberton, and the total was in the neighborhood of ten or a dozen. Broun had brought along a pun for the occasion, but neither he nor anyone else got far with individual talk until the question most frequently heard in drinking places all over the land was put to Frank Case.

Toohey made it formal. "Frank, are the bars really going out of business on the first of July?"

And Case gave the answer that public hosts were giving all over America. "It is the law."

Growls and gnashings of teeth followed, as everywhere.

Case folded his arms solemnly across his stomach. "Do you want to scoff the law?"

They did.

The pun which Broun had carried to the meeting was typical. It began, "Does anyone here know the true facts about Mrs. Reid's cast-iron fence?" There followed a gracious pause in case anyone happened to know about Mrs. Reid's cast-iron fence and cared to divulge his knowledge. After that, by slow stages, amidst heckling, the information was revealed that the *Tribune* desperately wanted money from Whitelaw Reid's fortune, while his widow was more interested in the construction of a formidable fence around her country estate.

"Millions for de fence," finally came the tag line, "but not one cent for *Tribune!*"

But it was Ruth Hale who carried off honors for the Broun-Hale household. She announced her intention of being psychoanalyzed.

That Ruth Hale had decided to accept the advice of any kind of doctor was news. She had dealt roughly with a vast accumulation of cures that Broun had laid in over the years. But with others of the *avant-garde* she was attracted to psychoanalysis. Since the baby's birth she had been ailing more than usual. It was not so much physical pain as a greater mental restlessness. She watched like a hawk over the child—blond and gray-eyed like herself—and was sometimes not even ashamed of being caught practicing the little affections of a doting mother.

But the wise old heads in the smatterings of the new mental healing nodded and spoke knowingly of Woman's Protest.

In his column Broun continued to block out a style of commentary. His literary tastes were broad. For reading pleasure he rather liked his novels sentimental and, if possible, short. Some thought the word fluffy more suitable. "Anybody who is not already in the middle of a book," he once insisted, "ought to lose no time in beginning W. H. Hudson's *Far Away and Long Ago*." It was a full-blown mass of nostalgia. He was fond of the romantic novels of Leonard Merrick, especially *The Worldlings* and *Conrad in Quest of His Youth.*

James Branch Cabell's *Jurgen* was a double-barreled godsend. He approved it for the symbols which the moderns thought charted the path of life. Suppression of the book at the behest of the moralists, who thought the symbols too sexual, provided an exciting, not to say titillating, cause. Broun rode gaily into battle. It happened that he pressed into service H. 3d (he had dropped the "the"), noting that any child could be expected to cry when living in a state that had banned *Jurgen.* A sharp note from John S. Sumner, successor to Anthony Comstock as master of the vice chase, inquired whether the columnist wished his son's mind to be molded by such a book. Broun said that he certainly hoped his son's mind would be. "We mean to have as little to do with the morals of H. 3d as possible. Let the child go out and find its own morals."

Broun was beginning to outline his program, or lack of it, for raising his child. Both he and Ruth Hale were enamored of the new progressive-school methods, which held that a child is best taught by experience, hit or miss. The shake was to be fair all round. H. 3d was urged—through the pages of the *Tribune*—not to make the Fifth Commandment his favorite. "Whenever he feels that he simply must honor his parents we hope that he will do it in an underhand way behind our backs. Although we hope never to spank him, he will be running a great risk if he makes his honoring frank and flagrant."

At the literary supper Broun had no intention of subsisting on meringue alone. He fully intended to fill up on the meat and potatoes of realism. Some of the helpings, it was true, had not been cooked long enough for his taste. When

F. Scott Fitzgerald's *This Side of Paradise* reached a panting public in the spring of 1920, Broun suggested that the publisher may have used overstatement in giving the author's age as twenty-three. He employed the adjectives callow and silly, called the young men of the book "male flappers," and labeled Fitzgerald "a rather complacent, somewhat pretentious, and altogether self-conscious young man."

The ancient Broun, thirty-one years old, could not be expected to join the League of Sad Young Men. Besides, the manic gaiety of the Algonquin crowd was ever a match for the manic depression of the literati of "The Lost Generation."

The *Tribune's* book columnist found himself sorely belabored by scores of his readers, some of whom, he said, planned to read Fitzgerald's book as a revenge on its detractor. But he stood his ground, not even granting the merit of good writing. "We fail to catch the glint in it of greatness not yet fully attained but on the way." In a kinder moment, though, he found the style "larded with fine writing," and suggested that with greater simplicity the young man had possibilities of going far.

Broun found evidences of immaturity, too, in the plays of Eugene O'Neill. He was irritated by the lad in "Beyond the Horizon" who yearned to visit the far places of the world but remained to drudge on a hillside farm until finally cut down by tuberculosis. "It is time," Broun wrote, "that playwrights realized that the most moving tragedies are those in which people go on living."

Sinclair Lewis' *Main Street,* on the other hand, got Broun's immediate and hearty approval. Besides its attack on smugness, he liked Lewis' handling of dialogue, and especially he praised the thoroughness with which the subject matter had been investigated. *"Main Street* is almost disconcertingly good," he wrote. "It will be a good many weeks, and perhaps months, before I can sit down again to the easy task of turning out copy around the familiar formula of wailing about the failure of American novelists to open their eyes."

At the same time Broun was gathering pay-dirt dislikes of individuals. The Reverend John Roach Straton, the fierce, gaunt fundamentalist who weekly wrestled the devil in the pulpit of sprawling, dingy Calvary Baptist Church on West 57th Street, served him well. After a night of forcing himself through Gotham's fleshpots, Dr. Straton had found New York to be "a feverish, unbrotherly, Sabbath-desecrating, God-defying, woman-despising, lawbreaking, gluttonous monster without ideals or restraint." Doom plainly awaited the city of lust.

Broun was sure that when departing the stricken metropolis Dr. Straton would chance being turned, like Lot's wife, into a pillar of salt for a backward look to see whether his name had been mentioned in the special five-star annihilation extras as having foretold the disaster. The city failed to tumble down, but Dr. Straton gave Broun his chance to stand forth as a religious commentator.

Nicholas Murray Butler was another antagonist. The prize intellectual of the Republicans wrote a whole book without managing to put in a single thing with which the *Tribune* critic could agree. Broun was taking liberties with the policies of the arch-Republican *Tribune*. To that newspaper Dr. Butler was nearly a saint, and, even if Dr. Straton happened to be somewhat gauche, newspapers were not in the habit of assigning writers to quarrel with ministers of the gospel. Broun went farther. He deprecated the ouster of five Socialists from the New York legislature, showed sympathy with imprisoned Eugene V. Debs, and protested Attorney General A. Mitchell Palmer's great Red Scare. Once he noted that it was the God-given right of every newspaper in America to have at least one page where "it may be chuckleheaded in its own particular way."

He was laying the groundwork for his major journalistic invention—the modern column of opinion which is sometimes at odds with the editorial policy of the newspaper in which it appears.

9

A Seat on the *World*

Broun mixed a pitcher of orange blossoms—bathtub gin and orange juice—and passed with it among the guests in his living room. Present beside himself and Ruth Hale were Harold Ross and Jane Grant and Oscar Bernstein and Rebecca Drucker. To have addressed them as Mr. and Mrs. Harold Ross and Mr. and Mrs. Oscar Bernstein would have been nearly as grave a social error as to speak of the host and hostess as Mr. and Mrs. Heywood Broun. The ardor of the Women's Righters had by no means been satisfied with the ratification a year before, in 1920, of the Woman's Suffrage amendment. They were now insisting vociferously on the retention of their maiden names.

Ruth Hale was, of course, the front fighter of this women's army. It was not long before that she had applied for a passport as Ruth Hale. The State Department, after some skirmishing, had agreed to issue one to "Mrs. Heywood Broun, otherwise known as Ruth Hale." She had said to hell with that. The trip had been canceled. The nearest thing to a concrete gain was the Waldorf Astoria's agreement to the registration of "Heywood Broun and Ruth Hale, his wife."

Broun was sympathetic with the aims of the women's struggle. Harold Ross had no exact position except irrita-

103

tion. He was nevertheless the father—a somewhat surprised parent, to be sure—of the Lucy Stone League. Because of the postwar housing shortage he and Jane Grant had lived, following their marriage, with Broun and Ruth Hale. That had resulted in a vast amount of talk around the house of Women's Rights, and especially the right to use maiden names.

"Aw, Christ!" Ross had exploded, finally. "Why don't you people hire a hall?"

The advice had been acted upon. At any rate they had decided to organize. On this early spring night of 1921, however, the conversation had been steered away from the woman's yoke of bearing her husband's name. Oscar Bernstein, husband of Becky Drucker (she was now Broun's assistant on the *Tribune* drama desk), had, since he was a lawyer, been asked to inquire into what legal details would be involved in the purchase of the three-story brownstone house at 333 West 85th Street, Manhattan. Ruth Hale had looked it over— Broun hadn't quite managed to keep the inspection date— with approval. It had the advantage of a floor for each member of the family.

Bernstein riffled his notes and began. "The first mortgage is for ten thousand dollars." He then proceeded into details about the mortgage holder, interest, and allied subjects.

Broun listened conscientiously, sipping his orange blossom.

Shifting the pages, Bernstein continued, "Now, for the second mortgage. It's for three thousand dollars. The holder ——"

Broun's eyes widened and his jaw dropped a little. Ross settled more comfortably in his chair to watch the show.

"The third mortgage," Bernstein went on, reading industriously, "as it happens is a little one. Only a thousand. Held by ——"

The fact that mortgages had something to do with real estate was not entirely news to Broun. But he had never confronted a mortgage head on. An expression of acute pain flashed across his face. He swung the pitcher of orange blossoms moodily and freshened his drink.

Bernstein started a new page. "This is a rather exceptional case, but since the third mortgage was small, there's a fourth. It's——"

Broun leaned forward, his face troubled. "Oscar," he said, "I've got just a thousand dollars cash. Could I get into that house on a thousand dollars?"

Bernstein glanced up from his notes. "As it happens, you can."

The clouds swept from Broun's face and he hauled himself to his feet and moved around the room with the pitcher of orange blossoms.

The fact that he had the thousand dollars ahead was owing to a run of good luck at poker. The stakes were getting higher at the sessions of "The Game," now becoming famous as "The Thanatopsis Literary and Inside Straight Club." They were not so high, however, as a kibitzer might have been led to believe. The final reckoning was always made at twenty-five cents on the dollar. After the war the game had been moved from Nini's in Paris to the homes of players, and later to the Algonquin. The first half of the title was taken from the Thanatopsis Club of Sinclair Lewis' *Main Street*.

The Lucy Stoners held their formal organizational meeting at the Hotel Pennsylvania on May 18. For it Ruth Hale had chalked up another victory. A few days earlier the *Times* had noted, as a Women's Rights victory, the issuance of the deed for the house on 85th Street to "Heywood Broun and Ruth Hale, his wife."

The League started with fifty members. The ladies broad-mindedly granted membership to males, though only Broun and Francis Hackett, book critic for the *New Republic,* knocked immediately at the door. Ruth Hale was elected president and Jane Grant secretary-treasurer. Other officers were Beulah Livingstone, vice president; Mary Pickering, editor of the League bulletin; Mrs. Grace C. Oakley, publicity director; and Rose F. Bres, legal adviser.

To some people, reading newspaper accounts, the "Mrs." before the name of Grace Oakley appeared to be wrong, since the general supposition was that the militants insisted on being called "Miss." Either way was perfectly all right. The patron saint had used "Mrs. Lucy Stone." It was pointed out that after Sarah Bernhardt married she became "Madame Bernhardt."

Ruth Hale outlined the philosophy of the Lucy Stoners in a booklet published by the League.

We are repeatedly asked why we resent taking one man's name instead of another's—why, in other words, we object to taking a husband's name, when all we have anyhow is a father's name. Perhaps the shortest answer to that is that in the time since it was our father's name it has become our own—that between birth and marriage a human being has grown up, with all the emotions, thoughts, activities, etc., of any new person. Sometimes it is helpful to reverse an image we have too long looked on, as a painter might turn his canvas to a mirror to catch, by a new alignment, faults he might have overlooked from growing used to them.

I am born female of a legitimate marriage, we'll say, and my brother is born male. Each of us takes our father's name. My brother grows up and does his necessary work, and I, because of the times I live in, also grow up and do mine. By marriageable age, each of us has come into a certain sense of personal identity, with which our names are inextricably bound up. Each of us has taken that name originally from a man, but each of us has also gone on from there, into an individual development which has welded us to our names in our own right. What would any man answer if told that he should change his name when he married, because his original name was, after all, only his father's? Even aside from the fact that I am more truly described by the name of my father, whose flesh and blood I am, than I would be by that of my husband, who is merely co-worker with me—however loving—in a certain social enterprise, am I myself not to be counted for anything?

The Lucy Stoners were taunted, but they rallied to their banner five thousand women, nearly all of them highly articulate. More than just the right to retain maiden names legally and without embarrassment was won. The powerful counterattack against male chauvinism helped break a path for women in all fields. They wanted no coddling and especially they hated any effort to treat them as a weaker sex kept on pedestals by possessive males. Ruth Hale never charged more fiercely into battle than when the city lawmakers tried to forbid smoking by women in restaurants. She was disgusted with Broun's invariable courtliness toward women.

Zealots are necessary for a vanguard, and Ruth Hale was passionate about the total cause. But private considerations exaggerated her views. At the time of their marriage Broun and Ruth Hale had stood nearly equal in their careers. Now Broun was advancing, while Ruth Hale had lost time in childbirth. For a while she had gone back to theatrical press relations. But opportunity was lacking for self-expression. Yet long ago she had been convinced of her want of talent for painting, her first love. And her serious writing, because she was a perfectionist, turned out prolix and opaque in contrast to the crystal, easy flow of Broun's prose.

The bitter irony was that she had superb equipment for complementing Broun. As a reviewer of books and plays his judgment, based on feeling, often resulted in flashing insights. But it was sometimes uncertain. "I have never," he admitted, "been able to learn the reasons for my enthusiasms," adding that it was much easier for him to function as an ethical than as an artistic arbiter. Ruth Hale was a surer, better-grounded critic. Concerning people, Broun's understanding was quick and remarkable, but his charitable enhancement of the good while tending to ignore the bad often threw him off balance. Ruth Hale was a swift executioner of phonies—though not always waiting until all the evidence was in before throwing the switch.

She wrote reviews for Broun and sometimes furnished whole columns or magazine articles. There was additional irony in her ability to write with greater ease under his by-line. Her most valuable critical function, however, was accurate judgment of his work. He came to feel that Ruth Hale looked over his shoulder as he wrote.

As eloquent prophet of the iconoclastic modern causes—for which a broad postwar public waited—she was helpful to him. After all, she had been advocating greater sexual, political, and cultural freedom for a decade. By now she hit Puritanism like a hunter shooting a wooden duck. She took pot shots at manifestations of Puritanism in Broun (and herself) and in effect acted as a teacher and a goad.

Some people said that Broun was mostly Ruth Hale—that

without her he might have remained a sports writer. Aside from her service as critic and advocate, the view arose from the impression Broun gave of being easily influenced. The false impression rose from his method of quietly feeling his way along—plus a habit of fishing about until he received advice to do something he intended to do anyhow.

He liked also to have near by a strong person who would tell him *not* to do something he wanted *not* to do. The value of the outside negative increased with the demands on his time, which brought sharply to the surface a constitutional disinclination to say "no" directly. Thus Ruth Hale served him also as a buffer.

Broun recognized that his wife poured much of her energy into him in spite of a desperate need to maintain her own identity. He tried to help in other ways than just support of the Lucy Stone League. The magazine *Judge* carried a movie column under his signature. Broun went to the editors and "confessed" that Ruth Hale had been its author all along—therefore her byline ought to be substituted. Broun had been writing the column himself and only wanted to get a place of expression for Ruth Hale. The editors were not misled, since Broun was always careful to lie ineptly enough at least to arouse suspicion. But they acceded. It happened that Ruth Hale was scornful of movies, never went to any, and consequently her reports were rather nebulous.

As Broun's outline grew and his marriage partner's diminished, Ruth Hale occasionally talked of regaining her identity through a divorce. This was rejected ostensibly because of their son, but friends were aware of the strong if tortured bond that existed between husband and wife. And so Ruth Hale compensated in ever fiercer feminism. As more people classified her only the wife of Heywood Broun, her scorn for the name conferred on her by marriage increased. The cat bore the title Mrs. Heywood Broun. Telephone calls for Mrs. Heywood Broun were referred to Broun's mother. If an invitation was directed to Mr. and Mrs. Heywood Broun, Ruth Hale took the position that she had not been included. She had toyed with the idea that separate apartments would be a solution, though finally compromising on separate floors in a house. And she held increasingly important the old marriage compact whereby they had agreed to nearly unlimited personal freedom.

One day in the summer of 1921 Broun telephoned Herbert Bayard Swope at the *World*. From his early successes on the Rosenthal murder case the immaculate and dynamic Swope had pressed rapidly onward and upward. He had been with the Kaiser's armies during their first great victories, and after the war he had scored a big scoop by publishing the secret covenant of the League of Nations. Now the job of executive editor of the *Morning World* had been created for him.

"Mr. Swope," Broun said, "I would like to work for the *World*."

Swope asked why.

"I think," Broun said, "the *World* has more independence than the other papers. A writer might find more freedom of expression on your paper."

"Come on over and we'll talk some more," Swope said.

Joseph Pulitzer, founder of the New York *World* papers—morning, evening, and Sunday—had been dead for nearly a decade, but under his eldest son, Ralph, they maintained a crusading tone. Below the masthead in heavy type stood the elder Pulitzer's charge to

Always fight for progress and reform, never tolerate injustice or corruption, always fight demagogues of all parties, never belong to any party, always oppose privileged classes and public plunderers, never lack sympathy with the poor, always remain devoted to the public welfare, never be satisfied with merely printing news, always be drastically independent, never be afraid to attack wrong, whether by predatory plutocracy or predatory poverty.

Broun did not look upon himself as a flaming crusader. Except for his brushes with war censorship, his major exposure to danger had been in a suit brought by an actor named Geoffrey Steyne, one of whose performances Broun had called the worst he had ever seen. Steyne lost the case on the grounds that a critic's opinion didn't have to be either accurate or intelligent. Broun had further revenge. After Steyne's next performance Broun wrote that it was not up to his usual standard.

The atmosphere of the *Tribune* nevertheless was smothering. Worse, Broun's pay for being dramatic critic, book columnist, special sports reporter, occasional feature writer, and the man to whom editors casually handed a "make this funny" assignment was barely more than a hundred dollars a week. Broun was generous and careless with money after he got it, but he liked to get it.

In the ornate Pulitzer Building on Park Row, Swope was scratching his red head over ways to improve the *Morning World.* There was plenty of opportunity for experimentation with the news columns. The editorial page's director, Frank I. Cobb, was the greatest of his day and perhaps any other. But the page opposite could stand improvement. Except for drama, written by Louis De Foe, and a short double-column feature by James J. Montague entitled "More Truth than Poetry," it was a hodge-podge of death notices and news items. The page might make a fitting receptacle for wit, wisdom, and criticism.

Broun had a definite proposal in mind when he came for the appointment, but his personal approach was as diffident and notoriously roundabout as Swope's was confident and direct. "It seems to me . . ." was Broun's customary preface to a statement of opinion. Swope got above the normal allotment during the interview.

Finally Broun came to the point. "It seems to me," he said, "that it might be a good idea if I were to write about what I think, maybe in a column that appeared every day in the same place."

Swope thought the idea held merit and after other discussions a deal was made. Broun's Sunday theater piece in the *Tribune* had been captioned "As We Were Saying." Under it, however, he had often shifted to the singular "I." When time came to choose a title for the new column, Swope suggested Broun's favorite diffidence phrase. The two-decade run of "It Seems to Me" began in the *Morning World* of September 7, 1921.

The Twenties were beginning to roar in spite of a depression that caused unemployment for six million, banks to fail, and the bushy red eyebrows of a young man named John L. Lewis to draw down ominously as he pulled the coal miners out on strike. The Red Scare was petering out, but over the land columns of bed-sheeted men marched and burned fiery crosses and whipped helpless people. The *World* delved deep into the mire and came up with the first major exposé of the Ku Klux Klan. The paper also sent a crack reporter, Sam Spewack, to Boston to get the story of two immigrant Italians whose conviction of fatally shooting two men during a payroll stickup had resulted in a general strike in Uruguay, a mob threat to the United States Embassy in

Paris, and bomb explosions elsewhere. Spewack reported that the prisoners, a fish peddler named Bartolomeo Vanzetti and a shoemaker named Nicola Sacco, were anarchists and had opposed the war, and that there existed grounds for suspicion that the conviction had resulted from their political views. In a dark little office Spewack found three zealots—Frank Lopez, a Spanish carpenter; Eugene Lyons, a youth just out of Columbia University; and Aldion Felicani, a linotype operator—who were just as surprised as anyone else that the protest letters they had sent abroad had brought such repercussions.

Broun took some note of political and economic developments. He lambasted the K. K. K. and came out for the release of Debs. But he was more concerned with cultural affairs and the quickening tempo of the jazz age. Having overheard a young girl call her escort a "dumb bunny," he was willing to grant the existence of flappers, although unsure which had come first, the flapper or Scott Fitzgerald. Hair was being bobbed, skirts were climbing rapidly toward the knee, and even Macy's displayed cigar cases that turned out to be flasks. Broun ranged himself on the side of greater moral freedom—though unable to bring himself wholly to approve of the flapper—and began to celebrate the drinking of illicit booze. He managed to find some good even in the most notorious drinking party of the period, that at which Roscoe C. (Fatty) Arbuckle was accused of fatally injuring one Virginia Rappe while raping her. To Broun, Arbuckle had been a lumpish, vulgar comedian whose films could be done without.

Broun became more firmly aligned with the modern school of realists. In a single paragraph he summed up his criterion for a writer while paying respects to old Harvard men John Reed and Professor Copeland.

Copeland had a great deal to do with the making of John Reed. Copey did not know, and no one of us knew, that this humorous, light-hearted youngster would burn himself up in a fever [*sic*] of revolution. We believe only a few things which Reed believed. As a political economist he did not inspire admiration, but he stuck as closely to the creed which an artist ought to have as any man we have ever known. He wrote what he felt. Copey did not groan in vain for this pupil.

Under the heading "It Seems to Me" Broun as readily dropped back to the editorial plural as he had exchanged the plural for the singular in writing "As We Were Saying." Sherwood Anderson's *The Triumph of the Egg* led Broun to call him perhaps the most promising of American fiction writers. He saw the literary merit of Ring Lardner's humorous sports stories and ran interference for John Dos Passos' *Three Soldiers.* "Nothing," he wrote, "which has come out of the school of American realists has seemed to us so entirely honest. It represents deep convictions and impressions eloquently expressed." Dos Passos was under attack as a near seditionist because of his less than flattering portrait of an American army that had been described by four-minute orators as the final word in nobility.

The censorship battle was stepped up by both sides. Broun led, and, keeping his Puritanism well suppressed, came out in favor of a certain amount of what was considered immoral writing. He defended the use of obscene words so long as they added to the truth of a book or play—a personal sacrifice, owing to his embarrassment by obscenity, especially when women were present. Short Anglo-Saxon words were just becoming fashionable among ladies of sophistication.

Broun's article "Censoring the Censor" ranked as the

classic on the whole topic of police rule of the arts. "I always feel," Broun said of the censor, "that if he can stand it so can I." A solution was proposed.

> If we should choose our censors from fallible folks we might have proof instead of opinions. Suppose the censor of *Jurgen* had been someone other than Mr. Sumner, someone so unlike the head of the vice society that after reading Mr. Cabell's book he had come out of his room, not quivering with rage, but leering and wearing vine leaves. In such case the rest would be easy. It would merely be necessary to shadow the censor until he met his first dryad.

About Eugene O'Neill, Broun was still unable to wax enthusiastic. His conclusion that "The Hairy Ape" was both dull and untrue led to a vigorous exchange of the kind that spiced his column. Mike Gold, an editor of the radical *Liberator*—successor to the *Masses*—suggested that Broun get a rough job of work and learn about life on the bottom. Such a course, Broun felt, might lead to a demand by producers of the current spate of bedroom plays that he take a job in a boudoir. Seriously, he sorrowed that O'Neill had become a propagandist. "Once a man definitely takes sides he begins to see a little less of the world." Yet Broun was hurt by the charge that the jagged facts of life were unknown to him. His most effective recollection was the terrible heat of the *Tribune's* composing room, where as sports editor he had helped make up the pages.

The Lost Generation got no increased allotment of sympathy. When the iconoclastic creed, *Civilization in the United States,* a group of twenty articles edited by Harold E. Stearns, appeared, he observed the whole with a jaundiced eye and leapt with unusual ferocity on the section dealing with journalism. "At first hand," he wrote, "we know of very few newspaper abuses." He set down the *World* as every bit as courageous as the British *Manchester Guardian*, which John Macy, the article's author, had held up as a shining example. Macy had quoted Walter Lippmann in disparagement of American newspapers. Broun pointed out that Lippmann had recently moved from the *New Republic* to the *World* without noticeable change of opinion.

Feeling his oats, Broun made a prophecy in answer to Macy's declaration that journalism in America was no longer a profession of real dignity. "We hate to abandon our inveterate modesty, but if he will agree to stick around for about twenty-five years we intend to prove to him that his statement is not true."

The opportunity for making a start on fulfilling the boast was not long in coming. One day Broun came into the Pulitzer Building, took the freight elevator as usual to the city room, and began the preliminaries to writing his column. These consisted of gathering an armload of mail off the floor (his pigeonhole in the office rack was never able to hold it), dumping the mail on his heaped-over desk, and then wandering about talking before sitting down to clang out twelve to eighteen hundred words of copy.

Freddy Benham, a smart, gregarious reporter, helped Broun off with his coat. It was the old coonskin, now cut off just below the waist. Broun had done the cutting himself with a razor blade, without managing to get it very even.

"Freddy," Broun said, "I've quit smoking, but I need a cigarette to get me started. Could you borrow a couple, in case you haven't any?" Broun's idea of cutting out cigarettes was not to buy any.

Benham set off on the mission—a customary one—while Broun looked in on F. P. A. Adams had come to "Op. Ed.," a few months after Broun. The saturnine little man sat at his roll-top desk in the only private cubbyhole afforded a writer. He disliked being disturbed.

Broun hunted for Deems Taylor, "Op. Ed.'s" new music critic. He wasn't around. As Benham came back with the cigarettes, someone shouted to Broun that he was wanted on the telephone. He took it at a vacant desk.

The caller was Lewis Gannett at the *Nation.*

Gannett explained, "We've set up a journalists' union. We want you to be president."

Broun tucked the receiver in his shoulder and lit one of the cigarettes. "Who's in this union? I hadn't heard about it."

"Well," Gannett said, "the truth is, we don't have many members on the dailies yet. Most of us work on liberal magazines and the like. We think you're the only byline writer on a big paper who has the guts to be president."

Broun crushed the cigarette under his foot and blew smoke contemplatively at the ceiling. "I've got a contract with the *World,* you know. Would I have to go out on strike against that?"

"No," Gannett said, "we'd never ask you to do that."

"All right, I'll be president if you want me to be. I'll have to warn you, though, I'm not very good at attending meetings."

And so Broun was a union leader. He knew little about unions, and he never did get to a meeting.

In his column Broun was creating a broad-stroked portrait of himself for public display. He became drama critic as well as columnist.

Audiences were demanding a look at the rising young journalistic star and getting it. The National Association of Book Publishers invited him to its convention, he debated

Will Rogers and Arthur Somers Roche for the Lucy Stoners, and cultural groups came forward with offers of fees. He loved it, after a couple of bad moments directly before hauling himself to the rostrum. His personality came through as easily to audiences as to readers. The *Bookman* described him at the Wanamaker's Fiction Day.

> Charming flappers all about. . . . Contrast—from behind a rich, dark curtain there came John Farrar, lithe and agile, featherweight John Farrar, editor of the *Bookman,* and the looming, rolling figure of Heywood Broun. Mr. Broun wore a very negligee collar. While Mr. Farrar was introducing him he sat relaxed forward, his elbows on his knees, and smiled in a quaintly intimate way at the audience. . . . Looks like a mammoth elf. Ambled up and down as he talked. And, much of the time, clasped his jowls in his hands.

Broun's dishabille occasionally disturbed the stuffier members of his audience. One lady carried a protest to his mother, who promised to take up the matter with him.

"Heywood," she said, the next time they were together, "the buttons were off your shirt. Those women could see your chest and even some of your stomach when you bent over."

Broun recalled the shirt and the meeting. "Now, Mother," he protested, "they paid me fifteen dollars for that appearance. How much do those women expect to see for fifteen dollars?"

One thing public speaking did was to lengthen Broun's voice until it became a drawl. He found it easier to stretch his voice than to raise it.

Little H. 3d, one of the most popular features of "It Seems

to Me," continued to labor hard to put bread on the family table.

H. 3d, our 3-year-old son, has created for himself out of thin air somebody whom he can respect. The name of this character is Judge Krink, but generally he is more casually referred to as "The Judge." He lives, so we are informed, at some remote place called Fourace Hill. H. 3d says that Judge Krink is his best friend. He told us yesterday that he had written a letter to Judge Krink and had received one in reply.

"What did you say?" we asked.

"I said I was writing him a letter."

"What did he say?"

"Nothing."

This interchange of courtesies did not seem epoch making even in the life of a child, but we learned later just how extraordinarily important and useful Judge Krink had become to H. 3d. Cross-examination revealed the fact that Judge Krink has dirty hands which he never allows to be washed. Under no compulsion does he go to bed. Apparently he sits all day long in a garden, more democratically administered than any city park, digging dirt and putting it in a pail.

Candy Judge Krink eats very freely and without let or hindrance. In fact there is nothing forbidden to H. 3d which Judge Krink does not do with great gusto. Rules and prohibitions melt before the iron will and determination of the Judge. We suppose that when the artificial restrictions of a grown-up world bear too heavily upon H. 3d he finds consolation in the thought that somewhere in the world Judge Krink is doing all these things. We cannot get at Judge Krink and put him to bed or take away his trumpet. The Judge makes monkeys of all of us who seek to administer harsh laws in an unduly restricted world.

On the day before Christmas 1921 Broun printed his first Christmas story. He rarely went to church any more and he was inclined to reject organized religion altogether. To define God, he felt, was to limit Him. Broun's meditations had led him to something near deism, a belief that God was a part of each individual's spirit, a something which raises man above himself. In "The Fifty-first Dragon," Broun's best fable, a young student is a famous dragon killer so long as he has what he thinks is a magic word. Upon learning that the word is not really magic he becomes helpless and is killed. In other words, man requires a faith of some kind. The New Testament was Broun's favorite book and the life of Christ fascinated and moved him.

Broun's first story was of three wise kings of the East who, learning of the birth of a new king, had gathered rich gifts of gold and frankincense and myrrh. Two of the kings were quite old. The other was young. At the very last minute, as the laden camels swayed and snarled, the young king went into a room which he had not visited since childhood. From the room he brought a black-and-white dog of tin with a key in its side. When the key was turned the dog leaped high into the air and turned a somersault.

"What folly has seized you?" cried the eldest of the Wise Men. "Is this a gift to bear to the King of Kings in the far country?"

And the young man answered and said: "For the King of Kings there are gifts of great richness, gold and frankincense and myrrh.

"But this," he said, "is for the child in Bethlehem."

10

Life Among the Literati

BROUN wandered slowly around Columbus Circle. Dusk was settling over the city. Half a dozen street orators had set up for business. Broun listened to each long enough to catch his topic. He was gathering material. The prime task of a good reporter, he thought, was to listen—to the big, the little, and even the fantastic.

Finally he settled on a husky red-haired man with a powerful voice.

"Michael Collins," shouted the speaker, "was a shame to the Irish." His stepladder shook with the violence of his emotion. The colorful Irish revolutionist had recently been assassinated, presumably by followers of the more fiery Eamon de Valera. Broun edged to the front of the little circle of listeners.

"That's a lie," he said.

The speaker paused. "And just how is it a lie?"

Broun saw no need for debate. Besides, he was due at home for dinner. "The whole thing is a lie. You're a traitor to the revolution."

The Irishman came down the ladder a step. "For two cents," he said, "I'd knock your head off."

Broun dug into his pocket. Never a penny pincher, he

121

flung a handful of change into the orator's face. Then, as the enemy descended to the battleground, he assumed his fighting stance. He planned to lead with his right and cross with the dynamite left.

But there was no time for protection of the flanks and rear. Partisans of the orator tore Broun's coat, bloodied his nose, hit him in the eye, and rolled him on the pavement before departing rapidly ahead of the cops.

Broun hailed a cab, feeling good for having demonstrated no lack of courage. Tow-headed H. 3d was sitting on the curb watching some sparrows when his father alighted in front of the 85th Street house.

"What's the matter, Heywood?" H. 3d asked, registering little surprise at his father's appearance. He was a very sophisticated four-year-old.

Broun handed the cab driver a dollar. "Hello, Woodie," he said. "Where's Ruth?" The chemical-formula-like title "H. 3d" was all right for print, but for direct address Heywood had been shortened to Woodie. Use of H. 3d's full name would have added confusion, since he had been instructed to call his parents by their first names.

"She was writing on her typewriter a while ago," Woodie said.

They climbed the tall stone stoop to the main floor—Broun's floor. Entrance was through a vestibule into a large sitting room containing a few pieces of ancient and heavy walnut furniture, a grand piano (equipped to play mechanically), and a huge kidney-shaped desk. This room was seldom used except for parties. Broun's bedroom, separated from the other by great rolling doors, was his center of operations at home. He was coming more and more to work at home.

They threaded among the stacks of books, past Broun's

big bed and his working desk, into an alcove off which opened a bathroom and the stairway down to the kitchen.

"Would you mind calling Ruth?" Broun asked Woodie.

Wetting a towel in the bathroom, he held it to the growing mouse under his eye. It was going to be a big one. He wasn't especially interested in diminishing the size, but it provided a fine opportunity for self-doctoring.

He called down the stairs. "Mattie, would you bring me a drink and a piece of beefsteak?"

In a minute Mattie came up with a glass of gin and bitters, but no beefsteak. That order required fuller explanation. For all she knew he planned to eat a piece of steak and nothing else for dinner. Broun was dieting, and every day he came up with an original system. He was also exercising. Calisthenics were done to the strains of the player piano, Chopin being preferred. Then he would run around his private track, laid out through the stacks of books and the heavy old furniture in the sitting room. Sometimes he ran for as long as an hour with only a few rests.

Pixyish brown little Mattie's eyes were big with concern when she handed Broun the drink. Mattie was already taking over the running of the house. Not that she knew much about running a house. Soon after her employment as a maid she had taken some expensive pongee, intended, eventually, for a dress, and made a set of curtains. That had amused both Ruth Hale and Broun. They had raised her wages and more and more gave her her head. Neither ever complained, ever wanted to look at a bill, or to order anything special for a meal—unless, when he was dieting, Broun hit on something not in the house.

Broun propped the pillows on his bed and lowered himself against them. "It's all right, Mattie," he said. "I've just got to have a piece of raw beefsteak for my eye."

Ruth Hale came down, followed by Woodie.

"Come on, Woodie," Mattie said. "We've got to run to the butcher's."

Woodie turned and dashed through the front room, his spindly legs flying. "Meet you out front," he called back. The picture of cozy, doting intimacy with H. 3d pictured in his father's column was not precise. Broun often romped with Woodie, but the progressive idea of raising children opposed display of affection. The child was expected to find his own way, which meant that sometimes he was ignored by his parents, or treated as a grownup.

He had a healthy respect for his mother's spirit. Once when Broun was reading aloud from a funny paper containing a snarling lion he asked Woodie if he would be afraid of it. "Sure," Woodie said. "Even Ruth would be scared of a lion."

Woodie's fame did not entirely please him. At kindergarten a visitor had laid a kindly hand on his head and inquired whose little boy he was. "You know damned well whose little boy I am," he had replied, disgustedly.

Ruth Hale, dressed in a blue wrapper, stood arms akimbo, examining her wounded warrior. "How," she asked, "does your opponent look?"

Broun caressed his eye tenderly. "Well, there were a number of them. They look all right."

"What happened?" She sat on the chair at his desk.

Broun told of the encounter. Ruth Hale listened sympathetically.

Mattie came back with a pound of sirloin steak. She had been taught to buy the best. Broun lay back his head and applied the cold, fine-grained meat to the injured eye. He winced, and in a moment took the meat away.

"Where's Pacifist?" he asked.

Ruth Hale whistled, and a tailless, mild dog with curly

hair came down the stairs. Broun tossed the meat. Pacifist tried to catch, but it was too heavy. He picked it up and walked unenthusiastically back to the stairs.

Ruth Hale noticed a rip in Broun's coat. "Too bad," she said, "to ruin the suit that fits your new svelte figure so prettily."

Broun nodded. He was in a dressing-up period, besides dieting and exercising, and he liked to be teased about it. He also liked to tease Ruth Hale with implications that he was becoming a gay blade among the girls.

"Oh," he said, "I'm liked for myself."

"You're liked by the babes that snuggle up because being a theater critic you can give flattering notices. Otherwise they wouldn't give you a tumble. Anyhow, a Saint Agnes' boy like you would never do anything even if you got a direct offer."

Broun lit a cigarette and took a long, contented puff. "You might be surprised."

"No doubt of that. But go ahead. It would do you good." She felt sure that she was not jealous.

Mattie called up the stairs that dinner was ready.

Broun's column in the *World* was catching on sensationally. Carl Van Doren, writing for the *Century*, placed him at the top of the Manhattan wits, above columnists F. P. A., Don Marquis, and Christopher Morley, and gave a reason. It was the good fortune of Broun, a liberal, to flourish in an age when enlightenment was a literary fashion and conservatism, though powerful, was extraordinarily dull. Hearing that the article was to appear, Broun, demonstrating that fame was in no way unwelcome, surprised Van Doren by journeying to the office of the magazine to read it in proof. For *Vanity Fair's* Hall of Fame, to which he was nominated because of the humor with which he laced his penetrating comments, Broun furnished a photograph of himself with face almost slender and hair well combed.

Broun did not forget proper remuneration for his work, and now he was able to escape the distress of negotiation. His custom was to address the executive editor as either "Mr. Swope" or "Boss," partly in deference to Swope's forcefulness, partly in affectionate jest.

"Boss," Broun said, walking into Swope's office one day, "I wonder if you would talk with Morrie Ernst?"

Swope, guessing what was in the wind, agreed. Morris Ernst, active as attorney in the censorship fights, had been at Horace Mann with Broun and now represented him legally. Ernst had negotiated his client's salary up to $250 a week.

Book publishers were rushing to gather Broun's columns and magazine pieces between covers. Harcourt, Brace published *Seeing Things at Night* and George H. Doran issued *Pieces of Hate*. For the latter Broun wrote a semi-serious introduction.

> Speaking as a critic of books, we are not at all sure that we care to recommend it. It seems to us that the author is honest, but the value of that quality has been vastly overstressed in present-day reviewing. We are inclined to say, "What of it?" There would be nothing particularly persuasive if a man should approach a poker game and say, "Won't you let Broun in; I can assure you he's honest." Why should a recommendation which is taken for granted among common gamblers be considered flattering when applied to a writer? Anyhow, it does not seem to us that Broun carried honesty to an excess. . . . We are prepared to wager nothing on him until we are convinced that he has begun to drive for

something. He may be a young man but he is not so young that he can afford to traffic any further with flippness under the impression that it is something just as good as humor. And we wish he wouldn't pun.

The editorial sanctums of the town evidently had large signs on their walls: GET SOMETHING FROM BROUN. Because of his block against giving negative answers his commitments were fabulous. Wiser editors simply pushed him down to a typewriter and stood by until the required number of words were on paper. In a way, Broun had small pride of authorship. He never hesitated to turn an assignment over to someone else. He passed on the checks, but the editors wanted his byline. The contributions were not always even read by him.

Of Broun's imaginative work Christopher Morley, prefacing a collection in which he had included "The Fifty-first Dragon" had said that he "is likely, in the next ten or fifteen years, to do as fine work as any living American of his era." Broun's ambition had been to write a great novel, and now he hoped he could write one that would keep John S. Sumner restless until he had suppressed it. George Putnam gave Broun his opportunity. Ruth Hale had rented a cottage near Westport, Connecticut, for the summer of 1922 and during his vacation Broun sat down to prove that Morley's judgment was sound. The cottage lacked screens and plumbing. Broun, having refused to be drawn officially into the venture, complained bitterly of living on the edge of civilization, where cows bellowed ferociously all night.

The book would not, he claimed, be autobiographical. But by some coincidence the hero, Peter Neale, turned out to be a sports writer and war correspondent, and there was an attractive foreign girl, Maria, a dancer and singer, who got on a boat and left him high and dry. Friends did not hesitate to read Lopokova into the dancer's part—though obviously some of Marie Doro was present also. In the novel, however, Peter and Maria are married and a son is born to them shortly before she takes the outgoing boat.

H. 3d was required, of course, to step into the child's role. The best scenes are between father and son, as in the columns. As the boy grows older, though, Peter Neale is unable to remain close to him and eventually Rufus Twice, an editor of abundant self-confidence (the book was dedicated to Swope), has to lend a hand. The boy, after becoming acquainted with his mother, decides against journalism as a career and sets off for Europe to become a singer.

Critics were relatively kind to *The Boy Grew Older*. "Light and amusing," said the *Bookman*, ignoring the hero's anguish. John Sumner raised not a little finger in protest. Sales reached ten thousand copies, a fairly large figure for the day, and Broun saw no reason why he shouldn't take a few weeks off every year to write a novel.

Others of the Algonquin crowd were having successes. George S. Kaufman and Marc Connelly had gathered laurels with their play "Dulcy." Alexander Woollcott moved from the *Times* to Frank A. Munsey's *Herald* at a vast increase in salary. Robert Benchley's humorous books caught on and so did those of a newcomer to the group, balding, bespectacled young Donald Ogden Stewart. John Peter Toohey wrote a novel. Dark, good-looking Art Samuels became editor of *Life* and Harold Ross got the equivalent job at *Judge*. The wry, masochistic love poems of Dorothy Parker —she drew heavily on real experiences—were enchanting the new generation.

Social philosophers have given no complete explanation for the sudden flourishing of the Algonquin set, the exact like of which had not been seen before and has not been seen since. Time and place were undoubtedly factors. The spirit of confidence and freedom—even abandon—in the air had its effect. Had not youth just finished fighting a war to expiate the stupidity of their elders? Why, then, should it listen to strictures on morals or politics or religion? As the disarmament conferences seemed to bode the end of wars the atmosphere seemed to become free from danger.

New York was still the center of the paying arts. All newspapers now permitted the byline, and bright and witty writers readily found places for their work. An aspiring wit sent his contribution to *Vanity Fair, Life, Judge,* F. P. A.'s "Conning Tower," or wrote a letter to Heywood Broun instead of becoming, as in a later day, a gagman for a radio comedian or a press agent exchanging a wisecrack with a gossip columnist for mention of a client. Some of the contrivance had been driven out of the theater by the experimental groups, aided by critics like Woollcott and Broun, while the movies were not ready with high fees. Book publishers made money on relatively small sales and consequently gave opportunities to fresh talent.

Algonquin host Frank Case had long since provided an actual round table, along with free celery and olives. It paid off in the luncheon checks of the habitués and of the humble and dull who were content to sit in the outer darkness and watch the sophisticates being bright and gay. Popular concept of the Round Table was an intelligentsia discussing the arts in weighty and well-shaped sentences, with here and there a glistening comment on the times, or perhaps a personal thrust. Instead of becoming sedate, the group in fact grew more high-spirited and rowdy. It contained, after all, most of the rising masters of nonsense in the era of wonderful nonsense.

Horseplay got precedence, usually, over the subtle *mot* and the savored morsel of wisdom. When Dorothy Parker's lethal drama criticism caused Condé Nast, *Vanity Fair's* publisher, to fire her, the other members of the triumvirate, Benchley and Robert Sherwood, immediately handed in resignations. In their two-week period of notice they conducted a rough-house which allowed little work by anyone. They pinned little green chevrons like those worn by discharged veterans on their arms and set up a picket line. Occasionally others of the Algonquin set, including Broun, marched in sympathy—although Broun was already a mental hazard to the magazine, sharing as he did part time an office with the editor of "What the Well-Dressed Man Will Wear."

Benchley and Mrs. Parker, deciding to write plays, had rented a tiny triangular office. "One inch less of space," said Benchley, "would constitute adultery." The door bore the legend:

UTICA FORGE AND DROP TOOL COMPANY

Dorothy Parker, occasionally lonely, entertained the thought of having the sign changed to read simply MEN.

The horseplay was sometimes as broad as it could get. One afternoon Broun and F. P. A. escorted tall, peaches-and-cream Margaret Leech and Beatrice Kaufman, a striking brunette, to a speakeasy. As show girls flocked in, the Algonquin gentlemen pretended to be ashamed of their companions. They edged away, ignoring the ladies. As a capper they crawled under the table.

The conversation was nearly always strictly roughhouse. No rule existed against insulting persons not present, but advantage of the lack was seldom taken because of the greater sport of harassing someone within earshot. A cutting instrument did all right for a weapon so long as it was an ax. The rapier was too light unless poisoned, or plunged between the back ribs. Habitués found the warfare exhilarating. But guests were often upset. Some regulars, especially Woollcott, were not above striking an innocent person for fatuousness or a lesser crime.

Broun made an excellent conversational butt. He was ridden for his puns, his usually careless dress, his occasional attempts to become a Beau Brummel, the ease with which a four-letter word shocked him when uttered in the presence of ladies. For years Woollcott had made fun of what he considered Broun's lack of knowledge of the drama, as well as some of his critical opinions. While unfriendly criticism easily wounded Broun, the Algonquin kidding was unlikely to go far enough over the line to bother. Besides, his own wit was an efficient equalizer when he wanted to use it. As a rule his humor was gentle, somewhat like his boyhood placing of his friends in allegories.

Broun was a great gossip in a nonmalicious way. He had to know everything about his friends and acquaintances. At one party, for example, he sat on a sofa with a psychiatrist and pointed to one guest after another, most of them famous, and related the history of his or her favorite neurosis. He talked as freely about himself. For a while he had a motto: "Sieve and let sieve."

One evening Newman Levy, a young poet-attorney, who was a summer neighbor of Ruth Hale's and Broun's in Connecticut, became shocked by what seemed to him to be disparaging comments. Ruth Hale spoke even more cuttingly than Broun, since she held many of the Algonquin set in low esteem.

Levy inquired, "Don't you people ever speak well of your friends?"

They were sitting on a screened-in porch. Broun puffed his

cigarette in silence and gazed at the ceiling. Levy began to think he had committed a *faux pas*.

"Well," Broun said at last, "I've gone over the field and it does seem to me that George Kaufman has avoided any reprehensible act for a while. As things stand now I don't see any objection to saying a good word about George."

The Round Table served as a sort of Chamber of Commerce for the Regulars. Many a log was rolled and back-scratched there, according to the Table's detractors. Frank Ward O'Malley once asked of Case, "The boiler room of the hotel is right under the Round Table, isn't it?" The ambassador of nonsophisticates, O. O. McIntyre, battered the Table relentlessly, and Burton Rascoe, who had become book critic for the *Tribune*, secretly vowed its destruction.

Broun noted in rebuttal that his back was raw from F. P. A.'s scratches, inflicted in the course of a book review, but openly confessed having received a Christmas necktie—of obnoxious colors to be sure—from Woollcott. A day after a *Follies* opening, Marc Connelly rose at the Table and rapped for attention. "Shall we," he inquired, "let it run?" Harold Ross could never recall having heard a serious word spoken there. But the Round Table was a clearing house for ideas. Regulars were, after all, more or less friends. They maintained a herd loyalty, and in addition really liked each other's work. Flying wedges were naturally formed as needed.

The fame of the Thanatopsis Literary and Inside Straight Poker Club grew with that of the Round Table. Woollcott maintained that the proper name was the Young Man's Upper West Side Thanatopsis and Inside Straight Club. Every once in a while Woollcott, who claimed to have fathered the venture in Paris, became embittered over losses and decided to do away with the child. He went so far as to write its obituary for *Vanity Fair*, death having been caused, he said, by the resignations of himself, Broun, and Marc Connelly. Broun, unaware of his departure, took the funeral no more seriously than anyone else.

Broun's ferocity as a poker player was not diminished by the opinion of a psychoanalyst—he was trying analysis in an attempt to get rid of his fear of having a bad heart—that in the poker battles he was working off suppressed sadism. He came off well on the whole, for his great powers of intuition allowed him to play the hands of others. There was profit to be had, of course, for anybody thoughtful enough to bring specie for the cashing of any checks which Broun was forced to take among his winnings. He allowed a 15% discount. There was always a chance, he explained, that he would die before reaching a bank.

When losing Broun was a monumental bitcher and moaner. He cried out without restraint under the adverse blows of fate. When sorest pressed he was not beyond intimating that heaven itself had set itself against him. But a minute afterward he would crook a sheltering arm over his head and look up and apologize, "I was kidding, God." Observers were sure that he was at least half serious. He still unashamedly feared thunder.

Broun was more apt to show anger at cards than anywhere else. Once Marc Connelly, who couldn't himself resist calling for a showdown, got up a movement to call Broun at a critical moment. Everyone had dropped out except Broun and John Toohey and they were bidding strong.

"It is the consensus of the group," said Connelly, "that Toohey call."

Toohey did.

Broun, who had been bluffing, rose, threw down his cards, and in departing came as near to stamping as a customarily ambling man could stamp. Connelly, though he didn't know what had been in the hands, was not forgiven for a while.

Broun always had trouble leaving a table when behind, especially if at grips with Woollcott. Between the two existed a warm regard. Broun talked perhaps more intimately with Woollcott than with anyone besides Ruth Hale, though Woollcott often complained, as did others, that Broun held himself aloof and was impossible quite to know. Woollcott charged that if a bomb were to kill every other member of the Thanatopsis, Broun would look upon the catastrophe first of all as a fine newspaper story. There was an inevitable rivalry. Each corpulent, or on the verge of it, each building a reputation as a wit, was a candidate to be the G. K. Chesterton of America.

One chilly autumn night Broun and Woollcott tangled in an after-dinner game of hearts at Robert Sherwood's apartment. Broun was supposed to catch a midnight train at near-by Grand Central Station in order to cover a Cornell football game. He planned to leave Sherwood's in time to pick up his coonskin coat—a new one—at his 85th Street house. When time came to leave, Broun was $7.50 behind. He decided on one more hand. It failed to catch him up. An hour later he hurried coatless to Grand Central, barely in time to make his train.

The Thanatopsis, like the Round Table, was a place for sporting the wisecrack and the pun, many of them carefully hoarded for the perfect opening. In his *Vanity Fair* obituary Woollcott recorded a few, none exactly side-splitting when embalmed with cold ink. One rainy night when drinking prohibition wine Broun, raising his glass, remarked, "Any port in a storm." Again, offering to go for some wine, he declared, "I'd walk a mile for a Kummel." Kaufman was credited with first twisting "trey-deuced" and "ace-nine" into something resembling "traduced" and "asinine." Swope's majesty of manner was illustrated by his remark after a Rumanian prince had failed to observe the table rules to the letter. "Boy, the prince's cuffs and hat," Swope had shouted.

Ranking as a place for high jinks with the Round Table and Thanatopsis was Neysa McMein's big, shabby studio at 57 West 57th Street. A striking redhead from Quincy, Illinois, Miss McMein had achieved a celebrated salon by the simple process of leaving her studio door unlatched and going right on with her work—she did covers and illustrations for the big slick magazines—while guests entertained themselves. They felt equally at ease if she happened not to be at home. Late in the afternoon people began to drift in for conversation and other amusements. Sometimes dinner was ordered from the Alps restaurant downstairs. Or perhaps the whole body moved suddenly to someone else's house for dinner. The round figure for dinner guests was twenty-five, and host or hostess of the Round Table-Thanatopsis-Mc-Mein set was expected to be able to get it up in a hurry.

Broun picked up a brief description of the McMein salon's atmosphere from an overheard telephone conversation between John Toohey and his wife. "The inevitable," Toohey was saying with a heavy sigh, "has happened. A poker game is starting."

Other recreations included a form of charades wherein one player acted out a role while others guessed who or what. It was more or less officially known as "The Game," which resulted in confusion with the poker bouts. Another recreation was a sort of truth game, in one of which Broun got his feelings hurt. The participants were rated on sex appeal, females classifying the males by secret ballot and vice versa. Broun came off with a low score. For some hours he worked on an explanation, without forcing a reversal. A serious doubt existed that he had the makings of a really great lover.

He was disappointed, too, at the musical evenings. Jascha Heifetz, though turned down for the violin section, had made good as part-time pianist, sharing honors with Irving Berlin and Deems Taylor. Robert Benchley played the mandolin, Dorothy Parker the triangle. Broun offered to play these instruments or any other. His talents were rejected. But he was allowed occasionally to sing. By this time he had the drinking song down pat.

> The mist on the glass is congealing,
> 'Tis the hurricane's icy breath
> And it shows how the warmth of friendship
> Grows cold in the clasp of death.
>
> Stand, stand to your glasses steady
> And drink to your sweetheart's eyes . . .

And in "No Sirree," a sort of under-a-single-roof performance of the Round Table-Thanatopsis-McMein Studio set, Broun was the master of ceremonies. The show, in which Robert Benchley rendered his "Treasurer's Report" for the first time, played only one night—April 30, 1922—at the 49th Street Theater. Broun appeared first as "The Spirit of American Drama," supported by a chorus harboring Woollcott, Benchley, Toohey, Kaufman, Connelly, and F. P. A. Later on Toohey showed up as Coal-Barge Bessie, a retired water-front prostitute, in a take-off on Eugene O'Neill's plays. In Kaufman's satire on current melodramas, Jascha Heifetz was allowed to get into the act—or near it—with Offstage Music, while Neysa McMein, because her studio had been used for rehearsals, had a speaking line.

Hit singer turned out to be baritone Robert Sherwood.

The young ladies of his chorus—Tallulah Bankhead, June
Walker, Winifred Lenihan, Juliet St. John-Brenon, Mary
Kennedy, Ruth Fillmore, Lenore Ulric, Helen Hayes, and
Mary Brandon—backed him magnificently, it was conceded,
and the subject was neatly topical.

> We've got the blues, we've got the blues, we believe
> we said before we've got the blues.
> We are little flappers, never growing up,
> And we've all of us been flapping since Belasco was
> a pup.

> We've got the blues, we mean the blues, you're the
> first to hear the devastating news.
> We'd like to take a crack at playing Lady Macbeth,
> But we'll whisper girlish nothings with our dying
> breath.
> As far as we're concerned, there is no sting in death.
> We've got those everlasting ingénue blues.

Nearly everybody got into the show. Cast here and there
through other numbers were Brock and Murdock Pemberton, Dorothy Parker, Alice Duer Miller, Beatrice Kaufman,
Jane Grant, Harold Ross, Dave Wallace, J. M. Kerrigan,
Kelcey Allen, Arthur Bachrach, and Sidney Miller. To insure a friendy audience the performers had bought up all
the tickets and had given them to tested friends.

There was great fun among the literati in those days.

11

Man About Town

THE plan to buy a farm had never aroused Broun's complete enthusiasm despite its role in starting him off as a columnist. Ruth Hale was the mover in the farm hunt. She liked to get away to the country's quiet, while Broun needed the lights and the crowds—as long as they did not hem him in—and the ability, if he felt like it, to move from place to place. And to him the fierce cries of the cows at night were still irritating. He managed to find an excuse for not buying each farm inspected.

And so Ruth Hale finally, in 1923, bought a farm out of her own savings. The kind of people who till soil for a living would not have called it a farm. A large portion was trees and brush and swamp and an acre or so of the rest was a shallow lake. It was in Fairfield County, Connecticut, a few miles north of Stamford. Broun bestowed the name Hale Lake on the body of water and Ruth Hale thought up the name Sabine Farm for the whole operation, borrowing it from Horace, who had fixed it upon a farm retreat given to him by a patron.

The original farm had three houses set a couple of hundred yards apart. Ruth Hale purchased the two smaller ones, along with a portion of the total acreage. The houses were dilapidated and unadorned by modern plumbing. The down-stairs of the best of the two consisted of four small rooms. Ruth Hale gave Broun an ax.

"Here," she said. "It's time you learned how to break down walls."

Broun stripped to the waist and, swinging mightily, had a wonderful time. Ruth Hale thought the psychological effect was good.

Not much was done in the way of remodeling.

The independence of the partners in the marriage was becoming ever more firmly established. Since Broun hadn't come in on the farm, it was necessary for him to make special arrangements to visit or board. There was a tiny house, or shed, near the house. He desired a retreat and the smaller house was put at his disposal, giving rise to the story, relished at the Round Table, that Ruth Hale had rented a chicken coop to Broun.

"It is perfectly all right to have your mail sent here," she told him. "Just make sure that it's addressed to Sabine Farm or in care of Ruth Hale."

For *The Sun Field*, Broun's second novel, which appeared at this time, he had used for the heroine a militant feminist named Judith, patterned obviously after Ruth Hale. The address of one of the characters turned out to be 333 West 85th Street in New York, and the narrator, George Wallace, is a plump ex-sports writer with a bad heart. The author nevertheless proved himself no slave to real-life studies. Wallace is short of stature. The hero, a home-run king and Yankee outfielder named Tiny Tyler, marries Judith, who climbs life's ladder, becoming a famous novelist, as Tiny slides down the baseball chute. Tiny makes a comeback, though, winning his way to Congress on a speech doubting the existence of hell.

The story was vague to those unaware that Broun was kidding his wife and maybe Babe Ruth. Funniest parts deal with the rivalry between baseball players' wives—social standings rise and fall according to each day's achievements of the players on the diamond—and the doings inside an intellectual magazine's office. Broun turned the clock back to Walter Lippmann's days on the *New Republic* (designated as *Tomorrow*) for the latter purpose. People around the *World* had quickly noticed that Broun and his old classmate bore no love for each other, with jealousy seeming to loom as a chief factor.

Muses George Wallace, *The Sun Field's* narrator:

> Hugh Coler, the editor, always frightens me. He knows so much, so many facts I mean. We were in college together and even then it seemed to me that he was all finished. There wasn't room to put any more education on him. That is one of the things there ought to be a law about. A city ordinance or a federal statute should lay down the principle that nobody shall be educated above the 23d story.

In summer, Broun spent much of his time at Sabine Farm, liking it better than he had expected. For one thing, he could exercise with greater ease. His favorite method was to take a paper bag of golf balls, purchased at the dime store, to the edge of the lake and try to drive them across. Sometimes he was successful. The handy man got a nickel for every ball retrieved.

The Round Tablers came for week ends, prepared for roughing it. No plumbing having been installed, those unhampered by Puritan modesty waded naked into the lake to make their toilets. The method presented difficulties, for the dog days' heat often left the water unpleasant. Sometimes it was called "Halitosis Lake."

The cows did not go beyond their blood-curdling night cries, but greater dangers presented themselves. On the Fourth of July of 1924 Broun and Ruth Hale and Newman Levy and his wife returned from a play in Stamford to find a fiery cross burning about equidistant from their respective lodgings. Broun thought the cross was an answer to a slashing column he had written against the Ku Klux Klan. Always frightened before going into action, he sweated beyond the demand of the season. For his part, Levy couldn't help thinking that the burning cross was a warning to Jews to keep out.

Broun answered the fiery cross with a column stating that he would be alone at Sabine Farm at midnight of the following Saturday. Let the cowards come and get him.

"That may have been foolish," someone suggested at the Round Table. "They may really go there and beat you up."

"Let them!" Broun replied. "I'll be at the Algonquin playing poker."

But on Saturday night he was at Sabine Farm. The Klan did not ride.

A little later Ruth Hale caught Levy and another neighbor, Gilbert Gabriel, sneaking into her yard dragging a makeshift cross soaked with kerosene.

"Do you want to kill a man?" she demanded. "Don't you know Broun has a bad heart?"

They had only hoped to lie concealed and watch him at last charge out to face the foe.

Broun much preferred his role as Man about Manhattan to the bucolic life. Swope, wanting to confine him largely to reporting the metropolis for metropolitans, syndicated only his Sunday article. The five daily columns (he was off Monday) were concerned more than ever with the city's night life.

Lack of syndication did not, however, keep Broun from demanding his share of each reader's two pennies. (When the *World* boosted its price, Broun was at first in doubt as to his ability to write the three-cent column.) As contract time neared, the inevitable question, "Mr. Swope, would you mind talking with Morrie Ernst?" came, and following it the well-groomed, bow-tied, persuasive young lawyer himself, lugging his client's weighty demands. Broun's magical future salary figure was $30,000 a year. That much would surely, he felt, satisfy him. After three years on the *World* he had neared the halfway mark.

Salary increases were essential, for Broun was now picking up all night-club tabs which came within his reach between 5 P.M. and 5 A.M. Ernst, keeping an eye on his accounts, estimated that roughly twenty-five per cent of his income departed in this way. Broun didn't know. The disfiguration of a check stub was opposed by him as much from principle as from indolence. It seemed that, while wanting to be treated as worthy of his hire, he had an active dislike for money. Once Ruth Hale found a hundred-dollar bill in her yard. When Broun was asked to count his money to see whether he had lost it, he refused on the ground that he wouldn't be able to tell. Some speakeasy proprietors naturally took the opportunity to raise his checks by thirty dollars here, a hundred dollars there.

Broun loved the secretive atmosphere of the speakeasies. At Jack and Charlie's 21 Club he watched like a boy playing cops and robbers as the huge camouflaged door to the liquor closets swung open. The peepholes fascinated him, and he knew the passwords for scores of places, expensive and cheap, even if no word was needed for his own entrance.

Over the years he had several favorite speaks and night clubs. At Tony's, a rendezvous of the younger and generally impecunious crowd, he was more or less the patron saint. He liked the singing waiters at the rough-and-ready Totsy-Totsy club. When the gangster Diamond brothers got mixed up in a shooting fracas at the Totsy-Totsy, Broun and Ruth Hale went to bat for a young Italian violin player who, held as a material witness in a police station cell, was reported near a mental crack-up. Often, he wound up the evening at the Dizzy Club. An Egyptian named Marbardey, a backgammon wizard, ran a speakeasy where Broun liked to play. He was fond of Madeleine's, on West Fifteenth Street, and the Lounge, on Fifty-first.

With others of the speakeasy era he liked the sensation of battling for freedom—without much chance of getting hurt. And he was far from despising the attention accorded him as a celebrity. He was gracious in the matter of autographing the secret speakeasy cards and other paraphernalia of the period. His courtliness increased, as a matter of fact, with his fame.

One night two young ladies slightly the worse for prohibition gin came over to Broun's table. He rose and bowed.

"You Heywood Broun?" one of them demanded.

He bowed again. "Yes, madame."

The girl stood off a little and surveyed him. "God," she said, "what a disappointment!"

Broun replied solemnly, "I'm sorry, madame," bowed, and remained standing until the pair had flounced off.

Above all Broun loved the speakeasy's intimate, clublike atmosphere. Everybody now wanted to talk with the celebrated *World* columnist, and it was his pleasure to talk with people of all kinds. It was also good journalism. He captured the mood of the times. Raking in specific information, testing ideas, he often composed his column as he talked. He had a habit of sitting hunched forward, chair pushed back, looking at the table, for his shyness remained. As he made a point he would look up, smiling, and then he would frown and talk off into the room. Or he would stare contemplatively at the ceiling, emphasizing his words with lazy flaps of his cigarette hand.

Despite the wall Broun seemed to build around himself, people talked freely to him of their personal problems. He was always encouraging them to spread their wings, try something new, do better whatever they were doing. Criticism of neither books nor drama was pure with him. If a writer needed encouragement, Broun might play down or write around an adverse opinion. Never having held it wrong for a drama critic and actors to mingle, he talked out problems of all kinds with the people of the theater. He did not confine his help to a passing suggestion. Many were started or materially aided in their careers by Broun.

One day, for example, Broun saw George Bye, a *World* reporter, sitting moodily at his desk after returning from covering a New York-to-Rio flight. The journey had made Bye too big for little assignments and no big ones were in sight.

"Why don't you write a book about your trip?" Broun asked. "Come on, I'll take you to my publisher."

It happened that while George Palmer Putnam was not interested in the book idea, he needed someone to look after the literary-agency part of his business. Bye took the job, and in time became an agent in his own right, handling the output of, among many others, Heywood Broun.

Broun was responsible in part for launching Paul Robeson

as a singer. The Negro ex-All American football player had scored in the title role of Eugene O'Neill's play "The Emperor Jones." Many outstanding Negroes—among them James Weldon Johnson, Walter White, Jules Bledsoe, Rosalind Johnson, and Florence Mills, besides Robeson—went to the dinners and parties at the Broun-Hale house on 85th Street. The house had become, in its way, a salon, notable for the great New Year's parties, where at the stroke of midnight everybody jumped off the undertaker's folding chairs brought in to accommodate the unnumbered throng.

Robeson had special value as a guest because sometimes he was the only one who could get Woodie to go to bed. Robeson's most effective stratagem was to sit Woodie on his shoulder and sing, usually a spiritual or some other folk tune. Broun insisted that Robeson try his songs in public, and for Robeson's debut at the Provincetown Playhouse on MacDougal Street loudly beat the columnar drums to insure an overflow audience.

For a while Broun and Ruth Hale had hopes of making a singer out of Mattie, whose voice they had heard raised in the kitchen. She was sent to study with Richard Hale, now pursuing his career in New York. Mattie worked diligently at her lessons, practicing at the grand piano every day when not in the country. She had to be content, though, with a few one-night stands in clubs about the city. Broun encouraged the acting ambitions of his chauffeur—tall, handsome Earl Wilson, who married Mattie. Broun did not drive himself and really trusted no one except Earl—and Earl up to only thirty to forty miles an hour. Earl liked to go on the stage when he had a chance and he preferred traveling abroad as valet to Jascha Heifetz to chauffeuring. But Broun always hired him back after a separation.

Life was expanding for Broun and his set beyond the

bounds normally allowed by their growing incomes. The houses of the very rich were being opened to them. An Algonquin wit was a garnish for a great table. Broun had become a member of the Racquet Club and in summer he wore a club band around his straw hat. But when invited to one or another of the city's plush houses he did not go to the inner reaches of the club to consult on proper dress with Heywood Cox Broun, who as the Twenties began had moved gracefully into his own seventies. In his column Broun had now built a solid reputation for his suits as "the gray" and "the brown," while caricaturists and fellow paragraphers had assisted in making his name synonymous with careless attire. He therefore encouraged such stories as the one in which he journeyed to a big house on Park Avenue to play bridge and was shunted to the service entrance.

For a dinner party given by Mrs. William Randolph Hearst, Broun had to borrow a dinner suit from Ed Mc-Namara, the cop-become-singer who sometimes shared the top floor with Woodie. Besides a fine story teller, McNamara was celebrated for the enormous steaks which he broiled, caked in salt, at Broun-Hale parties. The dinner jacket was all right, for its size.

"You'll have a bellyband of naked skin," McNamara said.

Broun admitted the truth of the statement, should he stand straight. "I'll just stoop a little," he said. "And I'll hold my arm across my middle."

F. P. A. was invited to the party, too, but owing to cuff-link trouble, most of it in finding them, he was tardier than his Op. Ed. colleague. By the time F. P. A. got there, Broun, bending from the waist, had established a reputation for Old World courtliness. He was ensconced beside an attractive, dignified lady while listening to an orchestra play "Tales from the Vienna Woods."

F. P. A. made at once for the only member of his own herd in sight. Introductions would have to wait for a break in the music. F. P. A. leaned over Broun, keeping his voice under the music.

"Who's the babe?" he asked.

Broun was unaware that "Tales from the Vienna Woods" halts with a crash which emphasizes the ensuing silence. The blast and silence came just as Broun launched his answer.

"The babe," he said, "believe it or not, is Mrs. Vincent Astor."

The silence lasted longer than usual. Then a general laugh cleared the air and everybody was at ease.

The Algonquin crowd went sometimes to the country house of Otto Kahn, banker and patron of the arts. The *World's* publisher, Ralph Pulitzer, a reserved but pleasant man, was a frequent host to members of the set, and they went to other great estates. But the chief summer oasis was Swope's place at Great Neck on Long Island. Nearly every week end they gathered at the big old wooden house for cards, conversation, and croquet. Broun stuck generally to the first two. The district had furnished F. Scott Fitzgerald, who lived near by, with the setting for *The Great Gatsby.* Another neighbor, Ring Lardner, joined the gatherings, usually in silence, without disturbing the impression of his syndicated readers that Great Neck was either fictitious or hicky.

Broun was a regular at the social functions, but Ruth Hale usually preferred the quiet of Sabine Farm, or, if in the city, a night at a neighborhood speakeasy. She liked to hold forth separately from Broun. By now the Broun-Hale theory of independent lives was well publicized, and every once in a while someone ground out a whither-whither piece speculating that separate residences, with the husband calling up his wife for a date as he would anyone else, were the coming thing. Setting off for home at the end of an evening, Broun would inquire courteously, "Are you going my way?"

He liked to squire pretty girls to speakeasies and night clubs. In that day of considerable sex emancipation—and totally unrestrained talk about it—he went to some pains in an effort to establish a reputation as a Casanova, upon whose approach wise men locked their wives away. A young matron inquired of Woollcott whether he thought an affair with Broun would provide her with joys compensating for the dangers of adultery. "My dear," Woollcott replied, "I know of no other way in which a struggling young girl can get so much free publicity." Broun professed to be deeply wounded when a girl whom he often escorted was reported to be saying around town that she had not slept with him. At the same time he was fond of dropping hints of impotency. In this latter propaganda he succeeded at least as well as in the first.

Broun took pleasure in making Ruth Hale jealous—it having turned out that she did not take the fact of his affairs quite as coolly as she had advanced the theory. One of Broun's favorite tricks was to write a letter in code and leave it where Ruth Hale was bound to run across it. The breaking of the code was easy, but a waste of time. Though pouring out journalistic words by the gallon, he could squeeze out only a few for the mail. Since Ruth Hale's philosophy forbade objection—rather, obliged encouragement—her anger had to seek another outlet. She was reduced to making fun of the secrecy, or charging him with juvenility.

Occasionally the lady of the code was treated to a piece of Ruth Hale's mind. It had also to be sent roundabout.

Once in a powder room she cornered a code addressee, a beauty new to the modern set's frank talk.

"Now look!" Ruth Hale said. "This silly little Sunday-school affair you're carrying on is bad for my husband. Do the decent thing and get into bed with him. Hurry up!"

Broun was equally jealous. Every once in a while he would shadow his wife, even though he was not of a size or of catlike enough gait for successful tailing of suspects. Or he roamed Sabine Farm in the dead of night, keeping the house under surveillance.

A boyish causing of jealousy and suffering its pangs ran through nearly all of Broun's relations with women. His rare letters or notes almost invariably mentioned one or two female rivals, real or fancied. His deceits were arranged to be as easily penetrated as his other falsehoods. "I've got to go to a man's bachelor dinner," he wrote as an excuse for breaking a date. Once in half-seriously accusing a girl of having tried to rape or at least seduce Robert Benchley, Broun elicited a letter containing a handful of Algonquin-crowd atmosphere. Broun had quoted Dorothy Parker as his source. Since fluttery-eyed, sweet-syllabled Parker had a reputation for the deadly thrust in the back, the accused girl wrote to Benchley for vindicating evidence suitable for showing to Broun.

Benchley, who always went out of his way to patch up differences, thought that one of Dottie's admittedly matchless figures of speech had doubtless been a major contributing factor. At any rate he could remember neither any incident or any remark of his that he could imagine would have led to such a misunderstanding. Dottie was given to telling wonderful tales of assaults by various ladies on men of her acquaintance. But heretofore he had never been cast in the role of hero.

149

He would take up the matter later on, he continued somewhat helplessly. But he had doubts that anything would ever be cleared up. Nothing ever was cleared up.

Having contributed at least half the story, and never having believed any of it, Broun accepted Benchley's disclaimer with a show of magnanimity. Later Dorothy Parker helped to involve Broun in a fist fight which resulted in the usual damage to his person.

Broun's old boyhood neighbors Gerald and Joe Brooks were a couple of the socialites who sometimes hung out with the Algonquin crowd. Joe was the only man of Broun's acquaintance who could wear his shoes. Brooks had, however, been an All-American football player and his weight came entirely from bone and muscle. One afternoon in a speakeasy the girl Brooks was with became insulted over some remarks another man of the party made and insisted that Brooks avenge her. The offender was of small size and Brooks gave him only a slight and perfunctory chastisement. But Dorothy Parker, also present, insisted that Brooks pick on some one his own size. Heywood was the only one she could think of who fitted. The party broke up, but Dottie continued to brood. Broun thought she had a point and, though dressed for dinner, he decided to drop by his friend's house and fight him.

Brooks tried to get out of it. "You know I'm in shape, Heywood," he said. "I'll lick you."

Broun took off his dinner jacket and insisted on proceeding. Brooks finally removed his own dinner coat. The bout was short and as sweet as Brooks could make it and yet assure Broun that he had fought the good but hopeless fight.

At the end they shook hands and redonned dinner jackets, and Broun departed. After a little while he discovered that by mistake they had exchanged jackets. In one pocket he found an address book well filled with feminine names and numbers. He rejoined Dorothy Parker and they happily tore the leaves of the book to shreds, certain that many of the telephone numbers were unlisted and therefore hard to replace.

12

The Gay Twenties Pall

N O MATTER that he symbolized to tens of thousands the hedonism of the Twenties, Broun never quite accepted or fully enjoyed it. For one thing, being basically a moralist, he had to weigh the right and wrong of things. The only job easier than a columnist's, he always maintained, was a preacher's. Intellectually he was against Puritanism. But even with the aid of Ruth Hale's stinging whip he could not exorcise it completely from himself. He had doubts that so much abandon was really for the best.

In joining with H. L. Mencken and the other iconoclasts against the bluenoses, Broun had found little space for economic matters. For him the depression of the early Twenties had hardly existed. Senator Bob LaFollette's insurgent run for the Presidency in 1924 struck no spark. Broun was for the Democratic candidate, Cox, mainly because he disliked the personality of Calvin Coolidge. Yet Broun's intuition, his inbred ability to sense the feelings of masses of people, was too great for him not to realize that America below the surface was not as content as the orators liked to purr.

He had hoped, like everybody else, that success would bring peace of mind. When it didn't, he began to search more restlessly than ever for a feeling of secure well-being. At first he suffered a setback. His claustrophobia got worse. It became impossible for him to go regularly inside a theater or to stay for long, which meant that he had to give up drama criticism. Woollcott replaced him in that department on Op. Ed.

For periods Broun eschewed the speakeasies and holed up either at the 85th Street house or Sabine Farm. He had bought the remaining farmhouse and a few acres of land. Technically, his property was not a part of Sabine Farm, a fact which Ruth Hale wanted made clear. But most people lumped them together and the whole was known as Sabine Farm or simply Broun's place or Ruth Hale's place.

Heavy depression sometimes settled over him. Yet his mental torture never showed in his column. One morning after Frank Sullivan, whose column "Out of a Clear Sky" ran on Op. Ed., and others had spent a night at Sabine Farm, Ruth Hale asked Sullivan to take Broun's copy to New York with him. Broun, ill, had not emerged from his bedroom since their arrival. Just before the party had to leave he came out, face haggard and drawn. Sullivan thought he had never seen anyone suffering so deeply. Broun sat down at his typewriter and clattered out his column. It was a humorous gem, Sullivan found when he read it on the train, about a zoo that Woodie had.

The middle farmhouse was occupied by the Murdock Pembertons. After becoming an art critic, Murdock had taken up painting.

One day when Pemberton was at work on a canvas Broun stood watching for a long time.

"Do you think I could do that?" he finally asked.

"Why not? Anybody can paint, whether it's good or bad."

Broun went over to Ruth Hale's house after some equipment. She still painted, though not often. Her favorite work was a hideous gargoyle over the fireplace on her floor of the 85th Street house. In self-jeering moments she called it a portrait of her mind. Broun rummaged through the art paraphernalia and came away with a handful of brushes, half-squeezed tubes, and a limp piece of canvas.

The rock at the edge of the swamp behind Broun's house seemed to be a good place for an artist to work. It was not a big rock, and in truth belonged to a black snake who sometimes came out of the swamp to sun. Broun felt friendly toward the snake and he hoped the feeling was returned, anyway to the extent that use of the rock would not be resented.

Lying on his stomach, he hung the canvas over the edge of the rock and began to work. It happened that he was wearing, in addition to the sailor straw hat he favored around the farm, a pair of striped flannel trousers which in their day had been very formal. The pants got nearly as much of the paint as the canvas.

The first picture was not recognizable as anything, but in fairness to himself he took into account the fact that he had not had anything specific in mind. Nevertheless he enjoyed his debut. Besides, the smeared trousers denoted him as something of a professional. He decided to continue with the career.

In a fairly short time total strangers were able to identify such objects as buildings and the sea. Some of his most relaxed, pleasurable hours were spent lying on his stomach next to his canvas. There was another gain. Readers of "It Seems to Me" were allowed to watch his breathless progress.

My first nude sold the other day for a price which was not made public, but which is reported to have been

25 cents. Personally, I felt that it was a $3 picture; but a creative artist may be too indulgent with himself and since 25 cents was the offer I let it go.

In this case the profit was not great, although I do believe in quick and frequent sales. My biggest money-maker is "Tempest on a Wooded Coast." This has never fetched more than $2.35 but I have sold it four times already. There is a point in almost every party at my house in which somebody gets the notion that he wants to buy "Tempest on a Wooded Coast" and pay cash. But it seems to be the sort of picture men forget. When the purchaser goes he always leaves the painting behind him although it is quite dry. Whether this is second thought or inadvertence, I don't profess to know. I merely stick it back upon the shelf and wait for another buyer to come along.

Humor had the added quality of defense. Broun did not maintain even to himself that his painting was fine art. There was always a chance, of course, that in his painting natural talent flowed as in his writing. Jo Davidson noticed a good sense of color. But whether good or bad was not important. Painting was an emotional outlet.

The humor inserted into *Gandle Follows His Nose*, which Broun considered his most—or only—serious novel, was less fortunate, only throwing most readers off the track and not standing strong as humor alone. The little fairy tale was intended to be somber and even savage in its total impact. Broun set forth in *Gandle* much of his philosophy of life and some of his feelings about death.

The shepherd boy Gandle has skin white as a rabbit—for which fact was coined his nickname Bunny—and hair black as a dragon's belly. In the hills near the hut of his uncle range many dragons feared by Gandle. Fortunately dragons fear sheep. If hungry they are tempted to eat one and wool clogs their teeth. When attacked Gandle has only to put a sheep between himself and the dragon. Because of his lonely life—his uncle is an uncommonly taciturn man—Gandle has learned almost nothing of the world when, aged eighteen, he is thrust into the inner room of the great sorcerer Boaz.

Together they gaze into a crystal ball. Boaz permits the image of Gandle to travel each of two roads. Up the one road lie many dangers. The other reaches straight and smooth ahead. But it seems to Gandle that on the smooth road his shoulders swing less free. The cold hand of Boaz, a man of small mind, weighs heavy on his shoulder, too, and he knows that upon the smooth road it will remain there. Gandle feels the hand even after Boaz puts on a cap that makes him invisible.

Boaz is determined that his client shall take the smooth road, but Gandle escapes, seizing before he goes a magic cap, and chooses the road of danger. Almost at once he encounters a knight who cries out, "Agatha is the fairest in all the world," and then, no reply being vouchsafed, wounds Gandle in the shoulder. Gandle whimpers and nearly faints, but at last he rallies and seizes his tormentor's throat. The pain from his wound grows less, he notices, as his fingers close tight. A little farther along the road Gandle battles another knight with the slain warrior's sword. But not being angry he quits the struggle and goes on his way laughing.

Despite his choice of the fearsome road, his rally against terror, his ability to depart from a meaningless fight, Gandle's tests continue. Now Gandle finds a lamp. He is unaware that all old lamps found in forests bring forth genii when rubbed. In removing the rust he accidentally produces a genie by the name of Yom. This Yom is several cuts above genii as a class. He is of a size to sit on mountaintops and is a philosopher as well.

Upon Gandle's order Yom quicky brings a palace, a poached egg, a dog, and two sheep. But when Gandle wishes the fairest and most virtuous lady in all the world, Yom boggles. He refuses even to attempt to define virtue and, since Gandle is of no help, that requirement has to be set aside. Yom wishes to reminisce of a girl he had in Chaldea a thousand, maybe two thousand, years ago. Gandle is bored. Finally Gandle settles on the image of a girl high as his shoulder, with black hair, black brows, white skin, and a fine curve of breast and length of limb. Yom brings her, gratuitously supplying a red ribbon in memory of the girl in Chaldea.

Gandle bestows on his maiden the name Agatha. She obeys his every wish, but in time he misses in her the salt of dissent, as he is bored with the cold formality of the dog and the two sheep. A son, he thinks, might liven things up. Yom deferentially suggests a flesh-and-blood woman to mother a son. But Gandle, learning that such a child must come out of ugliness and agony, and would not at once be able to run with him across the fields, decides instead in favor of the lamp. The son, called Flame, is beautiful, but he too is without fervor.

In his boredom Gandle requests Agatha to sing for him. She sings of love. Although this love is obviously sometimes troublesome, Gandle at last demands love from Agatha. Sadly she relates that, being a figment of the lamp, love is not for her. Gandle, irritated, orders Yom to bring love to him. But Yom's stock of goods beyond the mountains does not include love. In anger Gandle hurls at Yom the first thing handy, which is the lamp. It falls short into a swift river. At once Agatha, Flame, and the animals disappear.

Before setting off to a quiet life of eating poached eggs, Yom assuages as best he can Gandle's despondency over the loss of the lamp.

> It's my belief that nobody ever got much good out of the lamp. Somehow none of them could think up many things to wish for. A girl, a palace, and a bag of gold and that's the end of it. Wanting things is fun. Getting them ruins your appetite.

Gandle must go forth now with no other protection than the slain warrior's sword and the invisible cap. A single item remains from Yom: the red ribbon of the girl in Chaldea.

One of Agatha's love songs had told how Damien, the Prince from the Purple Land, had clambered up a mountain of glass to slay the dragon Gorgas who held his love captive. Coming himself to a glass mountain upon which stands a castle, Gandle resolves to slay, if suitable conditions exist, a dragon and release a fair maiden who will of course fall in love with him.

Broun's use of humor at this point illustrates why the story could not be truly somber.

> Cupping his hands, Gandle shouted up toward the castle, "Have you a princess held in foul captivity?"
>
> At once the answer came roaring back. "Twenty fair princesses held in durance most vile and unspeakable."
>
> This was rather more than Gandle had bargained for and besides the voice quite evidently was that of a giant and not of a dragon. Dragons invariably pronounce "v" as if it were "w." The word would have been "wile" if this were at all the usual sort of dragon.

The mountain is difficult of ascent and Gandle, deciding that the giant probably lied anyhow, continues on his way.

Now he comes to the land of Kadia in which a dragon said to be a god lies in a cave. The people believe that to speak his name, which is Kla, in his presence would be fatal. Gandle enters the cave and is afraid. But encouraged by a red-haired girl named Laida, he gathers the courage to cry out, "Kla, Kla, Kla!" The god crumbles to dust.

Gandle thinks at first that, having slain a god, he himself has become one. But in the arms of Laida he accepts, for a while at least, the role of a human being. Even when Laida burns up his magic cap Gandle is not angered and he does not mind when his reputation as a god killer dims. There is satisfaction and courage to be found in brotherhood with the Kadians.

> The hand of the old man who made him citizen trembled and, in fact, he cut rather more from off the ear than was the custom, but this time Gandle gave no sign of pain as when last he bled. Outcry he knew as something shameful and so he stood tightlipped and only Laida, who clutched his hand, shared with him the sharpness of the stinging steel.

Yet Gandle grows dissatisfied, wishing for new adventures and adulation. One night he goes to the glass mountain, this time climbing it without trouble, but the giant, Fo Fum, is dead of old age. The reputed twenty princesses turn out to be only one, and she is old and mourning Fo Fum. With his adventure turned to dust, Gandle hurries home to Laida before the morning. This time he does not depart until the mighty armies of King Helgas threaten Kadia from over the mountains.

With two others, Gandle runs to the mountaintop to meet the invading hordes. As there comes up the sound of King Helgas' elephants, trumpeting because the way is steep, the companions of Gandle talk of turning back and Gandle himself trembles. Then he cries, "It is no use. We have no chance. Let's go and fight them in the pass." The others flee.

In the pass, Gandle suffers a wound and comes near to fainting. But in Kadia he had heard the story of a god who had suffered himself to be crucified and yet stood forth the next day saying, "I am still here." In agony Gandle asks, "Oh, god who would not fight, help me to fight. I am still here." Now Gandle stands straight and blocks the path to Helgas. But the outlook seems hopeless. Gandle sends a desperate cry to Yom for help, pretending that he has a lamp. Then, weeping, screaming, Gandle's voice breaks upon one last cry, "Yom, I have no lamp." Racked with fear and pain, Gandle drops fainting to the road.

With thumb and forefinger and a gust of breath Yom routs the mighty armies. Gandle, regaining consciousness, thinks that he has been responsible for the victory.

Finding that after whipping an army it is hard to go straight home, Gandle lingers. In the Valley of Flying Death he finds Yom playing at being a god. Death's Angel on Yom's orders crushes men in the valley by dropping boulders. Yom confesses to Gandle that he is only acting as a volunteer for God, but insists that his death dealing is kindly. Most of it, anyhow. Yom is critical of God, thinking He makes a mistake by answering prayers. "When prayer is made and answered something is taken away from the glory of God. The man who prays to God seeks to belittle Him. He dares to jog the elbow of God. He says, 'This I have begun, now let God finish it.' "

Finding his own fortunes being slighted, Gandle inquires if Yom intends to kill him in the valley. Yom replies in the negative, saying that Gandle's life circle has not yet been run.

Laida is pregnant with Gandle's child when he returns. Angered by his tardiness, she drives him away. Remembering his beautiful Agatha, Gandle journeys to the swift river and, diving, finds a small piece of the lamp. A midget named Rif, a genie of whims, appears when the fragment is rubbed. But even tiny Rif has the power to bring Agatha. Gandle concludes that if Agatha is a mere whim he does not want her, and he smashes the lamp fragment. Now he must rely on his sword alone. He returns to Laida to find that his son has been born. Laida allows him to remain and he is happy.

But once more the armies of King Helgas approach. Gandle rushes to the pass as before. This time an arrow at close range thrusts near his heart. Soldiers toss him to one side that no passing elephant may slip and stumble. As a priest from the passing ranks kneels beside him, Gandle mutters, "I am still here."

"You will die," said the priest, "and come to a great gate where Peter stands and within those walls—"

Gandle motioned to him to be silent.

"I won't be told," said Bunny Gandle. "I want to know."

And so ends the tale of Gandle.

Broun was very fond of the novel.

When Deems Taylor based an opera on it he was pleased. Yet, when the Metropolitan decided not to produce it, he was not too disappointed. After all, Yom would have to suffer a reduction in size, and he doubted that an operatic tenor could do Gandle justice.

He admired Gandle's courage and his feeling for adventure and he did not think the less of him because sometimes along the difficult road he sought pleasurable and easy detours. Yom, too, received Broun's nearly complete admiration. Yom's contention that God should not answer prayers coincided to a large degree with that of Broun.

Yom's insistence that death could be kind recalled the Fat Man of "Death Says It Isn't So." The major thesis of *Gandle* was that man runs a circle, and when it is done there is not much point in running it again. And Gandle's last words, "I want to know," were very much a part of Broun. As a savorer of experience—and as a reporter—he wanted to see and experience for himself any life after death.

Broun's attraction to death was occasionally disturbing. Once Mildred Gilman, a night club companion—and for a while his secretary—fell seriously ill with pneumonia. He had her taken to the best of hospital rooms. He engaged specialists. And regularly he came to sit by her bedside. As she grew better he questioned her at length about her sojourn near death.

"No one I've ever known has been so close to death," he said. "No dear friend has died."

Sick as she was, and aware that Broun would do anything to save her life, Mildred Gilman could not help feeling that he would have relished even closer association with death.

In other ways he was interested in the possibility of passing into another world. When A. Conan Doyle had been in America, Broun had secured the assignment to cover his New York lecture, and, though unable to accept spiritualism, had written a sympathetic account. And he had a strong desire to pass beyond the pale through being hypnotized, though in the end he always drew back. "I might not be," he would say, "Heywood Broun any longer." For he recognized that the words came from his typewriter almost magically, seemingly as a result of the chemical reaction between brain and subject. It was generally believed that, although having paid more than once for the full or classical psychoanalysis, he had refused to go all the way.

Broun loved life too much, though, to dwell more than a fraction of his time on death or another world. And mystically inclined as he was, and relating Christ to the brotherhood of man, Broun could not help looking for brotherhood in his own time and place. Slowly over the years his respect for Eugene V. Debs had grown. Debs' statement, that when men were in jail he was not free, affected Broun deeply. Upon the death of Debs in the autumn of 1926, Broun wrote: "The Debs idea will not die. To be sure, it was not his first at all. He carried on an older tradition. It will come to pass. There can be a brotherhood of man."

Not many opportunities could be found in the America of the Twenties for observing man's brotherhood in action. People seemed content to contemplate the navel of Calvin Coolidge. Out in Detroit Henry Ford was casting suspicion on Jews in his *Dearborn Independent*. U. S. Marines were chasing Nicaraguan "bandits." The Ku Klux Klan had been powerful enough to defeat New York Governor Al Smith, one of Broun's heroes, for the Democratic Presidential nomination in 1924. Pussyfoot Johnson and the other Prohibition agents were making a mockery of men's personal freedom. Everywhere below the surface were signs of distress. Broun observed that if America were, as advertised, the finest of all the countries in the world, the rest were in fearful need of stalwart men with mops and brooms and shovels.

The only issue into which political liberals could get their teeth was defense of Sacco and Vanzetti, who had lain in Boston jails since the spring of 1920.

Broun, like other writers and artists, was moved deepest by the reading of the case's characters, leaving legal details to experts such a Felix Frankfurter of the Harvard Law School. The case had a perfect villain in the trial judge, Webster Thayer. Old, thin-faced, with skin pale and transparent, Judge Thayer became the symbol of death itself. Reliable witnesses swore that out of court Judge Thayer had used obscene language in discussing the defendants. One of the witnesses was Robert Benchley, whose whimsical humor had not kept him from being fired from the *Tribune* because of wartime pacifism. Benchley made a trip to Boston to tell the Governor that one day in the golf club of his home town of Worcester, Massachusetts, he had heard "Web" Thayer in a convivial mood boast, "I'll get the bastards good and proper." There were many such affidavits.

Broun, no more than most other Sacco-Vanzetti defenders, shared the anarchistic views of the two. But their life stories, their gradual growth of stature in the years of their ordeal, had established sympathy for them beyond the feeling that American society had convicted them because of their political views.

The younger of the two, Sacco, who had been aged thirty at the time of arrest, was a stocky, muscular man of vibrant energy. At thirteen he had come from tending his father's vineyards in southern Italy, already an ardent republican. A year later, while working as a water carrier on a construction job, he joined the Socialist Party. In company with his beautiful red-haired wife, Rose, he had put on plays to help finance strikes.

Later Sacco adopted anarchism as a political faith. When the war came he opposed it. He was well liked, but his views kept him in hot water.

A man such as Broun could not escape being impressed by Sacco's death-house adjuration to his son to care for his mother.

Take her for a long walk in the quiet country, gathering wild flowers here and there, resting under the shade of trees, between the harmony of the vivid stream and the gentle tranquillity of Mother Nature, and I am sure that she will enjoy this very much, as you surely would be happy for it. But remember always, Dante, in the play of happiness don't use all for yourself only, but down yourself just one step at your side and help the weak ones that cry for help. . . .

Even nearer to Broun's sympathies was big-mustached Vanzetti, the fishmonger, an intellectual and a deep student. As the years had worn on, Vanzetti's vast eloquence had stirred those who thought the two men unjustly accused. Vanzetti had come from the vineyards, too, from the Piedmont section of northern Italy, and his love for nature remained. "Some notes of bird song reach our cages," he wrote from prison. As a boy employed in a city pastry shop he had been labeled a bigot by Socialist fellow workers because of a deep religious streak. After years of toil he had gone home, sick, to care for his mother. After she died he had come to America. At first he was a dishwasher. "The drain clogged, the greasy water rose higher and higher, and we trudged in slime." In the following years of pick and shovel and other manual labor Vanzetti read when he could, enjoying especially Dante's *Divine Comedy* and Renan's *Life of Jesus.* A New England anarchist named Galleani converted him, and like his friend Sacco he opposed the war.

In his cell Vanzetti studied English by correspondence, read much, and wrote articles, reviews, and translations. A noted conservative Boston attorney, W. G. Thompson, who joined the defense because of a feeling that justice was not being done, described Vanzetti as "a man of powerful mind, of unselfish disposition, and of devotion to high ideals."

Broun rejected the view of those who defended Sacco and Vanzetti as symbols of abstract justice. "Take care of concrete wrong," he observed, "and abstractions will take care of themselves." Ruth Hale also took up the cause of Sacco and Vanzetti. She was opposed anyhow to capital punishment.

Broun wrote often of the case, and sometimes his copy was cut or left out. For the *World*, though editorially favoring a new trial, did not want to seem out of balance in defense of the two men. Broun sometimes argued. He thought that he should be free to voice opinions—that readers would accept them for his own, not attaching blame to the *World*. But the editorial prerogative of reducing or omitting was adhered to.

Broun's increasing concern with serious matters did not detract from his humor, any more than he entirely eschewed the warm and gay atmosphere of the speakeasies. There still remained pay dirt, too, in the fight against censorship. With Margaret Leech he wrote *Anthony Comstock: Roundsman of the Lord,* a biography of the old protector of the innocent.

Margaret Leech—her friends called her Peggy—did most of the research and half the writing. John S. Sumner, Comstock's successor, although advised that her partner was the old Sumner-baiter, furnished her with a diary that Comstock had kept during the Civil War. That, along with an official biography and Comstock's published books, were about all Broun had. But when Peggy Leech had sufficiently twisted his arm, he produced the required chapters without trouble.

They had for an adviser a young psychoanalyst who was supposed to ferret out Comstock's repressions. He gave the Algonquin crowd a fast analysis, anyhow. Conferences were held on the enormous bed that Earl Wilson had built for Broun. That was nearly inevitable because of the almost total absence of other furniture in the room. Half a dozen people sat on the bed at one time. Over this fact the analyst nodded and brooded. From it, they learned afterward, he concluded that the Algonquin set was a pretty promiscuous outfit.

Numerous crises arose during the writing of the book. For one thing, Broun lost Comstock's diary, as Margaret Leech had feared. In time it was found under the bed. Mattie Wilson had hesitated to look there because it was the favorite hangout of two horned toads sent by a Texas admirer.

Both authors—they initialed their chapters—were surprisingly kindly toward Comstock. Broun wrote:

> Certainly he sought to stymie the realists. Those who came through to the other side should pray in thankfulness to the fierce old prude who tried to set his heavy shoulders in the way of much truth and most beauty. But for the menace of Comstock they might never have learned to climb and blast and tunnel.

Comstock boasted of having convicted persons enough to fill a passenger train of sixty-one coaches, sixty coaches containing sixty persons each and the last nearly full. He had destroyed 160 tons of what he considered obscene literature. Broun had a sneaking admiration for the old man's tirelessness. Of the arrest of Madame Restell at her abortionist's palace and her subsequent suicide, Broun wrote, "Surely no one could hope to escape the charges of Comstock by carrying the case to God."

The book was the first selection of the Literary Guild and sold well. Everything Broun touched still turned to crisp new bank notes.

13

"Let's Go and Fight Them"

BROUN was trying to take life easy in the dog days of early August 1927. Three decisions had made newspaper headlines. In South Dakota's Black Hills Cal Coolidge declared, "I do not choose to run." There was the announcement that Jack Dempsey would have another crack at Gene Tunney's heavyweight title, and Governor Alvan T. Fuller of Massachusetts expressed a conviction that Nicola Sacco and Bartolomeo Vanzetti were guilty. The third decision got the least attention. And so the final nails were being hammered into the coffins.

Europeans were trying to help as before. Anatole France addressed the people of the United States.

> Listen to the appeal of an old man of the old world who is not a foreigner, for he is the fellow citizen of all mankind. . . . The death of Sacco and Vanzetti will make martyrs of them and cover you with shame. . . . Save them for your honor, for the honor of your children, and for the generations yet unborn.

Messages in similar vein came from John Galsworthy, H. G. Wells, Arnold Bennett, Mme. Curie, Alfred Dreyfus,

Ramsay MacDonald, and many more. In Paris, London, and other capitals the United States Embassies were stormed by mobs.

The average American paid little heed, and most of that was surprise and anger at the queer shouting of radicals over the probable execution of a couple of foreign anarchists. But in Union Square a crowd raised the ancient cry of workingmen, "Down tools!" Once the crowd surged as if toward City Hall, and at Hester Street police rode their horses into it.

A few bombs went off, and a package of dynamite was found in Governor Fuller's mail.

The *World,* trying to do its liberal duty, stated the Sacco-Vanzetti side for history's record. It did not print, however, a bit of journalistic history being enacted in its own offices. The trails of two great practitioners of the trade were crossing. Up in the *World's* gold dome immaculate, cool old-time Socialist Walter Lippmann, inheritor from Frank I. Cobb of the editorship of the editorial page, was tapping out the *World's* position, which was for commutation of the death sentence so that perhaps there could be a new trial later. The *World* counseled moderation to the liberals and radicals.

Said an editorial:

> We believe that he [the Governor of Massachusetts] was fully aware of the gravity of his task and that he sought with every conscious effort to learn the truth. Against his decision there may conceivably be other appeals at law. But there can be no appeal outside the law.

That final sentence seemed pointed sternly at Op. Ed. For Heywood Broun was showing signs of dangerous restlessness. Broun would not allow the possibility of doubt concern-

ing the innocence of the men. Vanzetti's exhortations alone
had been more than enough to arouse him. "To read the
speech Vanzetti made when sentence of his death was passed
is to realize that he holds within himself a very precious human spirit. The man who spoke as he did could not conceivably be guilty." One passage from Vanzetti's address has
been accepted as a passage of American literature.

If it had not been for these thing, I might have live
out my life, talking at street corners to scorning men. I
might have die, unmarked, unknown, a failure. Now we
are not a failure. This is our career and triumph. Never
in our full life can we hope to do such work for tolerance, for justice, for man's understanding of man as now
we do by accident. Our words, our lives, our pains—
nothing! The taking of our lives—lives of a good shoemaker and a poor fish peddler—all! That last moment
belongs to us—that agony is our triumph!

The galling fact that the man in the street cared nothing
about the issue depressed and angered Broun. On the very
day that Vanzetti appealed to Governor Fuller, the newspapers filled many pages with the testimony of a little corset
salesman on the appalling consequences of his gift of one of
his products to a woman named Ruth Snyder. The *World*
itself devoted four pages to Judd Gray's account of how,
armed with a sashweight, he had finished off Ruth Snyder's
husband, or nearly so. Who cared to read the eloquence of a
black-mustached anarchist when in the papers was reported
Judd Gray's anguished cry, "Momie, Momie, help me!"—and
how Ruth Snyder, responding, took the sashweight and finished the job?

If heroism was wanted, why consider two men who had
lived for half a dozen years in the shadow of the gallows

when Trudie Ederle had dressed herself in a coat of grease and breasted the English Channel? And out of the west had come a wind-blown youth, Charles A. Lindbergh, sometimes called "Lucky" and sometimes the "Flyin' Fool," to fly the Atlantic Ocean and set America wild.

The booming figures on the ticker tape showered down for Lindy were of no cheer to anarchists. As Lindy rode up the streets no waves of the future could be seen. Jimmy Walker, the playboy mayor, ordered the police to deal roughly with Sacco-Vanzetti demonstrators bent on roiling calm waters.

On the hot morning that Broun decided to go to Boston he lay on his stomach behind his farmhouse, painting. He was shirtless, wearing his old flannel painting pants and a straw sailor. Lately he had been doing crowd scenes. Sometimes he was able to create a large, even militant, audience with a few wiggles of the brush or a finger. He was finishing the third canvas in the short space of an hour, which was against his stated policy, for he had sworn to his column readers that he would cut down production and hunt the early Brouns out of attics and cellars. In a scarce market, he thought, it might be possible to ask as high as ten dollars apiece.

Murdock Pemberton came out of the back door of the middle house and wandered over to watch.

"Hello, Murdock," Broun said. "Did you hear Ruth say what train she expects to take?" Ruth Hale had taken up her station in Boston. Day after day she sat in the dim little office of the Sacco-Vanzetti Defense Committee, writing releases, typing, turning the mimeograph machine, running any errand. With her the crusade had taken on a holiness.

Pemberton sat down cross-legged on the grass. "I saw her

a while ago. She wasn't sure. I'll drive her to the station."

"I was wondering where the handy man is."

Pemberton was well aware that Broun was only hoping to get some fishing worms dug. Broun always said that he didn't mind digging for worms, but that they always heard him coming and burrowed too deep to find.

"I forgot to ask Mattie," Broun went on, "whether she had any bacon. I expect she has. The fish were biting pretty good on bacon the other day. Sometimes I think they bite better on bacon than on worms, and baiting the hook is much easier."

"Don't worry," Pemberton said, "I'll dig some worms for you."

"Don't bother," Broun said. "I can just as well use bacon, if there is any." He climbed to his feet, leaving the paintings and an empty flask. Mattie would take them in, eventually. "I think," he said, "I'll put on my rubber pants and take some exercise."

Pemberton got a spade and while he was digging the worms Broun jogged slowly about in his rubber suit, still wearing the straw hat. For reader consumption he was bringing himself down to two hundred pounds. His best private figure was 235. There remained some distance to go.

"Shall I bait the hook for you?" Pemberton inquired sarcastically. Broun was resting on Hale Lake's small dock.

"No, I'm becoming quite skilled at it. Thank you."

Ruth Hale came out of her house. She carried a small bag and was dressed for travel. Pemberton met her halfway, took the bag, and went to start his car.

"Where's Woodie?" Ruth Hale asked.

Broun cast the short fish line into the lake and secured the bamboo pole in a broken board. "He was with Mattie a little while ago. Probably getting ready to read one of the heavier philosophers." Woodie's precocity worried Broun.

Ruth Hale asked seriously, "Have you written anything more about the case?"

Broun watched hopefully for a nibble. "Well, not exactly. I asked Mildred to go around and talk to some Italians and get up a feature out of their reactions. It's to run in my spot Sunday."

Ruth Hale sat down on an old, backless kitchen chair. She clasped her hands tightly. "Heywood," she said, "you've got to keep on writing. You have a piece to speak and there's little time."

The cork bobbed and went excitedly under. Broun pulled out a three-inch bullhead, unhooked it carefully, and threw it back. "They keep cutting out stuff, or watering it down."

"Lippmann?"

"Well, Walter cuts a lot of ice. It looks as though Ralph Pulitzer is getting a real case of jitters, and Walter makes a fine court justifier. If Swope would come back from Europe it might help some."

"They're a batch of lousy sycophants around there caressing the ego of a weakling," Ruth Hale said. "Look, Heywood, you've *got* to keep on writing. You owe it to yourself, if nothing more."

Broun finished rebaiting the hook and threw it back in. "I was planning to see Ralph again. But it doesn't do much good. Maybe I'll go up to Boston and try some on-the-spot accounts. A news angle might get the stuff by."

"Good." Ruth Hale rose to go. "By all means. Wire me."

While Broun was dressing to go into New York, Mattie called him to the telephone. It was Mildred Gilman. The piece about the views of Italians on the Sacco-Vanzetti case was finished, she said, but at the *World* she had been told that it wouldn't be used.

"Did they say why?" Broun asked.

"Same old thing. Too much Sacco-Vanzetti. You've got to put up a battle."

"I'm going in to see Ralph. Cold contempt is my weapon right now."

"Oh, hell, Heywood," she said, "you're no good at cold contempt. You've got to hit them in the eye."

Mattie drove him to Stamford in the old Lincoln roadster which she owned. The day was growing hotter. He scrunched down in the seat, his shirt collar open, his coat on his knees, occasionally taking off his straw hat to flick the sweat from his forehead. The train was hot, too. At Grand Central he waited until the ramps were clear before alighting, and then he slipped through the back way, avoiding the crowds, and caught a taxi on Park Avenue. The gin in his flask seemed boiling hot when he took a nip in the *World* freight elevator.

Broun went directly to Pulitzer's office. He tossed his coat onto one chair and sank into another.

"Take your shoes off, Heywood, and be comfortable," Pulitzer suggested.

Broun didn't feel friendly enough to pull off his shoes, despite the heat.

"Why aren't you in or on your lake?" Pulitzer continued. "This is a hot day to travel."

"That's why I was afraid you might not be in. As a matter of fact, I nearly telephoned to see." Broun fished for a cigarette without luck and took the one offered by Pulitzer. "I'm thinking of going as far as Boston."

"That really is a long way."

Pulitzer waited. When Broun argued there was often a long and twisted route to the point. This was, however, a familiar road.

"Ralph," Broun began, "I just wanted to say again that I

174

think you have the wrong idea about my column. We won't debate the *World's* point of view on the Sacco-Vanzetti case. Basically, I think, we're on the same side. I've been around long enough to realize that no columnist can possibly have the right to say whatever comes into his mind. I merely contend that I express my own opinions and don't commit the paper. The title 'It Seems to Me' says that plain enough."

He finished his cigarette and crushed it in an ashtray on the desk before catching another from Pulitzer.

"Naturally," Broun went on, "I can't libel anybody. But I don't see that you're putting the force of the *World* behind what I say. Maybe we could have a duet with the editorial page carrying the air in sweet and tenor tones and in my compartment bass rumblings could be added."

Pulitzer settled himself in his chair, and his voice was a little stuffy. "Heywood, a separate entity within an entity," he said, "is what we call a cancer. Anyhow we've been over it before. It's the duty of writers to write and editors to edit. After all, in your contract you agreed, if I recall the words correctly, to 'carry out the directions of the party of the first part or its executive editors in the discharge of duties.' "

The inventor of the column of opinion not necessarily in agreement with the views of the newspaper ground out his second cigarette and rose. "It says that, all right. It seemed to me that I had some powerful arguments when I came up here, but they aren't taking hold."

Broun thought to be coldly contemptuous, but his smile came, and Pulitzer rose and they shook hands.

Several hours remained before Broun could take the sleeper to Boston. He tried to remain cool and calm in the neighborhood speakeasies. But whether talking with friends or sitting alone sipping his drinks, he could not get two things out of his mind. One was the final, clear realization that the press was not quite so free as he had once thought. The other item rolling around in his mind was a Biblical quotation. "When Pilate saw that he could prevail nothing, but that rather a tumult was made, he took water, and washed his hands before the multitude, saying, I am innocent of the blood of this just person; see ye to it."

The judgment of the world had been that Pilate had not done enough. In the same vein had been the cry of Gandle, "Let's go and fight them in the pass."

In Boston, Gardner (Pat) Jackson, the blond young chairman of the Sacco-Vanzetti Defense Committee, met Broun at the train. Years before, when Jackson was a cub reporter on the *Boston Post,* he and his bride, fresh from the Denver Junior League, had become convinced that Sacco and Vanzetti were innocent. At first they had given part time to the defense. Now they were giving full time, besides draining their purses.

Broun's clothes were incredibly rumpled and he had a good start on a beard. But he was in good spirits, feeling closer to the battle lines.

"We'll win," he said. "Don't worry about it. What's new on the reprieves?"

Jackson's face was drawn. "We're frightened. Any minute the date for execution may be set." He hailed a cab. "You can feel it in the air. The big fellows here want death and nothing else. It's a point of pride with them. Anyhow, I've got a hotel room for you. How about freshening up and breakfast?"

Broun settled back and looked at the old Boston of his college days. "Not if you've got a free typewriter at your office," he said. "I'll have to get the column out."

They climbed the two flights of dim and narrow steps to the defense office, and before they reached the top they knew that the worst had happened. A newspaperman had telephoned a flash. The reprieve had been rejected. In a week Sacco and Vanzetti would die!

Bedlam had broken loose in the crowded little office. Mary Donovan, vibrant and tireless, the scourge of the police assigned to break up demonstrations, was in tears. Aldino Felicani, the linotype operator who had helped begin the letter campaign throughout the world, seemed at last stricken. Young Joe Moro, Powers Hapgood, John Barry, and a dozen more were trying to decide on the next step. Ruth Hale strode angrily up and down. Tears came into the eyes of Broun. He was never ashamed to weep.

He sat down at Ruth Hale's desk. If the struggle seemed hopeless, now was the time to fight them in the pass! He rolled a sheet of paper into the typewriter and the keys began to drum.

When at last Judge Thayer in a tiny voice passed sentence upon Sacco and Vanzetti, a woman in the courtroom said with terror: "It is death condemning life!"

The men in Charlestown Prison are shining spirits, and Vanzetti has spoken with an eloquence not known elsewhere within our times. They are too bright, we shield our eyes and kill them. We are the dead, and in us there is no feeling nor imagination nor the terrible torment of lust for justice. And in the city where we sleep smug gardeners walk to keep the grass above our little houses sleek and cut whatever blade thrusts up a head above its fellows.

In searing words he charged that Governor Fuller's investigations had been intended but to put a new and higher polish upon the proceedings. One of a committee of advisers had been A. Lawrence Lowell. Broun remarked with bitter irony that not every prisoner had a president of Harvard to throw the switch on him. Savage respects were paid to Judge Thayer, and from the specific Broun proceeded to an indictment of American judicial processes. At the end he returned to the hunters.

> I've said these men have slept, but from now on it is our business to make them toss and turn a little, for a cry should go up from many million voices before the day set for Sacco and Vanzetti to die. We have a right to beat against tight minds with our fists and shout a word into the ears of the old men. We want to know, we will know—"Why?"

In the *World* offices the explosive document was examined with worried eyes. Then Pulitzer, against his wishes but trying to be fair, let it go through. On the following day there came another. It was not so eloquent as the first, but the blows were hard, and it ended with the bitter line, "From now on, I want to know, will the institution of learning in Cambridge which once we called Harvard be known as Hangman's House?"

Pulitzer and his editors were angry, but the piece was allowed to run.

When *World* readers next turned to Op. Ed. for new and perhaps fiercer strictures they found in Broun's place a harmless little item, "Whence Irish Whiskey?" Broun's column was absent again on the next day, and on the next and the next. Calls, most of them angry, jammed the switchboard at the *World* seeking a solution to the mystery.

14

Warriors Must Bleed

BROUN sent two more Sacco-Vanzetti columns to the *World*. The first arrived late and was omitted largely for technical reasons. Upon returning from Boston Broun had gone to visit at the estate of banker Otto Kahn. Another guest who promised to deliver the copy had turned it over to his chauffeur and there was a mix-up. Noting the column's absence, Broun telephoned and talked with a sub-editor, who said that it was the consensus that Broun ought to lay off the case for a while. The paper's editorial board then met and made the feeling official policy. A twelve-day reprieve for Sacco and Vanzetti, bound to excite Broun to greater efforts rather than cool him off, was a factor. For his part, Broun thought that his old classmate Lippmann carried too much influence on the board and with Pulitzer. The decision was communicated to Broun after the fourth column had reached the office.

He went back to Sabine Farm. He sat on his dock fishing, or he lay behind the house with his canvas and brushes. With Ruth Hale he discussed what to do. She suggested that he send a Sacco-Vanzetti column every day, thereby fulfilling his contract. But Broun wanted nothing that would indicate concern with money. He sent a simple telegram announcing that he was on strike.

The *World* offered no explanation to its readers. The editorial tone as the day of execution drew near did not allay the fears of Sacco-Vanzetti supporters.

> The *World* respectfully petitions the Governor of Massachusetts to commute the sentences of Sacco and Vanzetti to life imprisonment. We ask this on the ground of mercy.
>
> We do not question and we never have questioned the rectitude of the Governor and his advisory committee. We repudiate the notion that they could decide to send these two men to their death were they not convinced the men are guilty.

That could easily have been interpreted as an apology for a *World* writer who had gone crazy and was either reposing in a straitjacket or muttering incoherently in Union Square.

Finally, six days after the second of the Sacco-Vanzetti columns had appeared, Ralph Pulitzer put a sign in what Broun called "my old shop window." Customers were told that, straining its interpretation of full expression of opinion granted to its special writers, the editors had allowed Broun to express himself "with the utmost extravagance," after which instruction had been issued for selection of other subjects. The dictum having been ignored, the *World,* exercising "its right of final decision as to what it will publish in its columns, has omitted all articles submitted."

Broun had been up to see Morris Ernst about breaking his contract. It looked tight. They sent a couple of formal letters to the *World* asking, in effect, a contract burning. Broun offered to pay a bonus for his freedom. The *World* was not interested. The contract stipulated that if Broun quit he

Edward Thayer Monroe

CONNIE BROUN

WESTBROOK PEGLER, BROUN, AND QUENTIN REYNOLDS
SEATED AROUND THE POKER TABLE.

Russell C. Aikins

would be restrained from writing for another newspaper for a period of three years.

Unable to set up business elsewhere, Broun asked for a short stand at his old place. If not that, at least a place in the letter column for addressing his audience. He was let into the shop for a day.

No one, he wrote, had instructed him not to write about Sacco and Vanzetti. There had been only a casual suggestion before the fall of the censorship ax. But "even though my instructions had been definite I would still have been unable at that time to write about anything else." He had spoken "only to the limit of my belief and passion," which he agreed might have been extravagance.

His sense of humor had not departed.

> Once there was a pitcher on the Giants who was sued for breach of promise, and fortunately this suit resulted in his love letters being made public. The memory of one of these I have always treasured. He wrote, "Sweetheart, they knocked me out of the box in the third inning, but it wasn't my fault. The day was cold and I couldn't sweat. Unless I can sweat I can't pitch."

The *World's* treatment of him, Broun continued, had been fair, generous, and gallant. But—"Now I am willing to admit that I am too violent, too ill-disciplined, too indiscreet to fit pleasantly into the *World's* philosophy of daily journalism." And he did not find the phrase "fair, generous, and gallant" appropriate to the *World's* treatment of Sacco and Vanzetti.

Ralph Pulitzer was busy planning a big-game hunting trip, but he found time to letter another sign for the window. After recapitulating the differences, he concluded, "The *World* still considers Mr. Broun a brilliant member of its staff, albeit taking a witch's Sabbatical. It will regard it as a pleasure to print future contributions from him. But it will never abdicate the right to edit them."

Nor abdicate its right to forbid him to write for other newspapers for three years.

Broun was not softened by the flattering words. As the executioners in Boston rattled their equipment in final tests, *World* readers went without humorous comments on early Brouns or the size of Broun's girth. In his old place as Sacco and Vanzetti died was a little gambit called "Swat the Fly."

Broun retired to the mountains—his 85th Street house, hot as it was—to observe his wounds and search his soul. Poker and night clubs were given up. To reporters he said facetiously that he might live by his brush, or perhaps go on the stage. To friends he pleaded agoraphobia—fear of open spaces —as an excuse for his unwillingness to go to Sabine Farm, and claustrophobia for disinclination to go often out into the city.

With Horace Liveright, publisher of *Gandle,* he discussed the chances of founding a weekly paper. But even that might be subject to the contract. A tentative agreement was worked out with the *World* whereby he was allowed to write for magazines, and he accepted the invitation of Oswald Garrison Villard to write a weekly page—uncensored—for the *Nation.* Villard stood by his bargain. One of Broun's pages advised the strait-laced editor to relax at a few leg shows for the benefit of his publication. Villard printed the advice but could recall nothing in their agreement which forced him to take it. Dorothy Parker had told Broun, "You won't be able to hear a thing at the board meetings for the clanking of Phi Beta Kappa keys." Broun liked the meetings all right, and he was able to hear, but he could not for the life of him see why Villard objected to a man's refreshing himself with a drop of gin in the course of the proceedings.

During his exile Broun decided to write a short biography destroying the legend that he had so carefully nurtured. *The New Yorker,* founded by Harold Ross a couple of years earlier, had begun its "Profile" department. That looked to Broun like a good place for a full view of himself, and he asked Ross to come up to 85th Street and talk it over. Ross, so fond of anonymity that his own name did not appear on the masthead (he wished the passion would spread to vain authors) was a bit shocked by the idea, but he agreed to the self-portrait if someone else added details that Broun was bound to omit.

An incident of the visit demonstrated to Ross—others had similar experiences—that the public Falstaff was curiously dry on occasions. After the business had been concluded Broun suggested a drink. Ross was agreeable, and they repaired to the basement kitchen. Mattie was at Sabine Farm with Ruth Hale.

The iceless refrigerator yielded up one withered lemon.

"Well," Broun said apologetically, "I know there's some gin. We'll have to drink it straight."

He rummaged through cupboards and among empty bottles and finally got down on his knees to peer under tables. Ross did not expect much in the way of a drink, but he was a connoisseur of Broun in situations like this.

"I guess," Broun said, getting up, "that the furnace man drank up the gin."

Ross was halfway up the stairs before the absurdity of the remark struck him. "What in God's name," he said, turning around, "was the furnace man doing here in August?"

"Well, I think he sleeps here," Broun said, defensively.

Broun's autobiographical stint, written in the third person, was entitled "The Rabbit That Bit the Bulldog." Any courage ever exhibited by Heywood Broun, he wrote, was strictly owing to the stars, which sang at seven-year intervals. For proof he cited his various bouts at fisticuffs, sloughing over the exact spans to fit his thesis. The falsest item in the legend, he now said, was his reputation for amiability. "Heywood Broun is not in any fundamental sense a kindly person. He merely palms off timidity as something just as good as affability. Most of the people who read him have the feeling that he is Falstaffian. Hamletish would be closer, for his blood runs thinner than that of the fat knight and much more acid."

The autobiographer denied that he was a true humorist. "Broun's real interests lie in serious and even somber fantasy." To prove the point *Gandle* was cited. Broun ended hopefully, "In the secret places of his heart Broun is a crusader riding out to do battle even though he dreads it. Still, when his time and tide come round he may yet swing a mace and crack a skull."

The illustration for the piece was a genial, big-rumped Broun down on all fours looking for Captain Flagg's rubber ball. Most readers, having no independent evidence, took the new portrait in the spirit of the illustration. After all, Broun himself had not managed with all his trying to keep away from the clown's paint pot.

Broun continued his meditation of religious matters. Someone had given Woodie a fine big Bible containing much source material. The Bible was stolen outright and filled up with markers, lines were underscored, and altogether it was made such a prized possession of the thief that Woodie never was able to get it back. In the *Nation,* Broun hurled rocks at his old fundamentalist enemy Dr. Straton and added others. Bishop Cannon, Dr. S. Parkes Cadman, Canon William Shaefe Chase all got their lumps. Broun could find no quicker way of putting himself on the right side of a ques-

tion than by taking up a stand across the line from Bishop
Manning. By now Broun was a confirmed freethinker though
his faith in God did not waver. He kept repeating that he
thought a preacher's job a cinch. He was, of course, basically
a preacher concerned with the morals of the world.

His meditations extended to the effect of organized religion on freedom of the press. It seemed to him that churches
meddled far too much in temporal affairs, especially in censorship and in politics. "Personally," he wrote, "I would prefer to have my favorite candidate Jewish, Unitarian, or ag-
nostic. These are the denominations which meddle least."
But he blamed the churches less for trying to influence newspapers than publishers and editors for submission.

In the autumn Broun's good spirits began to return. He
was still on his "sabbatical" from the *World* and Mildred Gilman, her services not required, had left to work on a book.
He resumed poker. The speakeasies were once more alluring.
When Gardner Jackson, not yet recovered from the shock of
the execution of Sacco and Vanzetti, came to New York for
a visit, Broun resorted to tried and true doses of booze and
bright lights to cheer him. Jackson even absorbed one of the
devious jokes of which Broun was capable.

They sat pleasantly in a night club listening as Helen
Morgan, perched as usual on a baby grand piano, sang her
famous blues songs. The drinks had been many.

"Gardner," Broun suggested, "why don't you go over and
sit with Helen on her piano?"

Jackson turned the suggestion over with interest, but he
had reservations. "Maybe," he said, "it's against the rules."

"Nonsense." Broun blew smoke casually upward, a fine
example of a man familiar with the town. "She loves it. I
know Helen well. She'll probably even sing a song for you."

Jackson negotiated the tables and hiked himself up beside the singer. One second later his arms were seized from behind in vicelike grip. He was carried across the room and slammed down beside Broun. A few inches from his face, when he looked up, was the dark visage of Jack Dempsey. The visage scowled before departing.

Broun said soothingly, "That Jack really admires Helen's singing. I suppose he thought you were trying to flirt and that it would interfere with the music."

By Christmas Broun's mountain had grown cold and he was lonely. He missed the white heat of commentary on daily affairs. Besides, Herbert Bayard Swope had returned from Europe and was busy smoothing things over at the *World*. Certainly there was room for all in the happy valley.

And so on January 2nd, four and a half months after his departure, Broun, his rope and hobnailed boots and spiked stick slung over his shoulder, and carrying a large sign stating that he had in no way changed his views on the Sacco-Vanzetti case, was back. He did not promise to establish American sanity in a hurry.

On the day of his return, the papers reported that five United States Marines had been killed in Nicaragua as Lindy flew over Central America on a good-will mission. In Chicago, Mayor William Hale Thompson, otherwise known as Big Bill, threatened to bust King George in the snoot because of what seemed to him British propaganda in school textbooks. The speech of a famous English woman preacher had been concealed by the Methodist Women's Home Missionary Society when it learned that she smoked. Morning-after heads were reported smaller because Windy City authorities had barred the sale of ginger ale setups on New Year's Eve. Bad liquor had killed 770 in the nation during the year just closed.

Some people were happy. That day the *World* reported 228 individual incomes of a million dollars for the year before, on which Andrew Mellon planned to reduce taxes. An editorial, "Full Speed Ahead," noted that "the opening tomorrow of the business year 1928 will find the most honored prophets of industrial matters serene in the confidence that prosperity will continue. . . . Conditions will continue to justify enterprise and reward confidence."

Broun returned to the *World* stronger and more popular than ever. When had a mere writer ended at a stand-off in an encounter with a publisher? If, of course, Broun had come off even. He was not sure whether he had lowered his shield in returning.

One day while mulling over the matter he had a visit from a journalist who, when Mattie went to the door, described himself as the world's worst wishing to interview the world's greatest. The caller was a small, freckled highschool boy. Mattie, in command of the portals, let him into the big front room. After a little while Broun, dressed in ancient baggy trousers and a torn sweater, one of his socks blue and the other brown, came out and shook hands solemnly, plainly worried at not being able to offer a drink or a cigarette to put his guest at ease. They sat down.

"I'm William Lederer," said the boy. "I thought that if I, a novice, got an interview with the greatest journalist in the world I could sell it somewhere."

"What makes you think I'm the world's greatest newspaperman?" Broun inquired hopefully.

The boy, stammering more than usual from embarrassment, tried to explain that he considered Broun the most courageous of all.

Broun looked doubtful. "It happens," he said, "that I've been planning to write about New York papers for my column in the *Nation*. The *World* agreed for me to keep it going—I expect as a place to let off steam. But I've been wondering if a writer can really be courageous in any of the papers." He paused. "But go ahead with the interview."

And so for two hours the least experienced journalist in the world asked questions of his choice for the greatest, scribbling industriously in a five-cent notebook purchased in case his wild shot hit the mark.

At the end, as if, the boy said later, the roof had been pulled back and God had looked in, Broun said, "Bill, I don't know whether you will sell that story or not. And so I was wondering whether you would care to work after school as my secretary. You can work most of the time at home."

When the boy had pulled himself together and accepted, Broun started the customary jousting over money. "Do you think fifteen dollars a week would be all right for coming in for a while after school?" he asked.

The boy shook his head. "Mr. Broun, that wouldn't do. I wish to work for nothing, for the experience."

And so the greatest and the least newspapermen in the world haggled on. Finally Broun declared, "Twelve a week and I'll not go a cent less."

The boy gave in. Broun had failed to inquire about qualifications, and young Lederer, flustered, had forgotten to mention his inability to type.

Broun went to his desk in the bedroom and returned with a handful of letters. "You just write a couple of lines," he said, spreading out some of the pages. "Generally you can acknowledge and it's enough, or you can ask me what to say. No hurry. Take them home and see how it works out."

Bill borrowed a typewriter and by staying up all night managed to peck out a few replies. That went on until Ruth

Hale suspected the true state of affairs. She spoke to Broun and he gave Bill an old typewriter to practice on, cut down the work, and refused to accept a resignation.

Ruth Hale showed herself thoughtful in other ways, serving, as usual, as a supplement to Broun's eyes and ears. The boy hoped to be invited to Sabine Farm as spring opened. But somehow no one thought of him. But there was much talk of rats at the farm, which seemed a possible excuse.

"I would like to have a try at killing those rats," the boy told Ruth Hale. "I've got a plan."

She reported to Broun that Bill had worked out a new system of rodent extermination. Broun said he was glad to hear that, because the rats had become unbearable. Next week end the boy was invited to the farm, and nothing more was said about rats.

In his page on New York journalism, which he finally got around to writing for the *Nation,* Broun called for a liberal daily, thereby implying that none such existed. "No daily," he remarked, "has ventured into the vast territory which lies between the radical press and the *New York World.*" His mind had moved almost full circle since his vigorous defense of the press against charges of the Lost Generation. Now the *World* appeared to be only on the outer rim of the liberal target. On numerous occasions it had been "able to take two, three, or four different stands with precisely the same material at hand." It did not seem to him that the paper possessed either courage or tenacity, and in addition he thought it was squeamish. For proof he cited a recent squabble over a birth-control exhibit—mostly of charts and graphs—proposed by Margaret Sanger for the Parents' Exposition in Grand Central Palace. The *World* had opposed the exhibit on the ground that children would be present. Broun thought the swarming children would be a very good reason.

Getting warmed up, Broun moved to pressures exerted on newspapers by religious and racial groups. Most scurrilous postcards that came his way, he said, attacked the *World* as Jewish-owned and therefore Bolshevist. Broun doubted that the *World* had roots any longer in the Jewish community. Anyhow, his experience had convinced him that the New York Jews were not especially clannish. The Irish, on the other hand, he looked on as "the cry babies of the western world," ready to send resolutions and protests on the slightest pretext.

In greatest danger was the newspaperman who ventured criticism of the Catholic Church, Broun said. "There is not a single New York editor who does not live in mortal terror of the power of this group. Of course, if anybody dared, nothing in the world would happen. If the church can bluff its way into a preferred position the fault lies not with the Catholic Church but with the editors." As usual he ended with a snapper: "Perhaps the first thing needed for a liberal paper is capital, but even more important is courage."

If anybody had an idea of protesting, he had need to do it fast. Early copies reached the *World*. After hurried conferences Ralph Pulitzer seized his lettering brush.

Thus it was that on the rainy midnight of May 3, 1928, customers going to Heywood Broun's shop for meat, bread, and perhaps a mug to warm and cheer, found him driven back to the hills and the eviction notice firmly nailed.

The *World* has decided to dispense with the services of Heywood Broun. His disloyalty to this paper makes any further association impossible.

15

The Sword Mightier Than Before

Broun's fear that at forty he was finished proved about as groundless as it could be. Radio wanted him. Newspaper offers came from far and near. He talked with the executives at his old paper, the *Tribune* (merged with the *Herald* into the *Herald Tribune*). But Roy Howard, the pompadoured, mustachioed young chairman of the Scripps-Howard board, was more persistent than anyone else. Broun would be of enormous assistance in Howard's ambition to make good in his venture into New York journalism.

Huge, red-bearded E. W. (Lusty) Scripps had built his newspapers on shoestring budgets as crusaders for the underdog. But he hated New York and would neither buy nor found a newspaper there. On the other hand, his brash young partner, risen from a humble railroad brakeman's home in Ohio, had always wanted to crack the big time. Scripps had died in 1926 and a year later Howard had engineered purchase of the run-down *Telegram*. Then, flinging himself into its operation in the old Scripps crusading tradition, he had begun pursuit of the *World*.

Broun's basic demand was freedom of expression. While about it, he was hopeful of reaching his goal of thirty thousand a year. About freedom he talked copiously. About money he was, as usual, less explicit.

Finally Howard telephoned Swope. "I talk with this fellow a couple of hours about everything under the sun," he reported. "But when I get down to brass tacks of wages he puts his hand on his breast and says he can't talk about money because of a bad heart. Now what do I do?"

Swope advised him that Morrie Ernst would show up soon enough.

Broun's terms were met. After granting freedom of expression, Howard decided to take advantage of it for promotion. Turning to a typewriter—he had been an able working newspaperman himself despite an error responsible for the false Armistice—Howard dashed off a paragraph, to be run in a box in "It Seems to Me" (the *World* had released the title) which would run down the left side of the first page of the *Telegram's* second section.

> Ideas and opinions expressed in this column are those of one of America's most interesting writers, and are presented without regard to their agreement or disagreement with the editorial attitude of this paper.—THE EDITOR.

Howard added in a statement: "In the liberalism which is their cardinal creed, Scripps-Howard newspapers strive for the toleration which it seems to us is too frequently lacking. . . . The action of the *Telegram* in taking on Heywood Broun was more than a gesture." Added old Lusty Scripps' son Albert, the president: "Since Mr. Broun is writing under his own signature, we do not care what he writes as long as it is not libelous and as long as it is interesting."

In his turn Broun announced simply, "I hope and believe I am set."

The Sword Mightier Than Before

It was a famous day in United States journalism when a writer gained freedom to write as he pleased. And there was properly a degree of flamboyance—though other newspapers kept silence. "Evidently," said Broun, "when a dog is fired it's news. When the same dog is hired it isn't news." The *World* turned down an advertisement. But the *Telegram's* delivery trucks and billboards blazed with announcements of a fetterless Heywood Broun's emergence carrying an armload of thunderbolts. Newspapermen stood stock still in the streets to marvel. And on the day of Broun's first appearance —a little less than two weeks after the posting of the eviction notice—newsstands were quickly stripped of *Telegrams*. Broun was estimated to be worth a circulation of fifty thousand copies.

To boot Roy Howard got entree to the charmed inner circles of the big town. The tiny (five feet five) man in a pink or green shirt, a gaudy bow tie, and a checked suit was just another Odd McIntyre to the smart crowd. His habit of dodging hat-check girls and his ostentatious calculating of the minimum tip was further depressing. To Broun few doors or tables were closed. Consequently the editor-publisher was pleased to join his columnist on nocturnal tours.

"Here comes," the cynical liked to say, "Roy Howard and his tame bear."

Inasmuch as few Broadway wisecracks escaped Broun, the remark came to him. But he was not the one to snoot a man because he happened to be his boss. He remained on cordial terms, as a matter of fact, with Ralph Pulitzer.

Broun was happier in his new place. The *Telegram* seemed to him to be at least as honest as the *World*, even aside from his own special status. He had plenty of room, his space being double-column as far down the page as he wanted. While competing with F. P. A., Woollcott, and the others on Op. Ed. he had gained his share of attention. Now he was the lone regular feature on his page. The majority of his columns were as funny and intimate as before—even though ten-year-old Woodie now resisted invasion of his private life. Broun was still the recognized leader in censorship fights. Once Morris Ernst received a phone call from a judge who was considering a suppression case. "I don't find a statement from Heywood Broun," he said. "I would like to know Broun's feelings about the book before I come to a decision."

Now "It Seems to Me" dealt oftener with politics and social conditions. Broun vigorously supported Al Smith against Herbert Hoover in the 1928 Presidential race. The *Telegram* backed Hoover. Broun found space for the Socialists, too. From his old basketball opponent and friend of cub-reporter days, McAllister Coleman, he received witty and penetrating letters which he printed. He read Bellamy's *Looking Backward* and George Bernard Shaw's *An Intelligent Woman's Guide to Socialism*. More often he thought of himself as a sort of Christian Socialist. For one thing, he was becoming a passionate hater of war. And in Socialism he saw a possible realization of a society in which man was at last kind to man.

It was not hard for the enormously intuitive Broun, moving about, constantly talking with people, to get a "feel" of insecurity behind the façade of Hoover prosperity. He observed concrete evidence as well. Long before the 1929 stock-market crash he noticed that the breadlines were growing longer. Though lacking in the accepted specifications for a social worker, his habits of life equipped him for judging the breadlines. Going home from the speakeasies he drove past the lines and gauged their size against the hour. Men were queuing up earlier to be sure of a handout.

Broun's custom as his salary increased had been to alleviate distress with a lone if lavish hand. His administration of relief was not scientific. One of his physicians, Dr. L. V. Lyons, learned Broun's theory while walking with him. Broun was halted by a man obviously pursuing the life of a Bowery bum.

"Hello, Heywood," the man said. "Remember me? We were together on the *World* years ago."

Broun stuck out his hand. "Sure. How are things?"

"Not good, Heywood. Not good at all."

Broun reached into his pocket and handed out five dollars.

When they had walked on, Lyons inquired, "Newspaperman gone to pot, eh?"

"I wouldn't know," Broun said. "He was never on the *World* with me."

"That fellow will spend the money for booze and you know it. He's a bum. Why give him so much?"

"Well," Broun said, "you never can tell. If a man looks down and out I give him something. That way I can't go wrong."

Many importuning letters came to Broun, and, being unable to fill them out of hand, he was forced to conduct a certain amount of investigation. He was quick to penetrate to the essentials. Once he sent Lyons to investigate the needs of a former actress who, declaring that she suffered from arthritis, had requested medical help. Lyons found her to be no longer a pleasant person. After some further investigations he concluded that she was a chiseler.

"She's a phony, Heywood," he reported back, relating the circumstances.

Broun thought for a moment. "Has she got arthritis?"

"Yes," Lyons said, "she's got arthritis bad."

"Well," Broun said, "maybe chiseling is the only way she can get along. We better give her the money."

Broun signed up for a fifteen-minute program five days a

week on station WMCA. He did not take to the microphone like a duck to water. In the first place, it bothered him to be cooped up in a tiny booth. He had also, in company with many broadcasters, a fear that by some slip of the tongue he would utter an obscenity. Broun himself was a hazard to un-initiated guests. Studio officials frowned when he wanted to set his flask on the table in case a nip should be required, and a compromise was made on a Dixie cup. Frank Sullivan, Broun's old friend of Op. Ed., had plain water in his cup and was unaware that Broun's contained gin. During the fluster of a broadcast, Sullivan took a big swallow from the wrong cup. Being a long cool drink man, not a hot gin man, he barely maintained decorum.

Happier working conditions for Broun had not been matched by a smoother marital pathway. Ruth Hale stuck gamely to the war for her name and identity. By now the massive public figure of Broun was nearly suffocating. Her sporadic efforts to pick up her career after the birth of her son had not brought satisfaction. For a while she had written book reviews for the *World*. The *Brooklyn Eagle's* sugges-tion of a general column had been exciting. If not likely to grow exactly to the size of Broun, at least she would have a regular place for expressing herself. But she was expected, it turned out, to write as Mrs. Heywood Broun. That deal was off in a hurry.

Even her brother Richard, who had sung on the concert stages of Europe and with the big symphony orchestras of America, had to suffer from the Broun blight. A perfectly well-intentioned feature writer for the *Times* drama page could not decide whether Richard Hale was better known as a concert singer or as Heywood Broun's brother-in-law. (Ruth Hale's other brother, Shelton, had died after serving on Woodrow Wilson's peace mission and being launched on a brilliant law career.)

Ruth Hale now wrote under her own name mostly of divorce and other marriage problems. She still complemented Broun. She furnished columns, and the old paradox that under his name she wrote more freely remained. With a bit of pencil work Broun was able to make her contributions pass for his own. And yet when he wrote under Ruth Hale's byline, as he occasionally had for a *World* book column she had conducted, the product could be recognized fairly easily as his own. Ruth Hale served him still as a stringent but fair critic of his work. Together they thrashed out answers to ethical problems and affairs of the day.

Now, though, Broun had less need for outside bolstering of his opinions. He had gone into the thick of the battles and found himself adequate. And so, after Ruth Hale had helped to free him, his great natural strength sent him swiftly forward.

Unless Ruth Hale were to become irrevocably Mrs. Heywood Broun, or "the wife of Heywood Broun," there remained no way out, she concluded, except divorce. As a single woman she would not be bothered with the press of Broun activities. She would, she felt, be able to resume her career, to be the Ruth Hale of old. More than once she laid plans, and a few times she began to act on them.

Each time Broun argued her out of it. And yet now and then he weighed the possibility of picking up Ruth Hale's long-standing offer to dissolve the marriage should he find a mate he believed more suitable. The "Saint Agnes' boy," having with some reluctance slipped the leash of Puritanism, was having a good run, even if with not quite the speed that his appearance in the night clubs with girls seemed to augur.

He enjoyed the company of pretty girls and he was not displeased by show of affection.

With one noted beauty Broun was sometimes convinced that he had found the really great romance of his life. In turn she felt an affinity between them. It happened that she, too, was married, though the union was in the process of disintegration.

But at each critical point Broun discovered that he was bound to Ruth Hale by powerful thongs. And for himself he did not believe, basically, in divorce. The words of the marriage pact, on which had been placed the seal of heaven, were graven deep. "I take thee to be my wedded wife, to have and to hold from this day forward, for better for worse, for richer or poorer, in sickness and in health, to love and to cherish, till death us do part, according to God's holy ordinance, and thereto I plight thee my troth." His breaking of another portion of the agreement, to forsake all others, had cut its mark in half-buried feelings of guilt despite the private compact and opinions intellectually arrived at.

Ruth Hale found that her life was woven deep with Broun's, too, and so in the end they compromised on separate apartments when in the city, just as they had separate houses in the country. The brownstone on 85th Street was sold—the step hurried, it was true, by a series of heavy poker losses by Broun. The stakes at the Thanatopsis had skyrocketed with the inclusion of Harpo Marx and Swope and the continued successes of some of the original players. The food-and-drink bill in the upstairs room at the Colony Club, where the game had been moved, equaled a total night's losses of the old days. Broun was also playing in fast outside company. The legend arose that he lost the house at cards, complementing the story that he had won it the same way.

Broun took a penthouse apartment at 120 West 58th

Street, attracted by a pebbled terrace that allowed outdoor painting. Aluminum book shelves were built around the big living room, his huge bed was moved into the bedroom, and Captain Flagg assumed command. The place soon had a Brounian atmosphere. Books piled up. The wall near the bed became covered with telephone numbers—no names attached—in Broun's usual calendar-keeping manner.

Ruth Hale took a place on Fifty-first Street above The Lounge, one of her favorite speakeasies. Broun had a favorite speak near by also, Sherman Billingsley's Stork Club, which he helped to boost to fame.

An early morning March wind whipped Broun's overcoat around his legs and lashed sparks out of his cigarette as he descended from a cab at the Little Church Around the Corner. The men in the triple breadlines stood with their backs to the wind, like cattle bent on weathering a storm. The line had once been single-file, until people objected to the coils reaching out of 29th Street far up Fifth Avenue. They had not liked, as Broun put it, to come suddenly upon a worm that walked like a man.

Even the triple line extended far, and of the two thousand men in it, five hundred would have to be turned away empty-stomached. Six long months had passed since that day in the autumn of 1929 when the halcyon skies of Hoover prosperity clouded and rain began to fall. Had Hoover looked for prosperity around the corner where stood the famous little church he would have found only discouragement.

Broun started along the breadline, handing out cigarettes, asking questions, listening to stories, looking for a few men that he might send somewhere to apply for jobs. Nowadays he hoisted himself out of bed early for his journeys. It did not seem fitting merely to pass by huddled humanity while on the way home from warm speakeasies, and besides he often spent several hours a day hunting job leads.

Two young women were passing out Communist literature along the line. Broun took a leaflet. "The whole capitalist government is filled with fury at the refusal of the unemployed to starve in silence." It seemed to Broun that the breadliners were hungering docilely enough. Far too much so. Broun had no illusions that his charity was solving anything, and he was sure that eventually the lines only wrapped about and knotted their inhabitants.

When all the cigarettes were gone, Broun got back into the waiting cab and started uptown. On the way he picked up the late editions of the morning papers. President Hoover had exuded more confidence. The Communist leaflet had called for unemployed demonstrations. Broun wondered if something more concrete was possible. Of course, the slump might truly be of short duration. He had an idea.

At his penthouse Broun made a stab at patting Captain Flagg on the head—the sort of thing which infuriated the Captain—and went at once to his typewriter.

Give a job till June.

There can be no question that unemployment is acute and that millions are in want. Something should be done, and it should be done now. President Hoover's remedy seems to be a set of promises. Mr. Foster, the revolutionary, has offered the hungry a series of parades. Thus there has been little consolation from the right or from the left.

It is up to us of the middle class to stir ourselves. And so I say, "Give a job till June." This column will start immediately to act as a clearing house for unemployment. Naturally, its scope is small, but when so much

cries out for the doing even a scratch upon the surface
may not be wasted.

Specifically, then, I will start the movement by giving
one job, and I hope to enlist support from some readers
in this give a job till June campaign.

Broun repeated the plea to give a job till June on his
radio program.

On the day following the give-a-job appeal, Broun lay on
his bed waiting for his secretary to bring the first hamper of
mail from the *Telegram* office. He was not feeling well.
Several teeth were hurting. He stood in mortal fear of den-
tists. When finally a tooth hurt so much that the dentist was
the lesser of two evils, he had it pulled and allowed the blank-
ness to remain. There were several vacancies. He was distressed as well by a recent improvement made on the apartment. Painters had appeared in his absence and in the
course of their work had covered up the penciled numbers
on the wall near the telephone. That was the sort of thing,
he complained, that raised hob with a man's carefully ordered
life.

Tall, attractive Luella Henkel came in with an armload
of mail. She was another of his about-town companions who
had become his secretary. (Bill Lederer had joined the Navy.)
Broun took up the first letter.

"Do you suppose," he said, "that it will turn out fifty-fifty
on the nose?"

Luella Henkel pulled up a chair. "I won't be committed,"
she said.

They began reading. Whenever Broun came to a letter
marked "Confidential" he threw it on the floor, according
to his custom. In his experience letters marked in that way
were from girls wanting to work for him in order to get into

his "interesting circle," or else from people wanting financial help. The last he sometimes granted if approached in another way—perhaps by a letter not marked "Confidential"— or if the letter was opened by someone else and the case brought to his attention.

Broun and Luella Henkel made two piles. One was for the want-a-jobs. The other was for the give-a-jobs. At the finish the score stood:

Want-a-jobs, 400

Give-a-jobs, 4

Broun ran his fingers through his rumpled hair and down his unshaven jaw. "What can we do with four jobs?"

Luella Henkel shook her head. "This is no proper ratio. Do we answer these people?"

Broun nodded. "We can do that much. Anybody in the pile who would be good in an office? I'll give out my one job."

Luella Henkel shuffled until she found a letter from a secretarial applicant. Broun called the number and made an appointment for afternoon.

"I've taken on a big order," he said. But he persevered, in his column, on the radio, and by personal pleading. Before long the Give-a-Job Campaign was a major operation. The landlord donated an apartment and an office was set up with paid and voluntary help. Ruth Hale, vitally concerned, too, with the plight of the unemployed, took a penthouse to the rear of Broun's and helped out. She and Mattie Wilson shifted from wine to jelly making, and distributed their products on the Lower East Side

Broun threw all his energies into the drive, and as always when he moved it was with the force of three or four men. He listened endlessly to stories and went straight to the heart of problems. Sometimes new clothes were prescribed for those ashamed to apply for jobs in their old attire. Often cash was handed out directly. Broun never asked an embarrassing question, never preached. He went to the breadlines as before—a subsidiary office was set up near the Little Church Around the Corner—and much of his time was spent either in importuning people to give jobs or to contribute money. Most of the funds came, though, out of his own pocket.*

To get money he once went so far as to endorse a cigarette, though, since the incident was completely Brounian, the endorsement was never used. Broun didn't really approve of personal OK advertising, but after all, he did smoke the brand of his sponsor. Part of the ordeal was to submit to a blindfold test. He did—and liked least of all the brand of his sponsor, which was, of course, the brand he had been smoking. The advertiser suppressed the result, but Broun went right on smoking his old brand.

Soon more than a hundred persons were being placed in jobs every week. In addition, a Broun-organized theater benefit—stars included DeWolf Hopper, Rudy Vallee, Charles Butterworth, and Ruth Etting—for unemployed actors netted

---

* One of the office helpers was a tall, big-eared youth from the Pennsylvania coal fields named John O'Hara, who had written short stories and wanted to be a novelist. He recalls:

"When Heywood Broun was running the 'Give-a-Job-Till-June' Campaign in his column, I was out of work myself, so I wrote and asked him if there was anything I could do to help. Right away he called me up and said he had a lot of chores I could help out with, such as handling his mail and contributions from his daily WMCA broadcasts and some interviewing, etc. I ate lunch at his penthouse every day the first week I was with him, and incidentally it was usually the big meal of the day for me. At the end of the week I was genuinely surprised to receive a pay check for $35, which he gave me all the time I worked for him. And I know it came out of his own pocket, because I knew, through my job with him, quite a lot about his current financial situation, his checking accounts, etc. Until I got a regular newspaper job he kept me on his personal payroll (I may say there was plenty of work to be done) and also he used to take me out at night, always, of course, picking up the tab wherever we went.

twelve thousand dollars. Yet Broun was profoundly discouraged. All the jobs he found in a week were offset by the increase in a single day at one of the city's bigger breadlines. Society seemed unwilling to face the problems of increasing millions of desperate. In President Hoover he placed no faith at all and little more in Governor Roosevelt. To Broun, Mayor Jimmy Walker was a cheap and vain little man.

He brooded, and before the close of Give-a-Job-till-June he came to a decision. It was arrived at one afternoon as he lay on a rubbing table at the Racquet Club. His weight was up and, with little time for exercise, he was hoping to bring it down with steam baths. He dressed and went to look for his father.

Heywood Cox Broun was at backgammon when his son came into the club's game room. The elder Broun was now almost eighty, but of clear mind and good spirits. He rose from the table, greeted his son gently, and returned to his game.

After it was finished they took easy chairs in a corner.

"I wanted to talk something over," said the son.

"Yes." The old man put his fingers to his chin and with his thumb gently caressed his white mustache.

"You may be shocked, Father. I'm thinking of joining the Socialist Party."

He went on earnestly. About the Socialists he admitted knowing very little. But at least they believed in using the powers of the Federal Government to relieve unemployment. That seemed a wise thing to do. Somehow the people must stir to save themselves, and if capitalism were finished, as seemed possible, then it seemed to him that a Christian Socialism ought to take its place. Personally he felt the need to join with others in a closer brotherhood for the difficult days that lay ahead.

The old man was silent for a while. "You are aware, son," he said, finally, "that I can't judge the ins and outs of it. Are you certain that you want to take this course?"

"I am sure."

"Then you can't go wrong. I'm with you."

They walked to the door, the old man's arm in his son's.

16

A Leader of the People

THE stepladder shook and swayed as Heywood Broun crawled to the top. He was wearing a dinner jacket, but with a soft shirt because a stiff front would quickly have wadded up from sweat. Four Yipsils stood staunchly at their posts, steadying the ladder. Yipsils were members of the Young People's Socialist League. They were extraordinarily fond of their new comrade, especially for his habit of going to meetings in a spacious limousine hired at the Racquet Club. Returning to the car afterward, he would find it stuffed with Yipsils, as if ready for a hayride.

A good crowd was on hand, drawn by placards put up by the Yipsils. A sizable complement of police was present, too, as customary when Broun spoke.

Slender, bespectacled McAllister Coleman, at the foot of the ladder, waved his arms and shouted up to Broun, "No, no, no!" as Broun's big flask glistened in the light from the street lamps as he slid it from his pocket. But it did no good. Broun raised the flask to his lips. The Socialist position was against this sort of thing.

But the crowd roared its approval. Broun put the flask away. "I talk wet," he said, "and I drink wet."

Hecklers opened up. "Sun dodger," shouted one. That was a reference to the charge that he never came out of doors in the daylight. Another yelled, "Relief for the bartenders!" Broun held up his hands for silence as the cops moved about. After a little he was allowed to speak.

"Friends," he began, "most of you know I'm running for Congress on the Socialist ticket. It has been said that I'm just a columnist out for a lark. Don't you believe that. I'm in dead earnest."

The Yipsils cheered, some of the other listeners applauded, and others booed. The Communists, especially, made a point of sending representatives to heckle "this petty bourgeois clown."

"Why do I seek the office?" Broun went on. "Those who were on the soup line tonight know. So do those of you who pounded the pavements all day looking for work. And also do those who go to their job in fear and trembling that each day will be the last. We Socialists have a program. Indeed, the only program."

More cheers, more boos.

"The Republican incumbent, Mrs. Ruth Pratt," Broun went on in a courteous voice, "is reactionary and lacks initiative. My Democratic opponent, Judge Brodsky, is an old-line Tammanyite. They tell me that the Democrats, especially Governor Franklin D. Roosevelt, are endeavoring to steal our thunder. They may do that. They may steal our thunder. But, friends"—he raised an arm and his shirt billowed over his trouser front, but his voice rang eloquently—"they dare not steal our lightning!"

The Yipsils sent up a clamor, for phrase-makers like this were rare in any party. The hecklers, too, increased their efforts. One stocky man toward the rear of the crowd cupped his hands and in a powerful voice shouted, "Hey Gin Broun,

Hey Gin Broun, Hey Gin Broun," and would not stop. It was a familiar cry at the meetings.

Broun waited a few moments, and then he turned suddenly and shinnied down the ladder, the Yipsils hanging on for dear life. He shouldered through the crowd. The heckler took a few paces backward, then turned to stand his ground.

Broun reached out to shake hands. "Let's be friends," he said. "You're wrong to shout. We've got to talk things out sensibly. Look at it this way . . ."

And so it went on. Broun seldom stayed on the stepladder for long, even when no hecklers needed pursuit. Against the advice of seasoned street orators he chose to operate on the sidewalks and pavements.

When Broun set out on one of the more fabulous campaigns of American politics he faced many handicaps. Not the least was the electorate. His home district, the Seventeenth, known aptly as the Silk Stocking District, had been carefully gerrymandered to avoid the defeat of a Republican. Most of the district lay in the fashionable East Side above 42d Street. Republican Ruth Pratt was about as Silk Stocking as she could get, being the widow of a Rockefeller partner. (Broun sent a copy of Shaw's *An Intelligent Woman's Guide to Socialism* to her, without noticeable effect.) Magistrate Louis B. Brodsky, an old-fashioned Tammany orator, was not expected to count. Two years earlier the Socialist candidate had polled only a little more than a thousand votes out of forty thousand.

The Socialists themselves were not too sure about their new office seeker. Some even charged him with having muscled in. On the one side, cool to Broun's candidacy, had been the so-called Old Guard, led by Morris Hillquit. On the other side, favoring Broun, had been the younger element,

called "The Militants," of which McAllister Coleman was
one of the leaders. After a while Norman Thomas, the Presbyterian preacher who had made a good showing as Presidential candidate in 1928, swung over to the Militants.
Broun's credentials as a Socialist standard bearer were, after
all, rather slight. They consisted mainly of admiration for
Eugene V. Debs and George Bernard Shaw, and his recollection that he had attended meetings of the Socialist Club at
Harvard. Even Coleman was unable to report that a true
flame had secretly burned within his large journalistic colleague over the years. Now the Old Guard, irritated by
Broun's public gin drinking, was having a hard time giving
full-hearted support.

Clearance with the boss had been another problem. Broun
had gone dutifully to the *Telegram* office for debates, sometimes with Roy Howard, usually with big, shouting Lee
Wood, the executive editor. The meetings had never seemed
to get anywhere. Finally Broun settled the matter by simply
announcing his candidacy. Roy Howard learned the news
while on a Western air trip, and, though far from pleased,
contented himself with a sign in Broun's shop window, in the
lamented manner of Ralph Pulitzer.

Howard's objections broke down into four parts: 1. No
Scripps-Howard feature writer had ever gone to Congress
(or to jail). 2. The odds seemed overwhelmingly against
Broun's election. 3. The profession of journalism is more important than that of politics. 4. Independence of thought
precludes party membership.

Broun, replying in his column, was confident that if he
was elected the column would get better instead of worse.
That took care of the first and third points. As for the second
(and obviously Howard had never read *Gandle*), Broun expressed sincere doubt that lack of certain victory was suffi-

cient cause for not fighting. Sideline shouting of, "Hold 'em, forces of reform and decency!" he did not feel to be enough. "With all due respect for the cheering section, the man who gets down onto the field and tries to spill a few of the trick plays is doing a great deal more. I'm going to do all I can." As for party membership, he noted that Tammany, against which the *Telegram* inveighed, was run by men who operated a party on a year-round basis.

He readily agreed that use of his *Telegram* column for campaign purposes would be wrong. "Surely everybody can see how palpably improper it would be for me to solicit campaign contributions through the medium of this column to be sent to Morris L. Ernst, 285 Madison Avenue."

Other newspapers hurt less with outright attacks than by refusal to take him seriously. The *World* threatened to expose him as a poker player. The epithet, "Sun dodger," which irritated him considerably, was thought up by an editorial writer. Broun vowed to show them.

After the street meeting Broun and Coleman went to campaign headquarters in the Algonquin. Having furnished a special luncheon table and rooms for poker, Frank Case had decided that he might as well throw in space for Broun's crusade.

Broun asked, climbing to the second-floor suite, "How's the gin supply?"

Coleman laughed. "The closet's full, even if your pals have done their worst. And me on the wagon!"

"That's too noble for politics," Broun said. "Anyhow, we'll let go with a good one after we win."

"November is a long way off," Coleman said.

It was the middle of August. Broun had started his campaign early.

Officially the rooms were the headquarters of the Congress Non-Partisan Committee. Morris Ernst was chairman, but Coleman was in direct charge. The official Socialist headquarters was elsewhere. That was just as well, for the Algonquin crowd was strong both for Broun's election and the closetful of gin. The stern Old Guard Socialists might have been shocked.

Coleman sat down at his desk and Broun began emptying his pockets of handfuls of wadded bills. "Except for bad luck and maybe a little skulduggery on the final pot last night," he said, "we would have had a leg up on a sound truck."

Seeing the money, Harpo Marx ran over, eyes bugging, as in his stage roles. He fished a hundred dollar bill out of his own pocket, tossed it on the table, and, pretending to be dumb, whistled and pointed to it and to Broun. Others came over and tossed down contributions.

Alexander Woollcott made an entrance, carrying a handsome briefcase. Woollcott was head of the Arts Committee. "I have," he said to Broun, flourishing the case, "some replies. Come and look at them."

He sat down at another desk and with satisfied dignity took a sheaf of papers from the briefcase. Broun began to shuffle through them.

From George Gershwin:

Delighted to have you use my name in connection with Broun's campaign. Please nominate him for President or even Vice President some time. He'd be grand.

From David Belasco:

Your letter came to me just as I was about to write to Mr. Broun and send my good wishes for the success of his candidacy. I have always admired his keen mind and his style of expression. I am confident that Mr. Broun's integrity and clear thinking will make him a valuable member of Congress and I have every hope that he will be elected.

A somber handwritten note from Theodore Dreiser:

Dear Woollcott: Yes. Though why he wants to descend to Congress is beyond me. No power lies there. The power and direction comes from elsewhere. I have just signed for some independent committee of which Morris Ernst is the head & front. Committees, committees, committees. And still we sign.

Otto Kahn, the banker and art patron, had been asked to go a bit too far:

I do believe in Heywood Broun—very much so, both as to his head and heart—but I understand he is running on the Socialistic ticket, and I do not believe in the basic principles of that party, however well-intentioned its purposes and however sympathetic and worthy some of its exponents, and indeed, some portions of its immediate program.

Don Marquis, a professed conservative, wanted it understood that he thought Broun just something less than a wild-eyed anarchist, but:

It is my honest conviction that the salvage of what enlightened people hold valuable in this country hangs entirely upon more men of his type going in, men of conscience and talent.

At the bottom was scrawled a note. "So," Broun said, "Don is going to Hollywood and doesn't want you to tell anybody. All right, I won't tell."

Members of The Thanatopsis Pleasure and Inside Straight Club
caricatured by W. Cotton in 1929. See next page for identifications

Members of The Thanatopsis Club shown on the preceding page:

Leaning over the table from left to right are Dorothy Parker, Robert Benchley, Irving Berlin, Harold Ross, Beatrice Kaufman, Alice Duer Miller, Herbert Bayard Swope, George Gershwin, Joyce Barbour, and Crosby Gaige. Seated around the table reading clockwise are Franklin P. Adams (with the cigar), Heywood Broun, Alexander Woollcott, Harpo Marx, Paul Bonner, George S. Kaufman, Marc Connelly, Gerald Brooks, and H. W. Miller.

"Merely try to refrain from writing a column about it,"
Woollcott said.

William A. Brady, the theatrical agent and producer,
wanted to be excused from committee activity at the moment, but attached a check for a hundred dollars.

> I am sure that Heywood would be a great Congress-
> man. His sense of humor, his great humanitarian im-
> pulses, his independence of thought . . .

Woollcott whipped a lone, withheld sheet from the case
and, bowing low over the desk, handed it up.

Broun looked at the signature and bowed in return. It was
that of Mrs. Minnie Maddern Fiske, Woollcott's goddess of
the theater.

"The finest jewel in your crown, Aleck," said Broun.
"This insures my election."

When Woollcott had completed the list it contained the
names of Irving Berlin, Eva LeGallienne, DeWolf Hopper,
George Jessel, all the Marx brothers, Ed McNamara, Walter
White, James Weldon Johnson, Gilbert Gabriel, John
Dewey, Brock Pemberton, Frank Crowninshield, Emile Gauv-
reau, John Farrar, George Soule, Robert Misch, Clarence
Darrow, Lynn Fontanne, Alfred Lunt, Frank Sullivan, Helen
Morgan, Robert Benchley, Carl Van Doren, John Erskine,
Edna Ferber, Ursula Parrott, Katharine Cornell, Fred As-
taire, Robert L. Ripley, Stuart Chase, Floyd Dell, Elmer
Rice, Ed Wynn, Charles Butterworth, Harry Richman, Amos
Pinchot, Irvin S. Cobb, Fannie Hurst, Grace George, Ina
Claire, Helen Hayes, Charles MacArthur, Beverly Smith,
Richard Simon, Walter Frank, Alfred Hayes, Corey Ford,
Deems Taylor, Walter Winchell, Floyd Gibbons, and more.

Heywood Cox Broun died late in August after a short
illness. To his younger son it was more than the loss of a

father and counselor. Now for the first time, after brooding upon death for many years, he saw a loved one pass over. It brought closer the whole vast question of immortality. But he reflected, too, on his father's life and the impact on himself.

When reporters called to ask Broun for facts about his father's life, he recalled a few stock items: Heywood Cox Broun had been founder of a printing business, a member of the Racquet and Tennis Club, an ardent National Guardsman, and a crack shot. To Broun, when he put the receiver down, this seemed hardly enough. Even less adequate was the description in the paper of Heywood Cox Broun as "the father of the newspaper columnist."

Broun marked time on the first day by warming over an old column about the sea and cats. He was trying to escape. But later, brooding, he felt the need to write about his loss. For the first time he apologized humbly to readers for bringing in his personal record, hoping, he said, by including other fathers to escape the charge of bad taste. He wondered what the reporters who telephoned would have thought if, instead of relating the few items of ancient fact, he had said, "The most important thing to mention is that Mr. Broun was just about the most charming man anybody had ever known."

He added a tribute to his father for something which, often against somber inclinations, he had employed for his own benefit.

I take pride in the fact that my father was a gay man. That he liked to give and receive parties. For many years after he was well past 70 he kept, with all the ardor of a religious rite, a cocktail hour.

I have always felt that truly kindly people, like my

father, must be men who have themselves a flair for fun. Only from the exuberant is it possible to get an enlivening return in the execution of the commandment "Love thy neighbor as thyself." Nor would his tombstone have a better inscription than this: "He took and gave much joy in life."

After the funeral and a few days of retirement, Broun threw himself harder than ever into his campaign. The schedule of meetings was stepped up and, despite habitual inertia, Broun rarely failed to appear. The Yipsils had an old sedan covered with oilcloth signs which they parked at strategic points to help draw crowds. Broun continued to do most of his night electioneering in his dinner jacket, having come rather to fancy himself in it. The Algonquin headquarters grew no less bizarre. Broun continued to empty his pockets of wadded-up poker winnings on McAllister Coleman's desk. The gin supply remained at least equal to that of the average speakeasy—even though Broun occasionally invited entire audiences over for a drink.

Broun's experience was broadened by introduction to another style of street activity.

"Heywood," Coleman suggested one afternoon, "why don't you hit a couple of picket lines? That would prove your sincerity and give the pickets a boost."

Broun, wearing a huge straw hat and, despite the heat, a dark brown suit, was making his usual donation to the coffers. "Where is this picket line?" he asked.

Coleman began to smooth the bills. "I don't know. We can find a picket line."

"Maybe they won't want me." Broun went to the big closet and poured gin from a bottle into his big curved-to-the-hip flask.

215

"Of course they will. I'll call up one of the garment-worker outfits."

"All right, if they'll have me. I can't picket very long today, though."

Coleman telephoned and they set off by cab for a garment-district strike of makers of children's dresses. The picket line was desultory because of the heat. Coleman introduced Broun to the workers and one of them loaned him a sign. They walked up and down for a while without incident. The union had telephoned to the newspapers, which carried stories of Heywood Broun's introduction to the picket's placard.

The Broun family accepted the new crusade in various ways. When interviewed by the press, Woodie, who was spending his vacation from his Arizona school at Sabine Farm, at first tossed back his thatch of straw-colored hair and suggested rather coldly that the question was a waste of everybody's time.

"Heywood hasn't got a chance," he said.

That drew a hot column from Broun charging his son with stuffiness, if not downright Toryism. Woodie then let it be known that after a session in the woodshed he had changed his mind. Naturally, this led to a misunderstanding. No razor straps had been involved, it turned out. Woodie had been reading in a newspaper about starvation in China. In a near-by column was a story about a huge surplus of wheat that was breaking the backs of American farmers. Woodie discussed the paradox with his mother.

"Now," he said, "what would Heywood do in a situation like that?"

Ruth Hale said that he would try to work out a way for hungry people to get the wheat.

Woodie retired to the woodshed for political meditation.

Emerging, he announced his departure for the New York battlefront. He was welcomed, and a suit of armor, consisting of a sandwich sign advocating the election of Heywood Broun, was strapped on him. He also painted advertisements on his corduroy pants.

By this time Irving Broun was back from Mexico and moving up in the real-estate business. None of his associates favored Socialism any more than he did. But his suffering was chiefly esthetic. A politically confused painter, working on the walls of Irving's apartment, said that Heywood was a Communist, just as was the painter himself. Irving denied that Heywood was any such thing. The painter grew huffy and then morose. The paint job turned out badly.

Mrs. Heywood Cox Broun granted not so much as a tittle to Ruth Pratt in the matter of conservatism. But it seemed to her—and she so told reporters—that her son's efforts on behalf of the downtrodden were commendable. The reporters got the inexact impression that she was a Socialist at heart. She let it ride and ended out of loyalty to her son in making a fiery speech in his behalf.

Ruth Hale's attitude was even more involved. Having always been the greater rebel of the two, leading or pushing, she was disconcerted by Broun's reckless lunge forward. "Come on and be a radical," he would say. She balked. "Maybe Socialism up to here," she would say, drawing an imaginary line around the farm. "But this is mine." Besides, she did not much like the Socialists she knew, being inclined to resent the new visitors to Sabine Farm. At the same time she wanted to get into the campaign.

The gin closet at the Algonquin proved to be the catalytic agent that fulfilled her wish.

McAllister Coleman had immersed himself deeper in his task instead of following Broun's suggestion that the relaxing snifter is beneficial to the politician. One morning, alone at headquarters with the afternoon and the night stretching ahead, Coleman decided that the time had come to drop austerity for a round or two. He nipped, and the path of the teetotaler seemed not only thorny but ridiculous. As the route to the gin closet became more familiar, the world assumed a hue which, if not exactly of the Socialist millennium, was at least of rose color. The wisest thing being to eat, at last he set off for the dining room. Everything would have been fine had not a hundred lawyers been gathered in solemn conclave in one of the banquet rooms. Coleman was not fond of lawyers as a class. Moreover, these looked very self-satisfied—no doubt Republicans. He could not help feeling that a rousing Socialist speech would be good for their blood.

The test was not a fair one. He had barely warmed to his subject when angry members rushed out to get Frank Case. He came on the run.

Coleman realized at once that his enthusiasm—and Broun's gin—had carried him into dangerous waters. He apologized to Case, who was friendly but also firm. Coleman would have to go.

He went unhappily to his apartment in Greenwich Village. As the liquor wore away his distress increased, and, lying on a couch in the twilight, he easily imagined his action had ruined Broun's chances.

The bell rang from downstairs. Coleman pushed the buzzer and waited. There was no mistaking the slow, heavy pad of feet on the stair. When Broun rounded onto the last flight his smile spread across his face. Coleman's misery diminished by half.

"I had to get your idea on some things," Broun said.

He had come, as Coleman knew, to bring comfort. They

talked for a long time in the dusk. Broun genuinely shared Coleman's distress, besides blaming his own frivolous gin campaign for the trouble.

"Frank Case has raised quite a fuss," Broun said finally. "That is, he's pleasant enough, but adamant. Frank's a businessman, after all. I worked out a plan coming down in the cab. Ruth Hale is busting to get into the campaign. I thought I would put her in charge there at the Algonquin. You would handle the Village end."

"That sounds sensible," Coleman said. Broun wasn't running in the Village, but then he often spoke outside his own district.

And so Ruth Hale took over at the Algonquin. Inevitably she turned it into more of a feminist than a Socialist headquarters.

The political picture in the Seventeenth District was changing as a result of Broun's tireless if flamboyant campaigning, the rush to his banner of famous people, and the deepening depression. By late September Broun had come to be looked on as a dark horse. It was true that having a woman for his chief opponent was unfortunate for a man trained in the school of Heywood Cox Broun. The dignified candidate of the Silk Stockings took some advantage of the situation. At a debate before a Junior League banquet she stated a hope that before the campaign was over Mr. Broun would admit her to be neither unintelligent nor inefficient. Naturally he hoisted himself to his feet and declared himself already possessed of the proof.

Broun succeeded in overcoming part of Roy Howard's point that no Scripps-Howard writer had ever gone to Congress or to jail. As fifteen thousand striking dressmakers marched up Fifth Avenue, he trudged along at the rear of the column. After a while the police tried to clear the streets.

A patrolman suggested to the group near Broun that it repair to the sidewalk. No one moved in that direction, whereupon the cop remarked that arrests would likely be in order.

Broun was quickly embattled. "All right," he challenged, "arrest me."

The cop did.

Since a paddy wagon would have had to come slowly through the crowded streets, Broun invited his captor to share a cab to the station. The cop, whose name was Wilson, accepted. On the journey they discussed books and plays, not finding themselves far apart in taste, though Patrolman Wilson rated Eugene O'Neill higher than did the prisoner. Broun failed to learn anything of cell life, though photographers requested that he be placed in one if only for a little while. The desk sergeant refused. Nor did he make any move to have Broun's head shaved.

Broun's old country neighbor Newman Levy rushed to defend him. Afterwards Broun expressed himself as having been a little fearful about Levy's association with the case, for his counselor had written the burlesque of Police Commissioner Grover Whalen in the "Garrick Gaieties." But everything turned out well. Even Judge Brodsky got into the act, requesting that his opponent be given courteous treatment by any magistrate before whom he might be hauled. In something less than two hours after his arrest Broun was free, with scarcely a trace of prison pallor. In gratitude he promised Newman Levy all his criminal practice. But in one respect he was disappointed. "I thought," he wrote in the column inevitably squeezed from the experience, "that when they let you out you got $5 and a suit of clothes."

To battle-scarred agitators it was all just too damned gay. Broun was humiliated when they made fun of his adventure.

As voting day approached the crescendo rose steadily. The *Telegram* came out in his support. So did the *World*. Edna Ferber took the stump. Walter Winchell used "Vote for Broun" slugs between items in his column. Mark Hellinger rang bells. So did W. O. McGeehan and most other top-flight special writers. In a sharp letter to the newspapers, Robert Benchley, "a former newspaperman and bad dresser myself," attacked those who thought a newspaperman unlikely to be a good Congressman. Broun, he pointed out, had indeed been a reporter and baseball writer, and, while his stories had been the most readable in town, it happened that they had also been the most penetrating. Any celebrity who could resist the dead-serious Woollcott was of considerable fortitude.

At the end of a last-minute rally at which Floyd Gibbons, Winchell, Woollcott, and others had beat the big drums, a trodden, beaten, creased old brown felt hat was thrown into the audience. The campaign was over.

First candidate at the polls next morning, voting at 6 A.M., was Broun. To reporters he readily admitted not having had to get up for the privilege. There had been a party for hopefuls at Morris Ernst's.

The voters who marked for Heywood Broun numbered 6,662. They were not enough. Ruth Pratt squeaked through with 19,899 to 19,248 for Brodsky. Broun could console himself that the Silk Stocking candidate had run worse than expected. And elsewhere liberals carried the day: Fiorello La-Guardia, who once had run as a Socialist himself, went back to Congress; in Minnesota young Floyd B. Olson, Farmer-Laborite, won the governorship; thirty-three-year-old Phil La-Follette went into the executive's office of the Wisconsin State House; George W. Norris went back to the Senate from Nebraska; the electorate over the nation had taken away

President Hoover's majority in the House of Representatives.

Broun sent a telegram to Ruth Pratt: CONGRATULATIONS. LET'S FIGHT IT OVER AGAIN TWO YEARS FROM NOW. And to the press he promised to get up the next day—not before 3 P.M. to be sure—to start building a victory organization.

A few months later Broun sat in the home of Herbert Bayard Swope, waiting for news on whether the *World* papers were to live or die. The Pulitzers had gone to court to break the will in which their father had forbidden sale of the papers outside the family. They had been successful. Roy Howard had seemed to have the inside track for their purchase. That meant merger. And then desperately, in that terrible winter of 1931, the employees had begun to fight. They had sent an attorney to court while scouring the city for funds to effect a purchase. A million dollars had been promised and their hopes were high. Swope had left the gold-domed building on Park Row. So had Woollcott. But F. P. A., Frank Sullivan, and others had an acute financial interest in the outcome.

Swope took a phone call. From his conversation they knew the answer. Roy Howard had won.

F. P. A. looked mournfully at the fruit bowl as Swope turned from the phone. "Where," he asked, "are you buying your apples these days?"

The conversation was nostalgic for a few minutes. Then someone said, "Heywood, it will be the *Telegram-World* or the *World-Telegram* now. You've got your old paper back. You licked 'em. Why don't you cheer?"

Broun was deep in thought, his head sunk low on his chest. "That," he said, rousing, "is a victory I wouldn't give a nickel for. Mr. Swope, could I make a call on your telephone?"

He called Ruth Hale and asked her to go down to the

World with him. In a little while he picked her up and they drove to Park Row.

They talked for a while with Renaud, the managing editor, and, taking him along, joined the trek. *World* staff members, proud of their journalistic heritage, had been getting out the last edition—that of February 27, 1931—as if the paper would go on forever. But gradually, tasks done, they had drifted to the speakeasy. The air was thick with smoke and the fumes of Prohibition alcohol. Men and women had argued with each other and pounded tables. But they were beginning to relax. Here and there a song was going. At one table sat big-faced Jim Barrett, city editor, his steel-rimmed glasses in his hands, singing now after leading the tense fight of the employees to buy the *World*.

Now everyone was in the same boat. Renaud, spirit of restraint and dignity, heretofore entitled to "sir" from most, announced that no one need go back to work that shift. He was cheered. So whoop it up! No more titles. Just a bunch of newspapermen and women out of work.

There were speeches, more singing, more back slapping, some crying into beer. Shouts went up for Broun. He took the floor, swinging his drink gently, while playfully hissed as a spy. Then he spoke nostalgically, for he was an old, old man of forty-two with nearly a quarter of a century of journalism behind him. He could remember the old *Telegraph,* the *Tribune,* before it was married to the *Herald,* and the *Mail* and the others in their lifetime.

"I'm sorry to see the *World* papers die," he said. "Nobody's any more sorry than I am. But it's just as well that Roy Howard got them, if you couldn't. In the last few years I've felt that the *Telegram* was often more courageous and liberal than even the *World* papers. I feel that the *World* died because it lost courage."

Then the forty-thousand-a-year agitator debased himself before the rugged out-of-work individualists. "If there was a union, it wouldn't stand for what's happening. It would take some kind of action to stop it, and it would have the strength. I think that day of the union is going to come."

He went tactlessly on and spoke of the union of which he had been president—though admitting that he had not been a very good one. "Nobody would join us, because the average reporter carried in his knapsack the baton of a managing editor, or even the dim hope of being a dramatic critic. What did he want with organization? He stood on two feet."

They finally got the embarrassing outburst halted. Broun signed off amiably enough. Everyone was amiable. Ruth Hale even allowed herself to be called Mrs. Heywood Broun, in jest. Someone called for "Mademoiselle from Armentières," and Broun led them gaily through it into a dawn that was bleak for most of them.

And so in the end Broun preached the funeral of the *World* and sung a requiem over it.

17

"Shoot the Works"

BROUN'S place atop the heap of newspaper writing men
was firmer than ever on the day that the *World* papers
merged with the *Telegram* to become the afternoon *World-
Telegram*. His name was in type larger by several points than
the title of the column. As before, he was the sole columnist
on the second section's front. In a full-page advertisement the
World-Telegram threw a spotlight on Broun's journalistic
robes of glory: He Writes and Does as He Pleases.

The fiery crusades had made him persona non grata with
some people; the color of quite a few faces deepened when
he entered the Park Avenue portals of the Racquet Club.
But he fitted the mood of a changing era. Circuses were no
longer in demand, as a sullen Al Capone discovered when he
walked out of a court under a six-month jail sentence.

No one laughed with Jimmy Walker any more. When
Broun took an oath, "I'm going to get that man," after the
mayor, setting off on a vacation, said that he was "more or
less shocked" by accounts of the framing of innocent women
by grafting police, not many doubted that he was now of sufficient civic stature to make good on his word. However, as
citizens began to rally to Town Hall for the crusade's kick-

off, Governor Roosevelt seized the lead by appointing Samuel Seabury to make an investigation. Broun canceled the meeting and confined himself to columnar support.

Except for a degree of boyhood anti-Semitism more or less indigenous to his neighborhood, Broun's personal relations had always been free of religious and racial bias. Resolved after the rude shock of the Sacco-Vanzetti execution to fight publicly for tolerance of all kinds, he had signed a contract with Vanguard Press for a book to be called *For Christians Only,* an examination of discrimination against Jews in the United States, with something of overall history. This time he had as collaborator George Britt, a young newspaperman who had landed a job on the *Telegram* hoping to be near his hero, Heywood Broun, only to discover that he seldom appeared at the office. Britt was therefore happy when Vanguard Press hired him to research for Broun and also goad him. The latter task was as trying as had been Margaret Leech's. Britt had also to go through the money-haggling treatment. In a contract drawn 60 per cent for Heywood Broun, 40 per cent for George Britt, Broun took a pen and scratched the figure down to 50-50, and made it stick.

Britt hauled material regularly to the penthouse, was jumped on by Captain Flagg and vastly praised by Broun. Nothing much else happened. Finally Britt discovered that at Ruth Hale's suggestion Broun had commenced to dictate his columns, generally to Beatrice Norton, the first to be employed in the Give-a-Job-till-June Campaign. Broun would merely talk along for a while, then say, "Probably that will be enough," and when it was typed it would be a rounded column. Britt conceived the notion of having Beatrice Norton and her notebook attend book conferences. Kept hard at it, Broun dictated his share of the chapters—Britt did the more factual ones—at the rate of a couple of hours for each.

One night Broun was sitting in The Lounge speakeasy with Charlie Butterworth, the comedian—they were a great night-clubbing team—and other people of the stage. Helen Morgan and Helen Kane were there. The conversation turned to unemployment among actors, and there were many distressing tales. Broun began to talk of a cooperative play. Here was all the talent needed—actors, musicians, writers, artists. Why didn't they get together and put on a show? It had worked in England.

"Heywood," said Milton Raison, who had managed Broun's fund-raising theatrical benefit the year before, "would you help?"

"Sure," Broun said. "I'll give you publicity and maybe I can raise some money."

"That's not enough," Raison said. "Aren't you a man who's played the Palace? You'd be in the cast."

Broun had been billed for a couple of weeks at the vaudeville mecca following the controversy with the *World*. But he shook his head.

"I've got a job. Why butt in on some real actor who needs the money?"

The subject was dropped for the night. But from time to time it was picked up and examined. Broun repeated his suggestion in his column and began to make factual inquiries— what would this and that cost? Running into Irving Berlin or Ira Gershwin or Yip Harburg he would inquire about the donation of a piece of music. Dorothy Parker promised to supply a sketch. George Kaufman said he would help. Peter Arno had an idea that he could do something. Nearly everyone was enthusiastic.

People kept insisting, though, that Broun ought to play a role, maybe the leading role. What playgoer could refrain from laying out cash to see Heywood Broun the song-and-

227

dance man? But much as he loved the theater and especially its backstage, he doubted his courage to stay on the boards for an entire show. His singing voice might prove weak, and in some intricate, elflike dance step his ankles might buckle. Besides, many would call it self-ballyhoo and speak of an inflated ego drifting about the stage. Already Ruth Hale had provided strong backing for the point of view.

But finally Broun allowed himself to be convinced that his promotion and thespian talents were needed if the venture were to go beyond the conversational point. And so one warm June afternoon he sat with his mother on the stage of the George M. Cohan Theater helping to judge the pulchritude of maidens. Into a single powerful spotlight at the center of the stage stepped, one after another, the girls answering the chorus call for "Shoot the Works." The theater was filled with beauties, some already in the reviewing line, others gossiping.

Relaxed and happy in all this proximity to the folk of the theater, Co-producer (with Milton Raison) Broun watched lithe, pugnosed Johnny Boyle, the dancer and chorus director, put the girls through the necessary paces. Mrs. Heywood Cox Broun liked the excitement of it, too. The scene carried them back a decade and a half to Lopokova's graceful tread.

Suddenly Broun saw a small, black-haired girl standing in the wings. She looked very young and he thought that she might be afraid. "That girl would be a good one," he said to his mother. "Why doesn't she get in line?"

Mrs. Broun suggested that she may have been in line already.

"No. I'd have noticed." Broun motioned to Boyle. "Johnny," he said, "what about the girl standing over there?" He nodded toward the wings.

Boyle went back to the spotlight and snapped his fingers at the girl. "Come on," he called.

The girl looked startled, then walked reluctantly over to the light. She had round cheeks with traces of freckles and a slightly turned up nose.

"Take off your hat," Boyle said. He had a reputation for possessing a little more cantankerousness than the average director. But his voice was gaining gentleness under Broun's influence.

"I can't," the girl said. "I'm letting my hair grow out. Anyhow, I was only waiting for a friend."

"Time step," Boyle said, authoritatively.

She did, in the quick, professional joggle of the chorus girl. Boyle looked toward Broun.

The co-producer nodded.

"Report for the next elimination," Boyle said.

Mrs. Broun asked. "Heywood, what do you know about choosing chorus girls?"

He got up. "Let's go out in the alley and have a cigarette. Mother, there are some sides to me you simply don't know."

When they came back, Broun went over to Boyle and asked whether he knew the little black-haired girl. Boyle didn't, but he inquired around and in a minute had the answer. "Connie Madison, Johnny Dooley's widow. She's danced in shows before."

"Oh?" Broun, impressed, returned to his mother. "You surely remember Johnny Dooley in the 'Follies,'" he said. "He died a couple of years ago. Our little friend was his wife."

Mrs. Broun recalled her son's lightning crush on Lopokova.

Connie Madison, passing successfully through the eliminations, would have been surprised to know that she had caught the co-producer's eye. Broun's first approach was unorthodox enough to startle any girl, chorus or otherwise. He came up and stood by Connie's side as Johnny Boyle finished a lecture.

"Would you care," Broun asked, "to kibitz at a poker game tonight?"

Absorbing the shock, Connie looked up demurely. "I would love to kibitz at a poker game. But I have a date. Some other time?" The fascination of kibitzing at poker escaped her, but she was telling the truth.

Broun bowed once more and departed lonesomely for a gathering of the Thanatopsis.

Broun enjoyed the putting together of "Shoot the Works," despite its difficulties. Established skit and song writers were ready to contribute. But the maestro hoped that much of the material would come from unknowns. He sat hour after hour reading and listening and watching. Dancers rattled about on his roof. Frenetic-eyed young men and girls wearing the unmistakable mantle of Mrs. Fiske implored him. Old men pushed him into corners and offered Spanish tragedies in six acts. The hardest part was to turn them down. He usually left that to Johnny Boyle.

Broun was having trouble keeping up his political fences. He was still a Socialist and was even considering a run for alderman. The Old Guard suspicion of his lack of grounding had increased.

"It is being bruited about," McAllister Coleman reported one sunny afternoon as Broun sat in the alley off the Cohan Theater stage door, sipping a sherry flip while an ash-blonde chorus girl balanced on the arm of his chair, "that you haven't studied your Karl Marx."

"Those are big, heavy books, Mac," Broun said. "I've read

Shaw's book all the way through and *Looking Backward* almost twice."

Coleman shook his head. "It's not enough. You're under fire. You're charged with frivolity."

Looking worried, Broun set the sherry flip down. "You better bring me some home work, Mac. Maybe you can find some boiled-down stuff."

Coleman fetched books and pamphlets to the theater and penthouse and Broun did his best in the time at his disposal.

The contributions for "Shoot the Works" from the unknowns did not pan out, though a former *New York Post* columnist with ambitions for stage and screen writing, Nunnally Johnson, did proceed from his own contribution to operation on the dialogue for most of the show. A skit was made from Dorothy's Parker's story "You Were Perfectly Fine." Other authors were E. B. White, Peter Arno, Sid Herzig, Dorothy Fields, Harry Hershfield. And, of course, Heywood Broun. He brought out his old favorite, "Death Says It Isn't So," and enlisted Ed McNamara to play the pleasant Fat Man whose true identity was Death.

Music was furnished, as promised, by Irving Berlin, E. Y. Harburg, and Ira Gershwin. Among the principal players selected were George Murphy the dancer, Imogene Coca, Lee Brody, and Jack Hazard.

Broun went out to hunt backers and he bagged a few. But as usual the chief angel was himself. It was to be a "cheap curtain"—with an outlay of only five to seven thousand dollars before the opening. One chorus number was developed to utilize some enormous Mexican straw hats left in the theater basement from a bygone production. The girls danced around the brims of the hats—and picked up an itch from bugs making their home in the straw. Under the co-operative rules the backers were to take nothing out of the show beyond their original investments. The principal actors were to be paid after the chorus girls. Broun set the figure for the girls above the Equity scale. The chorus girls, accustomed to being kept long hours, sometimes at the petulant whim of dance director or producer, could not recall ever having had it so good.

"I think," Broun would say to Johnny Boyle, "we had better knock off early tonight." Or, "Who wants to work on a week end? Let the girls go."

The producers had chosen July 21, 1931 for the opening of "Shoot the Works," and it turned out to be the hottest night of the summer. But newspapers had been ballyhooing the show for weeks, using pictures of a happy-looking Broun surrounded by bevies of gorgeous chorines, and a big if sweltering audience was in the uncooled theater as the curtain rose. Even Jimmy Walker was on hand, just as happy that Broun had switched crusades.

Broun the dancer danced, Broun the singer sang, Broun the actor acted, and every once in a while Broun the producer came out and talked. A large percentage of the acts centered in or about (and sometimes under) a giant bed. That made for less scenery shifting, Broun explained, and he boasted that anyhow the show had no pansy or bathroom jokes, which was more than could be said for other current musicals. The best numbers, most people thought, were a soft-shoe dance by Johnny Boyle and the song number "Pie in the Sky."

At the end, Broun the critic came out for a curtain speech. "Just start off your review," he advised Walter Winchell, "by saying that 'Shoot the Works' is swell, and go on from there." When the critics got to their typewriters they could not quite go along with their old colleague. *Variety* thought Broun had made a fool of himself, and the man from the other trade paper, *Billboard,* was of the opinion that a BROUN FOR CONGRESS sign painted on the asbestos curtain would have been fitting. As a purely commercial venture, he added, the loosely constructed affair would not last a week.

The men from the dailies were not so destructive. John Chapman of the *News* liked it. The *Times* could afford only its second-string critic, who was this-a-way-and-that-a-way. Robert Garland of the *World-Telegram* was pleasant if not enthusiastic. Percy Hammond of the *Herald Tribune* bent double trying to do the right thing, calling Broun "the most versatile and brilliant of our public men," while noting that "I, for one, preferred his painting to his acting." Later on, defending himself against charges of overkindness, Hammond wrote, "When I see a Titan slowly stirring from his comfortable perch in order to ameliorate the distress of others, I am overcome by a desire to applaud. Also I take a pigmy's enjoyment in the discomfiture of a colossus trying to be a clown."

Broun had much stirring about to do, but he was having a wonderful time.

Alexander Woollcott stayed away, saying he didn't want to watch Broun's humiliation behind the footlights. But he commenced at once to scout around for a part, and soon was on the stage. Ruth Hale went to work on the dramatization of Elinor Wylie's novel, *The Venetian Glass Nephew.* "Shoot the Works" ran on despite the heat, though Broun did take care to add insurance with guest stars. The Marx Brothers came one night and wrestled him all over the stage. When early Broun paintings were presented, Groucho remarked that it was bad enough to work for nothing. Helen Morgan mounted a piano. Helen Kane was there with boop-

boop-a-doops. Even prize fighters Benny Leonard, Al Singer, and Jack Sharkey obliged. Among the other one-night-standers were Texas Guinan, Al Jolson, Eddie Cantor, Sophie Tucker, George Jessel, Harry Hershfield, Ted Husing, Bob Ripley, Morton Downey, Bill Robinson, and Harry Richman.

After a couple of offers to escort Connie Madison, Broun hit a night that she was free. It happened to be a non-poker night. They went night clubbing. As far as Connie was concerned, she might as well have kibitzed. Broun's entourage increased as they went from one speakeasy to another. Climbing into a cab with Broun, Connie would bid good night to someone, or a group just met, only to see him or them crawl into the cab. Everybody wanted to talk to Broun, which was understandable, but she couldn't see why he had to talk to everybody. They got few words said to each other.

At the evening's end she told him, "I live in Yonkers. But it's all right. I'll find my own way."

Broun looked incredulous. "Why, that's a short cab's run."

They had more dates, and it was the same—a dozen men and maybe a woman or two joining Broun for conversation. He seemed to be Heywood to everyone in town, whether acquainted or not. And yet to Connie he seemed hard to know. For one thing, she couldn't figure out exactly how to address him. It didn't seem quite right to call him by his first name. And yet was it fitting to call a date by his last name?

One night as a band struck up a number she hit on an idea.

"Come on, Commander," she said, "let's dance."

Broun was pleased with the rank, but shy about the proposal. "I haven't danced," he protested, "since the bunny hug."

Connie was on her feet and she snapped the fingers of both hands and did the time step. "Come on, Commander!"

Broun danced, and it was hard to get him stopped. After that they got in more words. She continued to address him as Commander.

Despite the guest stars, who donated their services, the show's deficit ran a thousand dollars or more a week. Most of it came out of Broun's pocket. More than that, the night-after-night grind was a terrific drain on his energy. He caught a heavy cold which refused to respond to treatment. Sometimes he was so ill that he asked Dr. Lyons to be with him at performances.

One night Connie received a note via Broun's valet asking her to come to his dressing room. She threw on a robe and followed, surprised by the request.

Broun was sitting before his dressing table, slumped over, his face pale as death. Dr. Lyons was laying out some pills beside a glass of water.

"I'm sick, Connie," Broun said.

She sat down on a canvas chair, not sure what she was doing there.

Dr. Lyons tapped on the table beside the pills. "Now come on, Heywood, you're a big fellow. Take your medicine." To Connie he said, "He's too sick to be doing this and after tonight he's going out to his farm and lie in the sun for a week."

Broun swallowed one of the pills and shook his head. "Not me. I'm in the old tradition." He struck himself a blow on the breast. "The show must go on! I brought you here, Connie, to protect me."

"In that case," Connie said, "I've got some news for you. You're going to do exactly what the doctor says."

They got him through the performance, Connie coming up between her own numbers. Afterwards they packed him off to Sabine Farm.

So ended "Shoot the Works," for the others decided that without Broun there was no show. He was in bed for several days and afterward was very weak. He did lie in the sun, but he was too sick and worn out for fishing and for more than a little painting. He missed the excitement of the show, especially the backstage camaraderie. Nunnally Johnson and Milton Lazarus, the show's publicity director, came out to report the gossip.

Connie Madison had interfered with a baseball game at the Polo Grounds. She had meant no harm. At a party she had met Ernie Orsatti, the handsome outfielder for the St. Louis Cardinals, who in off seasons acted in the movies. It was not her fault that when she went to a game Orsatti satisfied the manager of the Cards that he was more interested in the box in which she sat than the batter's box. He got benched. It was nevertheless the suspicion of Nunnally Johnson, who wrote a piece about it, that she was not greatly displeased. Broun did not think this a proper attitude to take toward baseball.

"So it isn't enough that I get sick and close the show," Broun said. "My cast has to go out and stink up other spheres of the arts."

He felt out of things. To make matters worse, several members of the cast, including Connie, were planning a cruise to Cuba as guests of a steamship company.

Broun grew restless. Ruth Hale thought he ought to get away for a rest, perhaps on the cruise. His doctors did not think he was ready to move anywhere yet. Broun paid several thousand dollars every year for the advice of doctors, and, having bought it, felt entitled to do whatever he wanted to with it. He studied the lining in his straw hat and picked out Connie Madison's number.

She lived, as he knew, in a house in Yonkers with her parents, who had come from Italy a few years before her birth. Not much of America's golden hoard having fallen into the laps of these immigrants, their five daughters had gone on the stage. Johnny Dooley, whom Connie married, had made big money, but none of it stuck, and when he died she and their small daughter, Patricia, had gone to her parents' home and Connie had returned to the chorus to earn a living.

Connie, happening to be near the phone, took Broun's call herself. She didn't recognize his voice because of the cold which somehow blanketed the long "Ah-a-a" that preceded Broun's entrance into any telephone conversation.

Broun convinced her that it was he. "I'm trying to duck the doctor," he said, "and I wanted to be sure you'll be on the boat."

"Are you well?" Connie asked.

"I'm pretty well. The doctor exaggerates."

"You stay," Connie said, "where you are."

Broun was on the boat, tucked away in a cabin, when the party boarded. He sent word asking if Connie would sit with him for a while.

"Your father would like to see you," one of her girl friends said, genially.

Connie and a girl friend sat with Broun until he had finished an old-fashioned and gone to sleep. Broun found Connie both pretty and hardheaded, a combination he liked. Later, on the beach, Broun was gay and relaxed, and his health improved rapidly.

Back in New York he began to escort Connie Madison around town regularly.

18

"He May Yet Swing a Mace"

AFTER nearly a decade and a half of filling a daily column, Broun on his forty-third birthday was feeling the approach, perhaps the arrival, of middle age. A touch of gray was in his hair. The lines about his mouth had grown deeper, and he was thinking of getting some china teeth to replace his rows of jack-o'-lantern pickets. His stoop was lowering toward a hunch.

For readers he was practicing a graceful entrance into old age. A column about the beautiful Mexican firecracker, Lupe Velez, starring in Ziegfeld's "Hot-Cha," portended his ability to bring it off. Seeing her in a restaurant he had, he said, tried a bit of staring, and, that failing, had resorted to the leer. Being rusty he had had trouble getting his back and shoulders into it. A little later he saw her again, happily this time with a man of his acquaintance. Thoughts of roses and soft Spanish music were interrupted, it was true, by the babble of his baseball-writer companions, debating the strength of Babe Ruth's ankles. But he persevered and at last mustered the courage to approach the table at which Miss Velez sat. Unfortunately, a baseball writer tagged along, by now on the subject of Tris Speaker. The actress lifted an eyebrow ever the slightest in acknowledgment of the introduction. The baseball writer rattled on. "In those days they didn't have dinky little fences. That Tris Speaker could go get 'em." Retreating, Broun replied testily, "Maybe he could go get 'em, maybe a lot of us could go get 'em. But that was twenty years ago."

The light touch was fitting only a little of the time, as he was becoming deeply depressed. In Washington Father James R. Cox of Pittsburgh led ten thousand unemployed to the White House asking for Federal relief. Herbert Hoover respected the cloth, if not the unemployed, and he allowed the priest inside, but informed him gently, "No chance." The President had, however, thought up a scheme to distribute $500,000,000 to banks through the Reconstruction Finance Corporation, and out of the mists came ex-Vice President Charles Gates Dawes, underslung pipe and all, to direct it.

Veterans began to drift into Washington, demanding the bonus. One band seized an East River ferry and commandeered a train. Huey P. Long received Washington reporters while dressed in lavender pajamas and later strode into the United States Senate to receive the oath of office carrying a lighted cigar, which was against the rules. Samuel Insull's utility bubble burst and he went on the lam. Abroad, Chancellor Bruening stepped down in Germany and President Hindenburg asked Franz von Papen to form a cabinet, while in the United States the wits demanded that Adolf Hitler, whose pictures were appearing in the papers, shave off his Charlie Chaplin mustache.

Governor Roosevelt said the social order was out of joint and the nation could use new leadership. Broun snapped that Roosevelt had never offered more than "a meal of parsnips and fine words," adding that, "If the choice next November lies between Herbert Hoover and Franklin D. Roosevelt it

239

will be rather more a Tweedledum and Tweedledee than usual."

There were enough thumps for all. Said the Communist *Daily Worker* of Heywood Broun: "Shooting may be deserved—and we do not exclude that from possibilities—but how about taking his gin away from him and putting him to work as a stoker in a steamer carrying workers to the Bermudas for their vacations?" Broun appreciated "this good-natured raillery," but thought that he was really the more radical, taxing the Communists with merely wanting to take the place of the financial masters.

Still a Socialist, Broun journeyed to Milwaukee for the party's national convention. With McAllister Coleman and other Militants he caucused against the Old Guard, and, something new for him, rose on the floor to points of order and other pleasures of parliamentary debate. In merry old Oscar Ameringer, editor of the *American Guardian,* he had found a comrade after his own heart—he was willing to bow to the rotund German immigrant as a raconteur—and together they boiled down the platform to a fast and punchy 267 words. It was rejected in favor of the customary long and profuse document with preambles attached. And it turned out that Broun, who some thought had joined the Socialists seeking discipline, was not easily held by the Militants within the roles assigned to him. Altogether, the Socialists looked to him as if they weren't going anywhere.

Broun watched the dolorous Republicans renominate the Great Humanitarian as expected. For the Democratic convention, as he journeyed to Chicago, he had higher hopes. Al Smith would, he said, take a place among the political truly great. Not that he intended to vote for Smith if nominated. He would stick with Norman Thomas. But he celebrated the Happy Warrior relentlessly. On Franklin D. Roosevelt he was nearly as rough as on Hoover, speaking sarcastically of him as "Fearless Frank." Finally, as the New York Governor forged ahead, Broun cried out bitterly, "If Franklin D. Roosevelt is nominated he will go before the country as the corkscrew candidate of a convoluting convention."

When Al Smith's name at last went before the delegates, it was to Broun like the old days with Matty on the mound and Home Run Baker at the bat. For a while he had merely stood in the press box and matched the cheers of the galleries, but it was not enough. Under the reproachful stares of objective reporters he clambered down and joined the parade, shouting, "Smith, Smith, Smith!" His eyes were hot with tears.

Far away other eyes were cold when they read about it. Julius Gerber, the Old Guard secretary of the Socialists, dispatched a telegram informing Broun that he ought to be ashamed, marching in other people's parades. Charges of disloyalty were prepared.

Though coming to think better of Roosevelt, Broun could not put his heart into the Presidential campaign. He did pick up a morsel of journalistic satisfaction from the *Herald Tribune's* careful explanation that the opinions expressed by columnist Walter Lippmann, who had moved there after the *World's* demise and was supporting Roosevelt, did not coincide with the editorial policy of the paper. Broun could not refrain from noting Lippmann's former belief that a newspaper ought to be an entity of opinion—and how he, Broun, had been asked to depart from the *World* as a result.

When Broun came into New York on an August afternoon during Roosevelt's first summer in office he had no way of knowing that the planetary bodies assigned to him had begun to shiver in their orbits while out in the ocean the tides were behaving queerly. Only six years had passed, it was true, since his description of the seven-year cycle in which his acts of courage ran. But then astrology was not among his stronger points. As the train pounded under Manhattan into Grand Central Station he was still searching the newspapers for a column idea.

In the upper corners of the newspaper blazoned the NRA's Blue Eagle, while in the news columns the rough-and-ready old cavalryman, General Hugh S. Johnson, alternately cracked a whip and cut with his saber at thrown dead cats. Broun had come to think well of Franklin D. Roosevelt and his New Deal. "I am smarter," he wrote, "than those who cannot perceive that his is an opening wedge into the creation of an entirely new state of society."

He was out of the Socialist party. Though acquitted in his trial for marching in the Al Smith parade, he had got into new trouble for addressing a Communist-sponsored defense meeting for the Scottsboro boys. Broun feared that the German Socialists might have failed to halt the onrush of Nazism because of their refusal to co-operate with the Communists. The Old Guard Socialist leadership had become weary of taking responsibility for Broun and he was tired of taking responsibility for the party leadership, so he got out before he was thrown out. Now, with faith in the New Deal, he planned to take care of his health in order to live through one of the most exciting periods of history.

Broun glanced through the NRA accounts for news of the Publishers' Code. The owners intended to ask that reporters and other editorial employees be classified as professionals, rather than as ordinary workers. The NRA codes set a five-day week for the workers. Professionals—anyone getting over thirty-five dollars a week—were exempt, being permitted to work unlimited hours. In New York, newsmen—those who still had jobs—had taken two 10 per cent cuts. Broun was contemptuous of the publishers, but he wondered if there was any limit to the number of kicks working newspapermen would take lying down.

He left Grand Central Station the back way and caught a cab to the 21 Club on 52d Street. Connie Madison was waiting. She was dressed in a flowered poplin frock and looked cool. Broun did not look cool. He was disarrayed and he walked carefully, trying to keep the bottoms of his trousers from revealing that his patent-leather shoes—he wore them for comfort—lacked strings. He was sorry not to look better than he did, and especially he did not want Connie to know that he had no socks on. There seemed a fair chance that his new Panama, sitting rakishly on the side of his head, would draw her attention.

"So," Connie said, "you're late and you haven't got your socks on." But she smiled.

"Well," Broun said defensively, "I couldn't find any socks. Today I plan to buy several boxes of them."

He dropped his newspapers on the table, still not settled on an idea for a column. Tall, loose-jointed Mac Kriendler, one of the owners, came over and discussed the progress of the repeal of the Eighteenth Amendment. Later Broun exchanged opinions with Karl Vireg, who usually served him, on the proposed NRA code for waiters.

After a couple of drinks and a hearts-of-palm salad Broun asked of Connie, "Would you mind holding tight for twenty-five minutes? I'll find a typewriter and tear off my column."

In the club's office he sat down at a vacant machine. The heavenly bodies jangled for a moment, then meshed and began to purr. In the air there was a whir, as of a swinging mace.

The type rolled over the paper. A letter had come to him, he wrote, from Reporter Unemployed. This Reporter Unem-

243

ployed expressed many of the ideas that Broun had spoken at the *World's* wake—and some thousands of other times. The "gentlemen of the press" were far too dignified to unionize. That was all right for dopes like printers, who, as it happened, were getting 30% more money than the smart boys in the city rooms. While agreeing with Reporter Unemployed, Broun hastened to add that he lacked self-interest. "No matter how short they make the working day," he wrote, thinking of his luncheon guest and increasing the tempo, "it will still be a good deal longer than the time required to complete this stint." Numerous people had assured him that columnists were overpaid, and he was willing to agree. A form of inertia, he felt, prevented editors from firing columnists oftener than they did. Looking back he could find no Legree among his bosses, and consequently it was difficult for him to accept wholeheartedly the conception of the boss and the wage slaves.

But the fact that newspaper editors and owners are genial folk should hardly stand in the way of the organization of a newspaper writers' union. There should be one. Beginning at nine o'clock on the morning of October 1 I am going to do the best I can to help in getting one up. I think I could die happy on the opening day of the general strike if I had the privilege of watching Walter Lippmann heave half a brick through a *Tribune* window at a non-union operative who had been called in to write the current Today and Tomorrow column on the gold standard.

And then he went back to his lunch date secure in the knowledge that two months lay between him and the day for arising to action.

The column appeared in the *World-Telegram* of August

7, 1933. The nation's publishers managed to get through the day with no jump in their consumption of aspirin. Even Roy Howard, harboring the great viper in his bosom, was undisturbed. That was Heywood. He started a lot of things and never got them finished. On October 1 he would probably be at the race track. Anyhow, newspapermen were newspapermen.

But the working journalists licked stamps on letters and jangled Broun's telephone. They talked action, and so he called a meeting at his penthouse.

According to Bill Bade, editor of the *Guild Reporter,* "There were 5,000 at that meeting, counting all the guys I've heard say they attended." The following are remembered by more than one as having been present at either the first or one of the subsequent three meetings held in the penthouse: Lewis Gannett, Joe Lilly, Carl Randau, Doris Fleeson, James Kieran, George Britt, Jonathan Eddy, Allen Raymond, Ed Angly, Frederick Woltman, Morris Watson, Leon Svirsky, Marguerite Young. There were, of course, many more. Morris Ernst attended as a friend and as counsel if needed.

Broun presided from behind his cluttered kidney-shaped desk in the corner. Others sat on the daybed or on piles of books or on the floor. Everyone agreed on the need for organization. The question was: What kind? The idea of a pure union was repugnant to many, who favored something like the American Bar Association. The union supporters charged sharply that this was more of the "gentlemen of the press" attitude and wouldn't fool the publishers a bit. Broun favored a frank union, but was willing to compromise, at least on the name. He suggested "Guild" and it was accepted in the discussions.

When the next three meetings covered much the same ground, Broun, the reputed great procrastinator, grew irritated. "What we need is some action," he declared. "Let's call a big meeting and invite everybody before we talk this thing to death."

Morris Ernst made arrangements for a hall in the City Club, near the Algonquin, and three to four hundred gathered on the night of September 17. Joe Lilly presided, Broun desiring freedom to speak from the floor. The debate was the same: professional group vs. union.

Meanwhile newspapermen in other cities, bearing the brunt of retrenchments and angered by the owners' code proposals, were beginning to stir. In Cleveland the Editorial Employes' Association had set up for business on August 20, noting with irony that newspapermen had previously submitted to exploitation "not only uncomplainingly but in fact quite happily." They now demanded something more than a byline and a pat on the back. Groups at Philadelphia, Camden, Rockford (Illinois), Newark, Boston, Buffalo, Minneapolis, St. Paul, Duluth, Tulsa, Cincinnati, and elsewhere began to meet.

At a newspaper-code hearing at which Broun appeared as the chairman of a committee of delegates, he said: "Quite inadvertently, I am sure, some of the publishers have allowed the feeling to grow and spread that newspapermen and women who join organizations of their own creation will be subject to penalties. The penalty may not be dismissal. All newspapermen know of an institution known as the Chinese torture room. A reporter who incurs the displeasure of the boss by organizing activity may find himself writing obits for the rest of his life." A press that rested upon "the fears and apprehensions of reporters who are frightened and who feel that they have good reason to be frightened" was not free, he felt.

And then he sent a chill into the hearts of publishers. "I

may add that if a news-writing guild cannot obtain those things which seem to us fair, then news-writing unions will."

A sharp counterattack came from Elisha Hanson, counsel for the American Newspaper Publishers Association. Those present, and especially the scarred Broun, knew that heavy battles lay ahead.

Back in New York, Broun threw himself into organizational work. Most of it was done in saloons. Broun's reputation for Homeric tippling, along with his successful scaling of other heights traditionally sought by journalists, was helpful in his pioneering task.

After work the newsmen and women would gather in their favorite bars to talk about the Guild. For the *Times* it was usually the bar in the basement of the Times Square Hotel. For the *Herald Tribune* it was Bleeck's Artists and Writers Club—where Broun usually held his business meetings, which consisted of one part business to five parts philosophy. *Mirror* staffmen gathered at the Pen and Pencil Club. Upstairs at Nick's was the meeting place of the *World-Telegram* crowd. For *Post* men and women it was John's. *News* staffers went to a little bar across the alley.

Broun's ability to create an atmosphere of good will at the pulled-together tables was his major asset. Personal and theoretical bickerings were forgotten. In an easygoing way he gave the feeling that here was something of historical significance, a practical but also idealistic crusade. Inevitably he would be asked the cynical question: "What's in it for you?"

To Broun it became a cue. "I'll get more out of this than anyone here," he would say. "If we win, I will have made my contribution to newspaper work."

It didn't come out corny because of his obvious sincerity— anyhow, what other reason could he have? Roy Howard had called a meeting of *World-Telegram* employees and warned

them that Heywood never finished anything he undertook.
But those who worked with him were sure that he was emo-
tionally and spiritually with the Guild. "This," he would
say, "is it." Sometimes Woodie had, of course, to be put into
the act. "I've been lucky," Broun would say. "My son may
not get the breaks. I want him to have the protection of organization."

Yet the Guild of New York Newspaper Men and Women
when it came formally into being, elected Broun to a post no
more demanding than the vice-presidency. A fear existed that
out in front he would irritate the publishers. Many still
hoped that the owners would accept the Guild in a sweet
spirit of reasonableness. A trysting date was made at the
Hotel Astor, and a few publishers showed up to eat a bite of
the buffet supper. But as for the Guild's demands—a forty-
hour, five-day week, collective bargaining, minimum-wage
scales, vacations—the publishers didn't even want to talk
about them.

Broun was secretly hurt and disappointed by the New
York Guild's action. He took Carl Randau, *World-Telegram*
rewrite man and a union advocate, to lunch and in his
roundabout way sought the reason, or anyhow corroboration
of his own analysis.

Randau told him. "They think the publishers will blow
up if you're at the head."

Broun lit a cigarette. "This is a historical thing, Carl," he
said, lazily flapping his cigarette hand in the smoke. "I don't
mind admitting that I want to be at the center of action." He
gazed thoughtfully across the room. "But it's all right what
they did. I'll be national president."

The New York Guild issued Vol. I, No. 1 of the *Guild
Reporter*, a two-page broadside, and scattered it through the
newspaper city rooms across the land. The groups were cor-

responding now, and a national organizing convention was
scheduled for the middle of December in Washington.

Broun got a neighbor across his page in the *World-Telegram*. Once in a while Alice Hughes and later Fleur Fenton
had appeared on that side with a woman's column. But the
newcomer was to live there regularly in a space extended to
a column and a half. At the same time Broun's girth was
pushed down from two columns to a column and a half.
Some people connected the new development with the Guild,
thinking that Roy Howard wanted to groom someone to offset Broun's militant liberalism. The new man possessed, according to his employer, "the drollery of Ring Lardner, the
iconoclasm of Henry Mencken, the homely insight of Will
Rogers." In addition he had perspective. Confidence he had
not. He arrived among the think-writers trembling visibly.
"I am scared of this place," he said at the end of his first
column. "I wish I were back where I came from already."

Broun had known the newcomer, Westbrook Pegler, since
they were fellow correspondents in France and had run into
him many times while covering sports events. Aware that
sports writers drew down the high salaries, Pegler, whose pay
as war correspondent had been twenty-three dollars a week,
had entered that field after the war. He had also noted that
most sports writers were members of the Grantland Rice, or
poetry-and-whimsy, School. He therefore had decided to be
rough, cynical, and rowdy. His method had worked out well.
As sports columnist for the *Chicago Tribune* and its syndicate he had reached a high salary before moving to Scripps-
Howard.

Despite the often brutal tone of Pegler's writing, a sulky
mouth, and sometimes angry defensive eyes, he was known as
a "fun guy." Broun liked him. He extended a warm personal
reception and advised Pegler, now that he was a think-writer,

to get a quiet place in the country. Why not up in Connecticut near himself? Fairfield County was getting to be a literary center. Harold Ross and Deems Taylor and George Bye were all there, besides Ursula Parrott, John Erskine, and many more.

Broun's public reception of Pegler was not quite so cordial. A few days before Pegler's arrival a mob in San Jose, California, had lynched and mutilated two men accused of kidnaping and murdering a Santa Clara University student, an action which Governor James Rolph, Jr., described as "a fine lesson for the whole nation."

About this Broun had written one of his angriest columns.

> In the beginning it seemed to me as if this thing were so monstrously and obviously evil that it would be enough to say calmly and simply, Here is one more sadistic orgy carried on by a psychopathic mob under the patronage of the moronic governor of a backward state. . . . Governor, I don't believe you can get away with it. There must be somewhere some power which just won't stand for it.

In his third column for the *World-Telegram,* Pegler in the rowdy, brutal style of his sports-writing days raked over the affair, finding himself in agreement with Rolph. The storm of protest from the liberal readers of Scripps-Howard papers almost blew him out of his new home. Broun administered a spanking in his own column. Afterward, feeling that Pegler's style had led to some misunderstanding, he blamed himself for having been unkind to a green hand.

In Washington in December for the Guild National Convention, Broun's first major act was to get into a fight with General Johnson, the NRA's boss. Angry because the publishers were having their way in the code, Broun hauled off with an armload of dead cats. The general, he thought, was a big bluff. Parrying the cats, Johnson replied, "Why don't you cast up results instead of bellyaching about interim methods? You don't know a god-damn thing about any obstacles. I know a hell of a lot about the best way to get results and you don't know anything. Give us a chance, you big brick thrower."

Broun charged that Lindsay Rogers, who was in charge of the newspaper code, was overfriendly to the owners. The forty-hour week and overtime, Broun said, had been in the code and were taken out under publisher pressure. Broun's indignation grew upon discovery of a memo from Rogers to General Johnson which seemed to indicate a move to name someone other than Broun to be Guild president. But Broun won, by an overwhelming margin, over a Scripps-Howard man from Cleveland. Most newspapermen were now aware that the fight would be long and hard and it was good to see Broun up ahead with his mace swinging free.

19

The Way Darkens

THE announcement came in January: the bonds of matrimony set that rainy day back in 1917 had, a few months more than sixteen years later, been rent asunder. Heywood Broun and Ruth Hale were no longer husband and wife.

The decision between the two had been made in October. They had moved from 58th Street to apartments in the Des Artistes Hotel at 1 West 67th Street. Broun had paced restlessly up and down Ruth Hale's apartment, lighting one cigarette after another. Ruth Hale had sat on a davenport. She was forty-seven now, and thin, almost emaciated. The hollows under her high cheekbones gave her face a tragic cast.

"I'm determined despite hell and high water to go through with it this time," she said.

The old arguments were worn out. But he tried them again. They were partners. He wanted no divorce.

"You'll have your freedom then," she said. "And I'll have mine." She took a cigarette from a pack and lighted it. " 'Ruth Hale, spinster.' I like the sound of it."

Broun sat down. "Don't talk about my freedom."

"All right, then, let the issue be strictly *my* freedom." She got up. "Woodie is in high school. He boards at Horace Mann. I can do as much for him single as married. After all, we have lived apart for five years. There won't be much change in our lives."

Broun lit another cigarette, puffed a few times, and threw it away.

Ruth Hale paced back and forth. "I like the sound of it better all the time. 'Ruth Hale, spinster.' I like it quite well. I can go back to my friends as Ruth Hale. At least I won't have that god-awful tag, 'Mrs. Heywood Broun.' "

She hoped that a return to the old status would bring peace of mind. Sometimes she talked of picking up the loose ends of her career. Her last rally, the dramatization of *The Venetian Glass Nephew,* had turned out dismally, with adverse criticism and a short run. Yet she might pick up the threads if she were determined. Broun saw that she really wanted the divorce and that was enough for him.

Ruth Hale went to Mexico for the divorce, to Nogales. It was granted—November 17, 1933—on the grounds that they had not lived together for five years.

Broun threw himself furiously into the Guild's struggles. Sometimes the events were dramatic, as when he roared out of a code hearing in Washington. But more of the work was of the kind usually performed by inconspicuous organizers. At the tiny Jamaica *Long Island Express* he participated in shop meetings, rising to dispute the management—and he offered 10 per cent of his own income to the workers in the event of trouble. He rode the ferry over to Staten Island for a legendary organizational stratagem.

In a saloon he had talked for a long time with a dozen members of the *Staten Island Advance.* The response was slight. Finally, he spread out his arms in exasperation. "Let one man raise his hand and you've got a Guild."

One man raised his hand.

Though in classical tactics the move was wrong, it was

the kind of romanticism that kindled spirit in newspaper city rooms. The hand raiser, Alexander Crosby, was fired and Guildsmen got a taste of the picket line and learned to climb the street orator's stepladder. Old war horse Broun showed them how and he gave a job to the discharged employe choosing columns for a collection.

During a trip to the Middle West Broun got himself gassed, was captured by state troopers, and lost the seat of the brown suit going over a picket fence, which he described as incredibly high. That was in Toledo, Ohio. Broun's great gift as a footracer was, he said, as a flat runner. He had never for a moment posed as a steeplechase man. When the gas began to float he fled to the wall, a good ten yards, he thought, in the lead. Since as in the old days of the folding bed Irving was not there to haul and Virginia to push, he hung half over the wall until the seat of "the brown" mercifully gave.

The troopers caught him later loafing around a street corner. The gray suit needed a press and his slouch felt hat also looked dangerous. A trooper had overheard a newspaperman say that Broun was a New York columnist.

"He's a big Communist from New York," the trooper recounted to his superior, handing over the captive.

"Columnist," Broun explained carefully.

The only credential he could produce was a key to a large downtown hotel.

"Oh," said the provost officer, "one of those *rich* New York Communists."

Other journalists finally identified Broun and he was released.

Broun lost an encounter with two old friends of the Algonquin set. The Round Table was a thing of the past now, and Neysa McMein's studio salon had disappeared with the building that had housed it. The regulars, most of them successful, were going separate ways.

One day a newspaper reported that at an Algonquin banquet Alexander Woollcott and others had donned aprons and replaced striking waiters. Woollcott, the story added, had carried the fun a bit further by trying to dump soup down Robert Benchley's neck.

Broun castigated his old pals, expressing unhappiness over Woollcott's failure with the soup.

Woollcott immediately answered. "I should be sorry to have my many old friends among the striking waiters believe me guilty of such repulsive didoes, and I am surprised that you yourself believed it even for the few minutes it took you to write that column of rebuke."

He also got Broun on the phone, in a towering rage, and a fine falling out was on.

Benchley's letter was even tougher. He felt Broun should have known the story to have been false. "They may sound the way you want them to sound for your column, but they aren't always true. And you know damned well that they aren't, but does that matter? I will go as far as you will for the waiters at the Algonquin and I'll thank you not to make a column out of a story which you know had no foundation in fact." And he made the unkindest cut of all—that Broun was a professional cross carrier.

Broun printed the letters without comment. But in a couple of days he was back with an indirect defense. Admitting no trouble in making a fool of himself, he resented the cross-carrier thrust and denied martyrdom. "I am, of course, subconsciously an exhibitionist. And not so very subconsciously at that." He told about having been driven to a meeting of striking cab drivers in a limousine. That had proved embarrassing when the chauffeur had called him from the platform to inquire how long he wished the car to wait. But, fool or not, he planned to keep on.

Both Ruth Hale and Broun were distressed by the failure of their marriage, though the divorce itself made no basic difference in their relations. They discussed Woodie's future and Broun's work. She still did some reading for him and furnished ideas. Broun spent much time at Ruth Hale's bedside, and they avoided recriminations. But sometimes she talked with Woodie about the past, of how she had often contemplated divorce, of the difficulties in being married to a public figure. After the divorce to get rid of being Mrs. Heywood Broun she had, of course, become the former Mrs. Heywood Broun. She was not quite sure that militant feminism had been, after all, the wisest thing in their case.

In the summer of 1934 Ruth Hale became very ill. The cause was not easily ascertained. She had never, of course, taken good care of herself. More than once she declared that she intended to will her own death. Old age seemed horrible to her. Now it seemed to her that she had lost Broun, despite the obvious remaining strength of the bond. Woodie—touring Europe that summer—was past the years when, she felt, he needed her. Broun stayed close to Sabine Farm and Mattie nursed her devotedly, but she declined, losing the use of her legs.

"After forty a woman is through," she told Luella Henkel. "I'm going to make myself die."

Broun's few excursions, except to Guild meetings—he was unanimously re-elected at the convention held in St. Paul—were mainly to the race tracks. Now the races had almost completely crowded out baseball. Woodie had become a horse player, too, though he worried his father by studying the dope sheets and showing disappointment when one of his choices lost. Woodie seemed to like to win money.

Broun was not sure that he could go along with many of Woodie's financial habits. When Woodie rattled off itemized lists of expenditures, Broun would frown. "Do you mean to say you know where the money went?" he would ask.

He would outline his own system of betting. "Now look," he would say, tapping his right pants' pocket. "I've put my betting money here. My winnings go over here." He tapped his left pocket. "If I end up the day with both pockets empty, then I'm even. It's wrong to go to the track to make money. You have fun, and you put as much in the right-hand pocket as you want to spend for it. Anything in the left-hand pocket at the end is like finding it."

He would then go to work on the horses, putting a two-dollar bet on each of several horses—usually long shots—in a race. That usually insured him a strong runner to cheer for. When he got a winner strangers got the impression that he had raised the horse on a bottle, trained it, and offered it and the jockey careful advice on the running of the race.

Betting commissioners raised their hands in mock horror at Broun's approach, claiming that in time his long-shot bets would ruin them. From Tim Mara he finally got a coveted 100-to-1 shot which came in winner.

That summer big, redheaded Quentin Reynolds stayed at Sabine Farm. Reynolds, sports writer for *Collier's* and a former football player, was now Broun's chief link with the behind-the-scenes of sports. A couple of years before Broun had noticed some humorous stories that Reynolds had written for the *World-Telegram* from the Brooklyn Dodgers' spring-training camp. Most of the stories were about Lefty O'Doul, a great hitter and a character. Broun had called Reynolds after the team came north, complimented him on the stories, and asked if there was a chance of meeting

O'Doul. Reynolds arranged it. Broun took them out drinking.

Late at night he became panic-stricken. "You have to play tomorrow," he apologized to O'Doul. It was to be a doubleheader.

Reynolds had known how to fix it. O'Doul was a mighty bettor. Reynolds simply bet him a dollar that he wouldn't hit a home run. He did, winning one of the games.

Ruth Hale sank steadily. She would not have a doctor, although she accepted a nurse. Her brother Richard came, and Woodie was home from Europe. One day in the middle of September, Broun brought a bouquet of orchids—Ruth Hale loved orchids—and Mattie fixed them beside the bed. Richard Hale sang for his sister at her request. Then she went to sleep and did not awaken.

The next day in a New York hospital her heart stopped.

Broun sat down at once at his typewriter, for it was at the keyboard that he could best let his emotions go.

> My best friend died. . . . Nobody else, I suppose, ever gave me such warm support and approbation for those afternoons when I did my best. She made me feel ashamed when I faltered, and I suppose that for 17 years practically every word I wrote was set down with the feeling that Ruth Hale was looking over my shoulder.
>
> It would be a desperately lonely world if I did not feel that personality is of such tough fiber that in some manner it must survive and does survive. I still feel that she is looking over my shoulder.

That night Broun and sixteen-year-old Woodie had dinner at a restaurant. They had some drinks. They talked only a little. Woodie wanted to be alone and he knew that his father could find release only in liquor where the lights were bright. He said good night and went home.

Broun telephoned Carl Randau, who had become president of the New York Guild. Then he called Jim Kieran, another Guildsman and friend. He asked them to meet him at the small restaurant on 49th Street at which they sometimes discussed Guild affairs.

Randau and Kieran and Luella Henkel were in a booth when Broun arrived. After a little he spoke of Ruth Hale, of his understanding of the inevitable bitterness of the person who projects herself through another. But it was hard for him to talk about it. Those with him felt a great sense of tragedy, as did all who ever saw Broun suffer and break for a moment.

They went to Ben Marden's casino. Broun played roulette. When the hour grew very late and the place closed, a table was kept in operation. It was a symbolic gesture to the man who for more than a decade had been a toast of the big city's life after dark.

Once Broun's great body collapsed over the table, for that night he got drunk. He pulled himself together and played on. The inevitable cab waited, but dawn broke before he was willing to depart.

That fall he stayed close to Sabine Farm, and urged Woodie to spend his week ends there. But he was terribly restless. He paced the floor like a caged tiger and could not sleep. Finally he would say, "Come on, Woodie, let's go to town." Sometimes they went only as far as Stamford, but more often to New York. Once after a holiday trip to Florida Woodie got a touch of the old column trouble. Broun wrote out an excuse for lateness, which Woodie piously delivered. And then he found tacked on the school bulletin board a column about lads, specifically on H. 3d, who kept their parents out to all hours. Woodie was furious.

Broun had also a job problem to solve. There had been personnel trouble at the *World-Telegram* and he had placed himself under the orders of the New York Guild—to strike with the others if a strike occurred. Now his new contract was coming up and he was not sure of the outcome. At the same time, Hearst had offered him a contract at a thousand a week, all money from syndication, and a $25,000 bonus. Hearst, supporting the New Deal, seemed for the moment more liberal than Howard. Broun was sorely tempted.

"I don't know," he would tell Woodie. "I can imagine myself sitting at the typewriter, my fingers beginning to move—and then I would think of that old man sitting in his palace out in California."

Woodie was introduced to a picket line in Newark, where the Guild was locked in a battle with the *Ledger*. It was the first major Guild action.

"It is time," Broun said, "for you to go under fire." He was spending much time on the picket line.

Woodie went bravely to the fray encased in a sandwich sign. Let the clubs of the dread cossacks swing free. And then he heard his father say in an aside to a cop, "Would you mind keeping an eye on my kid?"

But Woodie was genuinely thrilled as Broun swung into action. A newsman who had accepted higher pay as a strike-breaker came out of the plant. Two tight-lipped men in close-fitting overcoats escorted him. Broun swept the two gunmen aside.

"Here," he said to the newsman, "I would like to talk with you."

They crossed to a saloon, and Broun later admitted practicing intimidation, round after round.

Quiet—Fairly Quiet—Years

WHEN Broun passed through Arthur Brisbane's foyer he was pleased to note that the early Broun still hung there with a light thrown on it. The benign-looking old journalist took Connie Madison's hand and then Broun's.

"It is a nice picture," he said. "I prize it."

Broun said, "I've suggested to others that they emulate you in the matter of the light. The idea hasn't caught on as well as I'd hoped."

Brisbane beamed genially. "Perhaps in time. I believe we can go in to dinner at once."

The Hearst contract was still in the air—which, Broun presumed, was the reason why Hearst's chief editor had invited him to dinner at this particular time.

"You can congratulate us," Broun said as they walked to the dining room. "Connie has agreed to marry me."

Brisbane was between them and he pressed the arm of each. "I do indeed. When will it be?"

"Oh, several months from now," Broun said. They had decided to wait until a year after Ruth Hale's death.

After dinner they sat over brandy and coffee. It was December and a fire blazed in the fireplace. Brisbane steered the conversation around to the contract.

"Now, Heywood," he said in his precise way, "you will

put the bonus in the bank. You don't have any money in the bank? No. All right, you will have a nest egg of $25,000. Then each month you add a thousand. How old are you?"

"Forty-five. I'll be forty-six in a couple of weeks."

Brisbane calculated rapidly. "So you can easily have $200,000 in the bank when you are sixty. At 4 per cent interest—eight thousand a year. That is the minimum. Without doubt Mr. Hearst will raise your contract figure—"

Broun was studying a portrait over the fireplace. "Who is that?" he asked.

Brisbane looked pensively at the picture. "It's my father."

Rising, Broun stepped over for a closer examination. He was familiar with the story of Albert Brisbane, who had bought space in newspapers to support idealistic ventures.

"A fine head." Broun meditatively blew cigarette smoke upward.

The old man still sat in reverie. He said softly, "My father would not have worked for Hearst."

Broun delicately pretended not to hear. He went back to his chair and Brisbane once more became the precise editorialist.

Later that night Broun and Connie met big, florid Joe Connolly, head of Hearst's features, at a night club and Connolly made his final pitch.

"Here's an idea," he said. "Why don't you two go ahead and get married and after the signing we'll all go down to Florida for the races? All expenses on me."

Broun puffed thoughtfully. "Well, the money looks good. I suppose it's true that all columnists are whores at heart. Some merely find it easier to relax than others."

Connolly seemed hurt. "Mr. Hearst will give you freedom as a special writer. Look at Winchell. He's always getting off the reservation."

Broun said, "Hearst's *San Francisco Call-Bulletin* fired Dean Jennings a little while ago for Guild activities. That's two in one city."

"You've got those cases up before Government boards," Connolly said. "The main thing is, you'll have plenty of space and a bigger circulation."

Broun turned to Connie. "What about it?"

Connie shook her head. "If it were show business I would say grab the cash. About newspapers I don't know."

Broun got up. "I'll give you the answer in a minute."

He went to the washroom and took his courage shot. Half a minute later he started back with his decision made.

"You've been very kind," he said to Connolly. "I guess it's no." He smiled, but there was no question that the answer was definite.

Broun went to Florida, anyhow, to recover from a cold and see the races. The cold improved and he was as success-ful at the track as he ever was. But he was restless and lonely. He wrote to Connie, who was dancing in "Merrily We Roll Along." It was one of the only three letters she ever got from him.

I am losing more weight than money. Things are a little slow and I get to bed about 1 o'clock and don't sleep very well. I miss you like hell and am really anxious to get back and see you. You might start getting your trousseau ready and see if you can pick up something for a hope chest because if you haven't changed your mind I see no reason why we shouldn't trip pretty soon after I get back.

Back in New York, he took Connie to the 21 Club for lunch to discuss marriage plans.

"As I remember it," Broun said, "getting married is pretty

complicated. I better call Mac. People probably get married out of here every day."

Mac Kriendler, when he came over, suggested City Hall.

"That's where you get a license," Broun said. "I know that much. What do you do after that?"

"Why," Kriendler said, "simply call in Mayor LaGuardia and get married."

It sounded too simple to Broun. "If I can't get the straight goods here," he said, "I know where I can. The newspapermen down at City Hall are Guildsmen and they will tell me."

He meditated for a moment. "How about the Catholic Church?" he asked Connie. "Wouldn't you want to be married in Church?"

"Naturally," she said. "I always said I wanted to be married in Church."

"Have you found out about that part of it?"

"No. I thought when the time came we could go and ask Father McKenna at the Actors' Church."

"You do that," Broun said. "Find out what we have to do. Now we'll drive down to City Hall and get the score on that end."

He had been right about City Hall reporters knowing the marriage ropes.

"Why, of course," said Barney Mallady of *City News,* "we'll see you through. We wouldn't miss the story for the world. As a Guild brother I will be happy to stand up with you."

Broun held up a hand. "We hadn't expected such fast treatment. We're only investigating."

But he conferred with the bride-to-be. The church ceremony, she knew, could follow after the civil one.

"Let's go," Broun said to Mallady.

Mayor LaGuardia, as it happened, was not available. But after the couple had taken out a license they were quickly hauled before a magistrate and the nuptial knot was tied.

They decided to forgo a honeymoon, Broun being busy with Guild affairs. He took the required instruction from the padre of the actors, Father McKenna, liking the backstage touch, and the church ceremony was held a few weeks later. After school was out they took Woodie on an ocean cruise.

Broun at last felt the need for settling down. They gave up the lease at the Des Artistes, and after eleven years at Sabine Farm Broun took up seriously the task of transforming himself into a country squire.

He bought no tweed coat and feather-decorated slouch hat, nor did he sling a gun over his shoulder for a grouse. If on his way to shoot anything it would have been a hunter. The slaughter of hunters by each other was the only mass killing he ever advocated. But he did plant gardens of flowers and vegetables, he sat for longer hours fishing or painting, and a far greater portion of his columns went to New York via telegraph.

Connie went to work to put the place into shape. During Give-a-Job-till-June a big stone-walled room had been added to the main farmhouse. It had an enormous fireplace and hewn ceiling rafters and a stage at one end. But the house as a whole was in poor condition. The furniture consisted of an old gas stove, some heavy and shabby pieces from the 85th Street house, and the usual Brounian piles of books. The plumbing seldom worked well and often not at all. Cars had customarily driven straight to the front door, ruining any grass that tried to lift its head. The swamp, home of Broun's old friend, the blacksnake, was as unsightly as ever.

Under Connie's direction the house was renovated and new furniture was installed. The swamp, drained, became a

pond and was stocked with pickerel and bass. In warm
weather Broun did most of his writing at a desk on a small,
screened-in porch. He painted either on the steps or at a
stump, for both his rock and the blacksnake had disappeared.
Fishing activities were mostly shifted from the lake to the
pond, despite his feeling that the stocking had been over-
done. After getting four bites and two fish in an hour he
threatened to have the pond seined.

He laid out new and more fantastic holes for his golf
course. Everybody had to play him for the championship,
which rated a large cup originally won by the chorus girls
of "Shoot the Works" in a driving tournament. In its life at
Sabine Farm the cup was not presented unless filled to the
brim with champagne. Broun won it over and over again—
as often as half a dozen times in an afternoon—always sharing
the wine. The cup remained in his possession for the reason
that guests were not allowed to depart until he had beat
them. Sometimes this took as long as a week. Another form
of exercise was wood chopping, for in the winter he liked
to work at one end of a long, narrow table in the big room
while wood of his personal cutting blazed in the great fireplace.

It was true that Broun's new-found domesticity created
problems. He liked to take charge of the kitchen in the
cook's absence. Singing loud and clear, he would labor
mightily while family and knowing guests cowered. The food
would be delivered to the table as if presented by Oscar
of the Waldorf on one of his better days. Everybody had to
taste it. Broun was firm on that point. But upon rejection
he amiably ate it himself while the others fared for themselves, perhaps repairing to a neighbor's.

He remained something less than an epicure when partak-
ing of strong drink. Once Gene Tunney appeared at the

Broun house with some fine old wine and an ancient liqueur of beautiful bouquet. Rules of the gourmet were to be followed. Broun filled all requirements for the wine. He even washed out his mouth with black coffee, as told, in preparation for the liqueur. And then he dumped it nonchalantly over his ice cream and began to eat.

Tunney watched with round, shocked eyes.

"Very good this way, Gene," Broun said. "Try it."

Woodie couldn't figure out whether his father was kidding Tunney or merely wanted it that way.

Connie became secretary and chauffeur. After she had taken a course in typewriting Broun sometimes dictated his columns to her, and she answered the mail. As secretary she took down the column and as chauffeur she drove t to the station for telegraphing. She had selected a Buick when buying a new car and Broun came to trust his person in her hands—at a low rate of speed.

At the same time Connie went to work on his appearance. His figure did not become exactly slender, but under her urging he dieted and exercised in a more orderly fashion. The pounds disappeared. Though maintaining carelessness of attire at home—wandering around in the bottoms of pajamas or his painting pants or lying naked on the dock—Broun became a different man in public. Connie located a tailor near the 21 Club. When in the city Broun took a little time before entering or popped out between drinks for a fitting. He liked his new clothes, especially a handsome camel's hair overcoat.

The bright lights of the big town did not disappear entirely from Broun's life. With Connie he attended most of the big first nights and occasionally they toured the clubs together. Broun liked to spend evenings with the boys. When on the town he usually ended late at night with

Quentin Reynolds and Joe Brooks in Madeleine's Restaurant in the East Fifties, where a string trio knew Broun's favorite songs. Late customers never escaped the ringing

> Stand, stand to your glasses steady
> And drink to your comrade's eyes.
> Here's a toast to the dead already
> And a cup to the next man that dies.

One night at a party Broun met novelist Thomas Wolfe, who had a grievance. For years, he said, people had been mistaking him for Heywood Broun. They came up on the street, in the subway, and especially at parties. One thing they always seemed to ask was about night clubs. It was all right to be mistaken for Broun, but it was hard to answer the questions. After all, he had never been in a night club.

Broun apologized for the inconvenience he had caused. At least part of the problem could be solved. A guided tour of the bright spots started at once.

Winters Broun and Connie usually went to Florida, and sometimes they traveled from Sabine Farm for week ends. They never quite made it to Woollcott's Vermont island retreat, but they went to Swope's new place at Sands Point. For a great party every fall, Averell Harriman opened the family estate where as a cub Broun had crawled up the mountain. One of the noteworthy sights was Broun bowling. He could bowl well only in his sock feet. And he took care to bowl at his best. Broun and Alicia Patterson, daughter of owner Captain Joe Patterson of the *Daily News*, had become friends when she had been the wife of Joe Brooks. Later she had married Harry Guggenheim, and Broun and Connie visited at the Guggenheim estate in South Carolina.

In the main, though, the Brouns immersed themselves in the neighborly doings of Fairfield County's literary set.

Harold Ross' new house was only a few minutes away. Ross and Jane Grant had been divorced and he had married again. Even closer was Judge George T. Bye, known more familiarly to Broun in his columns as Old Ten Per Cent Bye because of his possession of a stable of fine literary properties. In the judicial field Bye had won a scintillating victory as the people's choice for justice of the peace, the sign for which hung above the bar in his basement. Westbrook Pegler had built a picture-book château among a grove of weeping willows only five minutes away. Quentin Reynolds either rented a place in the summertime or visited regularly. Ursula Parrott lived not far away and so did Gene Tunney.

They went back and forth to each other's houses for dinner and cards. Broun had given up high-stake poker after dropping a few less than a thousand dollars of a bonus check from the Book-of-the-Month Club—he was one of the judges —in a single sitting. Had he lost the entire thousand or even a little more he would not have minded. But he felt silly rising with only a few dollars remaining out of the check. Now he compensated mostly with bridge. As in the old days of partnership with Christy Mathewson he was an able player. He would spend a couple of minutes analyzing his hand, then play with lightning speed. With Connie he worked out a system that made them formidable.

There were also low-stake neighborhood poker games. Usually the players were Pegler and his wife Julie, Broun and Connie, Quentin Reynolds, Woodie if he were home from school, and Frederick Tisdale, now editor and publisher of the New Milford, Conn., *Times*. Broun permitted his love for inside straights full play. It was expected that Pegler would end up each time thirty-seven dollars in the hole.

One of Broun's poker habits disconcerted Pegler. The

Thanatopsis crowd had always known that when Broun asked to be dealt out for a hand or two he planned to hunt up a typewriter to do his column. Pegler was irritated when he found out where Broun went. Pegler required many hours of toil and sweat to finish his own daily stint.

Most *World-Telegram* readers would have been surprised to see the two columnists at play. For Pegler had accompanied Roy Howard into the camp of the extreme conservatives, where both busily stoked fires to warm Roosevelt-haters, while Broun was Roosevelt's chief friend among the columnists. Pegler in his column liked to call Broun "Old Bleeding Heart," and otherwise handled him roughly. Many thought Howard egged Pegler on.

Broun still looked on Pegler as a fine sports writer who was out of his element and therefore exaggerated his pose of cynicism. "It's too bad," Broun would say, "that anyone ever taught Peg to write at all. He's as sweet a fellow as you would care to meet until he sits down at the typewriter." Or he would say, "Peg's wife isn't well. He worries a lot about her and sometimes doesn't have time to think." Broun admitted that perhaps Pegler ought to have the hide taken off him—to reveal the better stuff underneath.

But occasionally he was rougher. He stated a belief that an income tax had bitten Pegler severely at an early age and suggested that the man who had named Pegler's column had also titled near beer. Once Pegler after a particularly cutting attack on Broun came up to him in a night club and suggested they forget what they wrote during the day and be pals at night.

"What I write by day," Broun said, "I live by night."

But he let it go at that and Pegler sat down.

The major neighborhood social event was Broun's picnic in the summer of 1937 for fellow-journalist Mrs. Franklin

D. Roosevelt. Mrs. Heywood Cox Broun journeyed from the city, adding a touch of Victorian formality to the otherwise free-and-easy journalistic atmosphere. The sharp editorial eye of Harold Ross noted that Broun dressed down for the occasion. In the morning Broun had looked rather natty for a trip into New York. In the afternoon he wore a sweatshirt and flannel slacks. Ross had personally made the chile con carne and he lurked in the background to overhear any comment Mrs. Roosevelt might make. "Very good soup," she said, and repeated, "Very good soup." Ross slunk away, happy. Pegler, who was beginning to disapprove of Mrs. Roosevelt as much as he did of her husband, sulked on the back porch, where the bar was, but kept his voice to a mutter. An old-time Brounian touch came when Mrs. Roosevelt got tangled in the broken back stoop, not yet replaced, and had to be extricated by Broun.

Broun was working hard to be a father and getting pretty confused about it. Woodie was attending Swarthmore. Broun had wanted him to quit after a year to be a journalist. Woodie refused. In the first place, he did not intend to be a journalist. In the second, he would have to go to college for a long time, inasmuch as he planned to be a teacher, probably of English. The exaggerated progressive education had affected both of them. Woodie, having been brought up to stand by himself, naturally was not demonstrative. He had fun with his father but kept his problems to himself. Broun wanted now to be protective and close. At the same time he was shy. He had known well enough, for example, that Woodie smoked, having seen him light hundreds of cigarettes. Though not disapproving, he had had trouble recognizing the fact by offering one of his own. Finally he had managed it. "Here," he had said, looking away while extending the package, "have a cigarette." Broun's father-to-son talks established a record even for him in tortured circumlocution. "Woodie," he would say, "sit down a minute." And then after embarrassed small talk he would suggest, "I was wondering if you'd like to go into New York." Toward dawn, after a round of the clubs, he would finally blurt out, "I had something I wanted to tell you . . . "

Broun had adopted Connie's daughter, Patricia Dooley, a slender child of nine, at the time of the marriage. He spoke and wrote of her as his daughter. She returned the compliment by worshiping him. Earlier, confused, she had addressed him as Mr. Broun. "You just call me Heywood," he had told her.

Middle age and domesticity in no way quenched Broun's spirit. The first stirrings toward organization in the mass workers industries after establishment of the Committee for Industrial Organization moved him deeply, for he saw not only the bettering of living standards but a step toward the brotherhood of man. His hatred for Hitlerism was more than intellectual and went deeper than sympathy for the victims of Nazism. Fascism could make him physically ill, and he attacked it with savage fury. Because he believed the United States should co-operate with Russia against Hitler's evident plan of world conquest, and because of opposition to political discrimination in unions, he was often called a Communist, or at least a fellow-traveler.

Sometimes Broun had moments of uncertainty about the Guild. Not the need, nor his loyalty—but there was a fairly large body of opinion that his leadership was actually harmful. The point of view was expressed in a frank letter by Allen Raymond, who had been elected president of the New York Guild at the time Broun had been named vice president.

You know as well as I that your position in news-
paperdom as a lively controversialist on all manner of
issues, notoriously prone to shock the bourgeoisie, has
made you and your personality so great a topic of dispute and discussion that a calm consideration of the
Guild in many influential quarters within the industry,
and in the editorial rooms of the newspapers among
persons who should be Guild supporters but are not,
is well nigh impossible as long as you are its flag or
figurehead.

Delegates at the national conventions carried home tales
of the whimsical giant sitting at the chairman's table sipping
from a water glass of gin. But that he was never tipsy. What
a man to hold his liquor! He was a good chairman. Even
Editor & Publisher, which accused him of trying to kidnap
the Guild and all manner of other crimes, admitted that he
was a superb handler of fractious meetings. His intuition
allowed him to get the feel of a gathering in a hurry. And
he was always re-elected by acclamation.

While Broun welded together various schools of opinion,
he was anything but a compromiser. Given the role of helms-
man, he intended to steer. And being of an impetuous
nature he sometimes, his friends charged gloomily, handled
the Guild as if it were a canoe instead of a ship. He led the
fight to get into the American Federation of Labor, feeling
the need for outside support for newsmen in time of trouble.
But by the time William Green arrived with a charter Broun
favored industry-wide rather than craft unionism and consequently preferred the climate of the C.I.O. When in his
presentation speech Green attacked industrial unionism,
Broun rose and answered. Afterward he admitted to the
canoe charge. A big Broun-Green feud got under way, with

Green threatening a rival union. The Guild went into the
C.I.O., began to take in employees of business departments
and other noneditorial workers, and sloughed off altogether
the "gentlemen of the press" ideology. Walter Lippmann
quit paying dues and dropped his half a brick. Other "name"
writers did the same.

Many of the city Guilds had, of course, risen almost spon-
taneously and nearly all of the early ones had grown without
paid organizers. Broun never collected a salary, which was
beneficial to the treasury, but lack of a full-time president
threw a strain on Executive Vice President Jonathan Eddy
and others. Broun, being hardly a detail man, tended despite
strong guilt feelings to withdraw from the smaller problems.

In this he did not hesitate to employ deviousness. Because
of his constitutional difficulty in saying "no," Connie was
put forth as a sort of outer guard. She felt herself gaining
a reputation as a block in the pathway of progress.

But when Broun's help was essential, he took down his
mace and sallied forth. In such a campaign he once more
saw the inside of a jail, though the truth was that he had
been tagged as expendable before the battle ever started.
In 1936 Guildsmen of Hearst's Milwaukee *Wisconsin News*
struck—the wage scale was fifteen dollars a week for reporters.
The struggle dragged out. Something dramatic was needed.

Police had been rough and local Guild leaders thought
they would arrest Broun should he insist on making a speech.
And so Broun was called upon to journey to Milwaukee.
A platform was set up across from the *News* and at the
appointed time a crowd of Guildsmen and sympathizers
gathered. Broun began to speak as advertised.

The police told him to desist. He proceeded. In a minute
the police and the crowd were battling and Broun and others

were arrested. There was more fighting when the crowd marched to the jail, shouting, "We want Broun!"

Afterward he maintained that he lost his case—he was fined a few dollars—through either the overenthusiasm of a local attorney or his own inability to look gallant. Conducting his own defense, he was about to win, he thought, when the attorney made a glowing speech describing him as a white-plumed Sir Henry of Navarre ridden out to right the wrongs of the oppressed. Disheveled, unshaven, face and clothes streaked with dirt, Broun felt that the court didn't put any more credence in the description than he did.

The arrest had its effect. Victory came after a national crusade had been raised.

Broun stood in danger of sacrificing economic security, as he neared fifty, for the sake of the Guild and the views for which he stood. Pay scales and shorter hours won by the Guild had cost Roy Howard money.

"A fine thing, Heywood," he had said, "to do to a friend!"

Broun told Carl Randau, "Roy hates me now. I can feel it."

The little "He writes as he pleases" box and its philosophy had long since departed. Broun's column was often mercilessly slashed—ostensibly to improve its reader interest—but the first to go seemed always to be the guts. Sometimes it was left nearly unintelligible. Around the *World-Telegram* office the general opinion was that Lee Wood, the executive editor, was out to "get" Broun at Howard's instigation. All manner of insults, such as notes to Broun accusing him of deteriorating, were resorted to.

The deadline for Broun's copy was moved up from 6 P.M. to 4 P.M. on the day before publication. The reason given was need for earlier distribution through the syndicate.

The change severely handicapped Broun. It was hard to adjust his thinking to a new schedule, for more than ever he wrote from hot news. Without the afternoon papers to work from he was thrown a day behind the news.

Though his claustrophobia and psycho-cardiac condition were nearly cured, there came over Broun occasional fits of profound depression. He needed companionship and sometimes it was unbearable to be alone. Often he would cook up involved—and completely unnecessary—schemes to avoid being alone. Stopping off at Saratoga Springs once, when returning from a Guild convention, he telephoned Frank Sullivan, who lived there, asking if he had a free typewriter and if so could he bring it down to the hotel? On the train Broun, suffering a bad attack of depression, had considered wiring ahead for Sullivan to meet him with a car. But he had gotten a little better. Sullivan quickly perceived that not a typewriter but company was wanted.

Heavy colds continued to strike Broun down despite a more regular life. At such times he spoke gloomily of death, often calling Woodie to his bedside. "It looks as though my insurance money will be about the size of it," he would say. "I won't be able to get much ahead between now and the time to go."

The big blue Bible filled with new markers as he meditated on religious matters. To fulfill a desire to write more fully of religion he contracted for a book on Pontius Pilate. His idea of God was changing. God was less abstract.

To Carl Randau he said, "It is inconceivable to me that no hereafter exists. Except for belief in the future life, I couldn't keep going."

The Catholic conception of a brotherhood of man in the fatherhood of God interested him, and so did the security found by many in the Church. The mystical side of him had always been impressed by the ceremony and pageantry of the Catholic Church. And he was not unaware of the value of absolution of sins, if such were possible. He asked Frank Sullivan for the name of a priest with whom he might hold religious discussions. Sullivan didn't think he was serious. He asked Connie to scout around for a priest with whom he could discuss theology.

21

Halfway Home

Wᴴᴇɴ spring came to the rich, greening farmlands of
Fairfield County in 1938, seven stalwart sons of the soil and
one daughter gathered at New Canaan in ancient pioneer
fashion. A barn-raising was not the purpose. All those who
wanted barns had them. The meeting was a "literary," in
the tradition of early settlers who foregathered to consider
sustenance for the brain. Country folks plainly needed a
country newspaper.

Those present to fill the gap were Ursula Parrott, Deems
Taylor, Stanley High, Gene Tunney, John Erskine, Quentin
Reynolds, George Bye, Heywood Broun, Jack Pegler, and
Colvin Brown. The last two, advertising executives when
away from the soil, would be handy in the case of any busi-
ness. The meeting place was in what Jack Pegler's brother
Westbrook (who offered to contribute words but no cash)
called "a love bower over a grocery store." Already a name,
Connecticut Nutmeg, had been supplied by a factual type
who recalled that Connecticut is known as "The Nutmeg
State."

Scribbling furiously, George Bye, trying out for gossip
columnist, got down a flavorsome stenographic report.

278

HIGH: I have to meet my wife in Stamford, and if the others are going to be late I had better be getting on.

BYE: They all said they would be here.

ERSKINE: Good afternoon. I think there should be a note of substance in the publication.

BROWN: We must hold these meetings later. I'd like to stay in my garden until five.

PARROTT: Good afternoon. Speaking of gardens, I am going to grow all my own vegetables this year.

BYE: If any of you have manuscript I will be glad to put it in our hope chest.

PARROTT: My secretary has my copy in a portfolio and she will be along in a few minutes.

REYNOLDS: Howdy. How long do we have to be here? I have some friends waiting downstairs.

BYE: Just about an hour—after Broun arrives.

TUNNEY: Hello, all of you. Has anything been decided?

HIGH: I would like to meet Mr. Tunney.

REYNOLDS: Get the pen for an autograph.

PEGLER: Excuse me for being so late, please. I just sold my place in Pound Ridge and am moving up to Lewisboro.

BYE: Need any more land there? My wife has a nice 60 acres—high, dry, flat, cleared, with a stream.

PEGLER: What do you want—?

BROUN: Sorry I am late. I would like to persuade Gene to be our sports commentator. Now, now, now, don't say you would rather be in the business department. We are all for all here and if you would only tell everything you know about sports, our fortune would be made.

PEGLER: I understood this was to be a benevolent

enterprise where none of us was out for a fortune.

BROUN: Well, we want to see the paper satisfy, don't we? Gene has the dope that sells. If he is bashful, I propose we retire—he, Quent and I, with the stenographer—and get started on his first column.

TUNNEY: I'll do my own column, thank you.

PARROTT: If you will come up to my place I will telephone my butler to have a drink ready.

BYE: Have any of you such a thing as a piece of manuscript?

PARROTT: My secretary will be along in a few minutes —or are you all coming to my house?

PEGLER: If it isn't a newspaper, what is it? I think the subscription rate outside Fairfield County should be the same as inside. How are we going to have national advertisers?

HIGH: Are we going to have national advertisers?

BROWN: Sure, and it's just a matter of our decency in setting the rates.

BROUN: I move these matters be left with a business committee consisting of Brown, Pegler, and Tunney.

BYE: Is there a second?

PARROTT: Shall I telephone my butler?

JANITOR: Good evening. I have to be paid extra. It's not in the rent. Now, if you are going to have carpets, it will be $10 a month. Without carpets, $5.

BROUN: We must be fair.

PARROTT: My butler says he is ready.

BYE: Please, isn't there any manuscript?

Deems Taylor either maintained a dignified silence or said nothing that Bye considered newsworthy.

Halfway Home

In the first issue of the eight-page tabloid *Nutmeg*, Broun turned up in charge of nature notes, writing of his garden, where Connie was doing the heavy work albeit with brilliant guidance. Tunney did appear with a sports column; Bye whispered county gossip; Ursula Parrott handled Beauty, Diet, and Etiquette; John Erskine did Men's Furnishings and doubled as heavy-duty thinker on local problems; Stanley High made Americana notes; Quentin Reynolds was unrestricted. Plainly *Nutmeg* would be a scurrilous journal. A rival editor, Harold Ross, was to be profiled and all having seen him with low companions were invited to correspond.

Broun loved the horseplay. After all, nowadays the *World-Telegram* was cramping him into six hundred words underneath Pegler and, of all people, General Hugh S. Johnson. In the *Nutmeg* he could be corny in his fashion of the *Tribune* and the dear, dead *World*. Once in pursuit of material for his Nature Notes he encountered a gigantic rabbit. While they stared at one another fiercely he allowed himself a soliloquy.

One does not like to seem sentimental about inanimate things but I remembered spring and the good earth and the scent of lilacs. And when I had finished my planting Connie and I had gone to New York for dinner at the Stork Club. And she joshed me about the fact that at last I was a farmer with half a row of beets in the bank.

"Just the same when summer comes you'll laugh out of the other side of that pretty little mouth of yours," I told her. Always I must have my joke.

"When these vegetables ripen we will turn them into soup," I continued, "and this time the meal will be absolutely free."

"What do you mean, free?" replied Connie who is a sucker for a cue.

"Because," I answered with a dead pan, "this is to be beet soup and it will be borscht and paid for."

And just as easily he wrote words of unmatched eloquence and flashing insight. After the Munich Pact, Gene Tunney, writing in the *Nutmeg*, defended Neville Chamberlain's action as the only way out, saying that he had secured peace and anyhow the Germans would win a war if it started.

Broun's tossed-off answer recalled a discussion among *Nutmeg* editors before the second Louis-Schmeling fight. They had expected Schmeling to win again. Tunney the expert had at first listened in courteous silence. "Gentlemen," he had finally said, "you're forgetting the imponderability of spiritual fortification." He was thinking of Schmeling's Nazi insults to Louis' race. And Louis had won by a ferocious first-round knockout.

Broun ended:

> The Gargantuas of the world make a most fierce appearance and when they thump upon their chests the forest echoes to the sound as if great drums were beating. And yet it is a hollow sound although in sheer volume it may almost deafen those who stand by the good word. And Tunney should not forget the lesson which he himself expounded. Remember well, Gene, before you surrender the world over to the fury of the Fascists that there is such a thing as "the imponderability of spiritual fortification."

Except for the gathering war clouds, nearly everything was pleasant that summer for Broun. He had hoped, it was true, to step aside as president of the Guild. In only five years it had become a solid working institution. Guildsmen decided that he was still needed, and that was heart-warming. Relations with his boss were still bad. But how could anyone expect them to be otherwise? Anyhow, his contract had more than a year to run. His health was better. Diet, exercise, and the eschewing of old-fashioneds and sweet cocktails had brought his weight down forty pounds.

He was having a good year on the ball diamond. True enough, his arm was gone. Never again, as at a Madison Square Garden benefit, would he make Babe Ruth pound the air as thousands cheered. The Babe had struck the empty air only two blows and on the third try had struck the baseball—well, softball—for a home run. That sort of thing could happen to any pitcher. Now Captain Gene Tunney was on the mound for the *Nutmeg* team. Like Babe Ruth before him, Broun had gone to right field, and now was looked upon primarily as a slugger. He was also a popular base runner, though his proxy shared honors. Connie ran the bases—including from the plate to first—in shorts.

The Nutmegger Club was just a little tougher than the rowdy St. Louis Cardinals' Gashouse Gang. The lineup against Lowell Thomas' Nine Old Men was Westbrook Pegler c, Honorable Michael A. Connor 1b, Deems Taylor 2b, Jack Pegler 3b, Quentin Reynolds roving ss, George Bye ss, Bernard Gimbel cf, Harold Ross lf, and Broun rf. Substitutes included H. T. Webster, R. E. Simon, Colvin Brown, John Erskine, John Gunther, Hendrik van Loon, and Humphrey Doulens—a notably strong bench. They played hard and neither asked nor gave any quarter. When Hendrik van Loon suffered a grievous injury, breaking a toe while getting into his uniform, they merely laughed heartily. Since Lowell

Thomas' team had usurped the proper garb for sons of the soil—overalls—they played in T-shirts, duck trousers, and a paint company's white give-away caps.

When December 7 rolled around and Broun awoke knowing that fifty years had passed since the great day on Brooklyn's Pineapple Street, he called for a mirror and had a look at himself. The triangle lines had cut deep around his mouth and other lines in his face had deepened. His hair was shot with gray, and at the top back of his head was a bald spot the size of a dollar.

"Halfway home," he said cheerfully to Connie, sitting down to his poached eggs.

"You look very youthful on your birthday," she said, tactfully.

"The second half they say is the hardest." He tried his coffee but it was too hot.

Connie said, "You can use a sun tan. Florida will do you good."

Broun nodded. "We'll have fun. But I'd like to take along some studying matter when we do go. Have you found any priests?"

Connie poured more coffee for herself. "I thought you'd been talking with Quent."

"Quent's no theologian."

"Well, why don't you go and see Father Kelly at Stamford? He would be happy to talk with you, he told me. Or Father McKenna. Do priests have to run after you?"

"No," Broun said. "I've been thinking of going for a talk. They must have some reading they could steer me to."

After breakfast Broun sat down at the long table. He decided not to fret about age, either to mourn the past or mull over whether he had done right or wrong. He began to type.

Halfway Home

At 50 I have more faith than I had before. People are better than I thought they were going to be—myself included. In mere physical exertion there may be some let-up. Instead of the daily constitutional of a hundred yards it will be 25 from now on. But at 50 I'm a better fighter than at 21. I'm more radical and things which once were just a sort of sentimental solace are now realities. Brotherhood is not just a Bible word. Out of comradeship can come and will come the happy life for all. The underdog can and will lick his weight in the wildcats of the world.

On the day before Christmas, in the late afternoon, the atmosphere in the big room at Sabine Farm was tense, despite the roaring fire, the Christmas tree, a flowing bowl, and other signs of relaxation and good cheer. The ear of Patricia was glued to the radio. Connie hid her nervousness. Woodie, home from college, made a fairly successful effort at nonchalance. Broun paced, lighting one cigarette after another. In the city Mrs. Heywood Cox Broun had been alerted.

For President Roosevelt would soon deliver his Christmas message, and Broun had reason to believe that he might be due for a signal honor. The two men, besides being warm admirers of each other, had become fairly well acquainted. Broun had been a guest on the campaign train two years before, though it was true that he had lost his nerve after picking a bouquet of sunflowers, Alf Landon's emblem, for presentation to his host. In the end he had worked up courage only to give them to Mrs. Roosevelt.

On the other hand, Broun had been guilty of a startling *faux pas*. He had been invited to Hyde Park with a few others who might know how to bring peace between the A.F. of L. and the C.I.O. After the main discussion, the President, relaxing, had begun an anecdote. The President's anecdotes could be long, and Broun's column deadline had already passed by. The rule of protocol is that no one shall interrupt the President of the United States. Broun was not familiar with it. He had found a pause, wedged into it, excused himself graciously, and departed.

Shocked upon learning of his gaucherie, Broun had boned up on such matters with the result that a little later he had been able to look down his nose at Connie. George Bye, visiting with his wife at the White House, had telephoned an invitation from the President and Mrs. Roosevelt to dinner. Broun had been at work on a magazine commitment.

Connie said, "Just ask for a rain check on that."

"When the President commands," Broun said, importantly, "one goes." The typewriter began to roar.

Roosevelt and Broun possessed the same habit of slyly drawing people out through baiting, and with plenty of time the two would have had many pleasant hours of gossip. Once at a luncheon on the Hyde Park lawn Connie, offered a place next to the President, had been fearful that some discussion of gigantic affairs would snow her under. Her endeavor to change with Broun had failed. Hendrik van Loon had started the conversation with four loud harrumphs and a "What do you think of your chances of re-election, Mr. President?" Roosevelt, stating that he lacked the foggiest notion, had launched into a story about William Randolph Hearst's jealousy over his friend Marion Davies.

Now, out of the radio, clear as a bell, came the celebrated voice.

Last night before I went to sleep, I chanced to read in an evening newspaper a story by a columnist which ap-

pealed to me so much as a Christmas sermon that I am
going to read it. Here is the parable.

Still Broun was not quite sure.

The voice continued, "We were sitting in a high room
above the chapel . . ."

Broun knew that it was his, and he rushed into the hall
and wept. But he listened, pacing up and down.

The story told of the narrator, Broun, sitting with an old
dominie who was pondering his Christmas sermon for the
morrow. It must be of peace and good will toward men, in
a world filled with hatred and sorrow. "You may laugh at
me," the old man said, "but right now I am wondering how
Christmas came to Judas Iscariot."

He requested his visitor to grasp his fingers and with them
open the Bible at random. It was a gentle trick of the old
man's, but his hand was less subtle than of old. The verse,
when he ran his finger down the page, turned out to be the
twenty-fifth in the twenty-sixth chapter of Saint Matthew.
"Then Judas, which betrayed him, answered and said, 'Master, is it I?' He said unto him, 'Thou hast said.' "

And so the dominie seemed to have arrived at a dead end.
Then, face brightening, he asked for the twenty-seventh
verse: "He took the cup and gave thanks and gave it to them,
saying, 'Drink ye all of it.' "

"Mark that," cried the old man exultantly. "Not even
to Judas, the betrayer, was the wine of life denied. I can
preach my Christmas sermon now, and my test will be
'Drink ye all of it.' Good-will toward men means good-
will to every last son of God. Peace on earth means peace
to Pilate, peace to the thieves on the cross, and peace to
poor Iscariot."

I was glad, for he had found Christmas and I saw by his face that once more he heard the voice of the herald angels.

When the President had finished and the announcer had given credit to the proper columnist, Broun came back into the room. He was gay now. Picking up the phone he called Western Union and sent off a message to his old friend, Steve Early, White House press secretary: PLEASE CONVEY TO THE PRESIDENT MY APPRECIATION FOR THE FACT THAT HE READ MY STORY. AND TELL HIM, ALSO, THAT HE DID IT EVEN BETTER THAN I COULD HAVE DONE MYSELF.

Brotherhood in God

IN FLORIDA, where they went in January, Broun and Connie stayed at the Miami-Biltmore in Coral Gables. Broun swam and played golf and went to the races. But old friends noticed a change. He was not in the ordinary sense morose, for his smile would come quickly enough and his courtesy was unflagging, but he brooded more than ever and he was not quite spontaneous.

Staying at the Miami-Biltmore, too, was Alfred McCosker, publicity director for the Mutual Broadcasting Company, and his wife. A quarter of a century before, Broun had nicknamed McCosker "Hollywood" for his bringing about of "a meeting of the whispers and the shadows"—early radio and movies. McCosker, a stocky, hearty man with a pink face and white hair, was in possession of a special pass admitting its bearer to special preserves at the Hialeah Track. He lent it often to Broun.

Broun's habit was to attend the races in the afternoon, usually with Connie, and then go back to the hotel and swim in the pool or play golf, or both. Afterward he wrote his column. Then they dined and spent the evening at the dog races, at roulette, or merely sitting around talking.

One night they ran into McCosker and his wife in the dining room of the Roney-Plaza Hotel. In the quiet, residential Miami-Biltmore no more than a hello would have been exchanged. But the gay, whirling Roney-Plaza seemed far from home. It was like Main Streeters running into one another in the city.

McCosker got up. "Old friends, greetings," he said as if they had been long parted. "Join us. We're having a beer. What will you have?"

Broun and Connie sat down and ordered. The conversation fitted the gay atmosphere, except that Broun entered it but rarely.

"What's the matter?" McCosker asked. "Why do you brood?"

Broun shrugged. "I'm not brooding, Hollywood."

"You were brooding until something more like brooding comes along." McCosker looked around the room. "Here are people drinking, eating, being merry. God can't be such a bad feller, after all."

Broun nodded slowly. "You know, Hollywood, I've been interested in your church. Maybe I will study the catechism."

McCosker didn't want to start a religious discussion. On the other hand, he did not want a suggestion of patronage to pass unnoticed.

"What makes you think the Catholic Church would even be interested in you?" he asked.

"Probably wouldn't be." Broun sipped his Jack Rose, a tall pink iced drink. "But I could study. They wouldn't mind that."

McCosker started to turn the conversation to a new subject when Connie, carrying out her research orders, motioned to him to keep going. She said aside, "Heywood is really interested."

"Where do you plan to study?" McCosker went on.

Broun puffed his cigarette idly. "Oh, Connie's been hunting around, talking with priests, and I've been doing it some, too. Probably I would study with someone up in Connecticut."

"That's fine," McCosker said. "I'm sure you can get excellent instruction there. But why don't you see Monsignor Sheen?"

Broun glanced up. Monsignor Fulton J. Sheen of Catholic University, Washington, D. C., was already a famed preacher and church philosopher. "Sure," Broun said, "and I'll bring along Franklin Roosevelt to keep me company."

"No, no." McCosker shook his head. "I'm serious. If you say the word I'll get in touch with Monsignor when I go back North. You'll owe a favor to no one and no one will owe you a favor."

"I would appreciate it," Broun said.

"Done and done," McCosker answered.

Almost immediately after returning from Florida, Broun and Connie made a swing through another section of the South. At San Antonio, Texas, Broun toured the slums—some of the worst in America—with Father Tranchese, pastor of the Church of Guadalupe. Father Tranchese said to him before they started, "It may be dangerous if you go with me, for there are many who have made threats because I am in favor of a housing project." Broun was impressed by the priest's fight for better homes in the face of danger.

In St. Louis he pursued his investigations of Catholicism in talks with Father Edward Dowling, who had been a baseball player and newspaperman before studying for the priesthood and now as editor of a local Catholic paper was an enthusiastic Guildsman. These three things—ball player, newspaperman, Guildsman—were as fine qualifications for a confidant as Broun could think of. They talked for many hours.

The burning question in Broun's mind was: Is there anything in Catholicism which stands in the way of a person who believes in political and economic liberalism?

Father Dowling said there was not. "Don't you realize you're a little naive, Heywood?" he asked. "You like to call yourself a radical, but the doctrines of the church are far more radical." He pointed out that one of the top C.I.O. leaders, Philip Murray, was a Catholic. And in the big C.I.O. drives the local priests had generally helped, not hindered.

Broun sighed. "You remember, I didn't want to run last year for the Guild presidency? Now, if I should be taken into the Church, I'll have to prove I didn't change my ideas by running again."

Back in New York, Broun was at once embroiled with another priest. Father Charles E. Coughlin's admirers marched on 52nd Street before radio station WMCA, which had stopped carrying Coughlin's speeches because of anti-Semitic content. Some of the signs carried by the pickets read, CHRISTIANS AWAKE, BUY CHRISTIAN, and EMPLOY CHRISTIAN. Hundreds of policemen were on the alert.

Broun hunched his shoulders. "Come on," he said to George Britt. The police opened a gap to let them through. Broun hauled out a copy pencil and the twice-folded copy paper of the professional reporter.

"We know you," shouted one of the leaders. "You're Heywood Broun." A chorus of boos backed him up.

Broun was, said Britt later, like an old fire horse loosening his muscles. He looked happier. He approached the Coughlin leader. The cops hurriedly formed a circle about them. "Keep moving, boys. You can't block traffic." They tried to move Broun gently forward.

"I'm not blocking traffic, officer," Broun said. "I'm asking this man about his anti-Semitic posters. I'm a newspaperman and I've got a right to be here."

"All right, Mr. Broun. Don't get excited."

The picket line marched down Broadway to WOR, which had also barred Coughlin. Broun, having assigned himself to cover the story, went along. In his honor the Coughlinites switched to an anti-Broun demonstration.

"Don't read the *World-Telegram,*" some of them shouted, parading before a newsstand. "Heywood Broun is around the corner."

And there he remained until it was over. He refused police protection, but since they were on hand to prevent trouble they gave it anyhow.

Albert McCosker returned to New York early in March, and hearing that Monsignor Sheen was to preach at Saint Patrick's Cathedral the following Sunday, made an appointment to see him. On Sunday afternoon McCosker was sitting in the Plaza Hotel at a late lunch with a friend when he spied Monsignor Sheen crossing the plaza. Since it was almost time for their appointment he hurried out and encountered the tall priest. By a coincidence, Monsignor Sheen had been thinking about Broun, composing in his mind a letter he intended to write about publication of some material in the Chicago Hearst papers, against which the Guild was striking.

"Please hold the letter up," McCosker asked. "Broun is very interested in the Church and if he gets the letter now he might think he's being solicited."

Monsignor Sheen agreed. McCosker had been active for some decades in human-relations work and he wanted to make sure that this meeting would be under the best of circumstances.

Monsignor Sheen telephoned Broun the next time he was

in New York and on Broun's invitation went to Sabine Farm. Not long afterward weekly instruction sessions were begun. A little later Broun asked that the sessions be increased to two a week.

"I have a strong premonition of death," he told Monsignor Sheen.

In April the *Connecticut Nutmeg* was turned into *Broun's Nutmeg*. The publishers had not worked smoothly together. But the major enemy was inertia. Broun had been writing most of the paper under his own byline and such pseudonyms as Barton Bruce, Howard Campbell, Blake Hemphill, B. K. Atwood, and sometimes contributed letters denouncing himself. Now he bought out the others. Right away he printed old favorites like "Death Says It Isn't So." A supplement carried *The Boy Grew Older,* after which his sports byline became Peter Neale. Serialization of *The Sun Field* was not long in coming.

Broun's plan to enter the Catholic Church was carefully guarded. Few were aware of his move when he was received into the Church on May 24. On the following Sunday, Pentecost, he received his first Holy Communion at Mass in the beautiful Lady Chapel of Saint Patrick's Cathedral. His confirmation was the first by recently installed Archbishop Francis Spellman. Albert McCosker stood as godfather and the name Matthew was chosen, since the evangelist Saint Matthew had been as near to a journalist as there was in Biblical times.

While deeply moved, Broun when he walked out on the street thought of himself as only another man in the street.

"Hollywood," he said to McCosker, "come on, let's get a drink."

He was unprepared for the storm of criticism and abuse that broke over his head as soon as his entrance into the

Catholic Church was announced. Some of it came from people calling themselves free thinkers. Those he did not mind. Others, many of them friends, said or intimated that he had forsaken liberalism. These cut him deeper than they realized.

Suggestions that he make an explanation, because he was a public figure, angered him. Obliquely for the *Nutmeg* he denied having changed his economic or political views. In the *New Republic*—to which he had shifted his weekly page from the *Nation*—he noted the flood of letters. "Indeed they seem to ask not so much a statement of belief as an immediate apology." He added, "Some morning there will come to me a feeling that the time has come and the words will spring up in such a way that what I want to say will be done with some measure of eloquence and dignity."

But he talked privately about his motives. Of Carl Randau he inquired, "Frankly, why are they saying I did it?"

Randau gave him a list of reputed reasons. 1. Connie influenced him. 2. He wanted to scare Roy Howard to make sure of a new contract. 3. Fear of death. 4. He was just plain religious.

Broun answered them one by one. Connie was a good Catholic but had not proselytized him. The business about influencing Howard was beneath contempt. He did not, he claimed, fear death. The real reason was the one he had stated publicly—that the Catholic Church gave him a sense of security in life. "I wanted the brotherhood of man. I have found it now because its full fruition can come only under the Fatherhood of God."

He had hired blond, long-jawed John Groth as cartoonist and illustrator for the *Nutmeg*. Groth painted too, and at Sabine Farm they painted together. At first embarrassed in the company of a famous man, Groth, trying to be chatty, had blurted, "What's all this stuff about you becoming a Catholic?"—not knowing that it wounded.

Lying in the sun, painting, Broun spoke for two hours of his reasons. He admitted the appeal of the ritual and told of a time in Caracas, Venezuela, while on a cruise, when he had been deeply moved by the expressions on the faces of the Indian worshipers. They had seemed close to God and Jesus, as if coming to ask, "How go things at Calvary?" He spoke at length of security and brotherhood. As for his social views—well, there were many points of view in the Catholic Church. He could strengthen, he believed, the liberal faction.

Broun had talked with Morris Ernst for hours about entering the Catholic Church. Ernst's analysis of Broun was that he wanted to be told—that he had sought authority in his mother, in Ruth Hale, in the Socialist Party, and now in the Catholic Church. Broun agreed that he had sought authority. (He had, of course, never accepted it.)

There were, as with everything Broun did, some humorous aspects. For years many of the old Algonquin crowd had expected Alexander Woollcott to enter the Catholic Church, believing that he awaited the psychological moment to step forth as America's G. K. Chesterton. Learning that Broun was about to enter the Church, Woollcott had telephoned asking George Bye to tell Broun to wait. Now the role of American Chesterton seemed safe in Broun's hands. They could not imagine Woollcott playing second fiddle.

Broun invited Woollcott to a lavish luncheon at the 21 Club. Woollcott's tastes, all expensive, were carefully catered to. Corks popped. Waiters carried heavy and varied loads. Over the last wine course Broun began to speak of Catholicism. Woollcott had seen it coming since the soup.

"My dear old friend," he said, fixing Broun with a baleful eye, "one literary fat ass is enough."

Old friends were divided as to whether Broun had been serious, was baiting Woollcott, or both.

Broun had a hand in making one convert to the Catholic Church, though he didn't know about it for a while. When Mattie Wilson, who had opened a beauty shop in Harlem, read in the paper that Broun had become a Catholic she took instructions and was received into the church.

That summer Broun took turns having fun and planning and worrying about the future. One thing he did was to go along with Harold Ross and sign up to be a Connecticut citizen. Broun thought he would have another try at Congress, this time on the Democratic ticket. Woodie worked on the *Nutmeg* and Broun privately asked John Groth and Harold Yudain, the young managing editor, to interest him in making a career of journalism. As contract-signing time—in December—drew near, Broun's worrying increased, and the war with Howard and Pegler was stepped up.

Pegler called up Harold Yudain. "Are you a member of the Guild?" he asked.

Yudain started to explain that the national office was trying to work out a way to allow a man in so small a shop to carry a card. He was drawing more pay than Guildsmen of the same experience.

"Please answer," Pegler said, "whether or not you are a member of the Guild."

Put that way, Yudain answered, he was not a Guildsman.

Pegler wrote a column denouncing Broun for being the owner of a newspaper that was not a Guild shop.

The charge that Broun was slipping lacked basis. One day at the race track between races, while Yudain helped him select horses, Broun sat in a Western Union booth and wrote a column about a shipload of Jews who, not being allowed to land anywhere, seemed destined to return to Hitler's torture. The column won the Headliners Club award for the year.

As the summer waned Broun watched the European crisis with little hope, for he did not trust Neville Chamberlain. The Moscow-Berlin pact, with the obscene embraces of the Nazis and Communists, was a sickening blow. He had believed with most other liberals of the Thirties that Russia stood as a powerful bulwark against Hitlerism, and for his belief in a united front and collective security he had taken the charge of Communist or Communist stooge in his stride.

He wrote sorrowfully, "The masquerade is over. The dominoes are dropped and it is now possible to look at the faces of the various ones who pretend to be devoted to the maintenance of democracy."

And with the rest of America he sat at his radio while Adolf Hitler donned his field-gray uniform, saying, "I'll win or die," and the Panzer divisions crashed through Poland.

Death Says It Isn't So

BROUN sat in the big room at Sabine Farm. It was an afternoon in late November and a strong, cold breeze swirled the fallen leaves across the yard. Connie had driven into Stamford to shop. Harold Yudain was with Broun and they were discussing the next issue of the *Nutmeg*. The paper was costing Broun money, but he liked the free-and-easy style of it.

The telephone rang. Broun, answering, seemed gay and he laughed with the party at the other end of the wire. But when he shuffled back across the room his shoulders hung dejectedly.

He smiled at Yudain. "That was Roy Howard. Roy was in favor of making me an offer, he tells me, but the board won't go along. They don't want to sign the contract."

"They're crazy," Yudain said.

Broun looked out the window. The wind had died and a few flakes of snow sifted down. "Harold," he said, "I've been fired in the spring, in the summer, and now in the winter. I like it best in the summer." As with his astrological cycles, Broun was not always autobiographically accurate. Technically, he was never fired in the summer. His disagreement with the *World* started in August.

299

He reminisced how at twenty-one on the *Morning Tele-graph* he had tried to ante his twenty-eight dollars a week to thirty and had been fired. Only the other day at the Harri-mans' Thanksgiving party he had told the story of his adven-ture climbing the mountain at Tuxedo Park for the *Sun*. He spoke of landing the *Tribune* job, and of the *World* and the trouble there.

The Buick drove up and Connie bustled in carrying sacks of food, her cheeks red from the cold. She went into the kitchen and Broun lit a new cigarette.

"Connie," he said when she came out, "I talked with Roy. I'm fired."

Connie was pulling off red mittens. She stood stock still. "So . . ." And in a minute, "They'll be sorry. Let them wait and see! You just don't worry. You'll have your say some-where else, and get along as well or better, too."

Broun tossed his cigarette into the cold fireplace. "Yes." He nodded slowly. "Yes, I will. Tomorrow I'll go in and see Roy and I suppose there's a chance of a change of mind. But I don't think so."

"Don't take any more guff," Connie said.

The next day was harder. Howard was genial and they laughed as of old. No offer was made, none had been ex-pected. The price of newsprint was going up, Howard said, and the place to cut salaries was in the higher brackets.

"I've made that speech to Guildsmen a thousand times," Broun said. "I won't take it back because I'm the one to be chopped off."

Broun was actually deeply hurt by the dismissal. The money he could get along without. But he felt that he had failed. And he was distressed by the mergers and the failures which inevitably destroyed independent thought among jour-nalists.

Much deeper was a cut that was the more tragic because of a misunderstanding. The habit of *World-Telegram* staff members was to treat Broun, when he came into the office, as just another newspaperman. It was a point of pride with them—a greater deference than if they had gathered round. The rumor had gone about that the contract would not be renewed. But the decision was attributed as much to Broun as to Howard. In the journalistic war to come they could not imagine Broun losing.

But he needed, walking through the city room, the men and women to rally round him and bolster him in his time of trouble. They had no way of knowing that he did not feel the bold, confident journalist that he looked. He misconstrued their attitude as callousness.

He went to the Guild's clubrooms and the scene was repeated. Few there knew that he had been fired. Once more Broun thought that he had been cut—that his beloved newspapermen had turned against him. John Groth was waiting at 21. They sat in a secluded spot and Broun wept.

Another job offer waited. But the depression, by accelerating the trend of mergers and fewer newspapers, had left New York journalism more tightly in the hands of those who found Broun's work either despicable or unsuited to their publications. He had come full circle since the battle with the *World*. Now he was tired and, he felt, his health was no longer able to bear a heavy strain.

He had told George Britt, "It's about all I can do nowadays to get my column out"—though he was writing reams for the *Nutmeg* and refurbishing old magazine pieces and writing new ones. But it was hard to set out on a new circle.

The new haven was offered by George and Dorothy Backer, who had recently purchased the *New York Post* and were renovating it. The salary was only about a quarter of his

$49,000 figure at the *World-Telegram*. Despite independent syndication his readership would at first be much lower.

But it was a place to speak. "Besides," he told Connie, "people forget your name when it's out of sight."

The *Post* wanted him to go abroad and report the war. He decided to wait a while. But in the spring he would tour the baseball camps as of old, picking up light stuff. Though disliking radio, he might work harder at it. Hollywood was interested in *The Sun Field*. Perhaps he would try something else in that direction. And he had the *Nutmeg*—losing money, to be sure, but one could never tell! His new agreement was, in a way, a merger of publishers, for the *Post* would distribute the *Nutmeg*.

Broun was pleased, on his fifty-first birthday, as friends gathered in the Roger Smith Hotel at Stamford for a joint exhibit of the paintings of himself and John Groth. As for the year closed, he did not feel that he had changed very much. In the *Nutmeg* he had run the birthday piece of the year before, merely changing fifty to fifty-one.

The crowd moved slowly about the room, admiring Broun's and John Groth's more professional work. Showing the pictures—trying to sell Groth's—Broun was like his old self. It was the cocktail hour, and songs began. He gathered Quentin Reynolds and George Bye and Harold Yudain and Joe Brooks and Groth and others who had sung the old songs with him.

The moment arrived. "Come on," Broun said. "The big one." Voices rang out strong and clear:

> The mist on the glass is congealing.
> 'Tis the hurricane's icy breath
> And it shows how the warmth of friendship
> Grows cold in the clasp of death.

For more than three decades Broun had been leading it, and in the chorus he got a powerful response.

> Stand, stand to your glasses steady
>   And drink to your sweetheart's eyes.
> Here's a toast to the dead already
>   And a cup to the next man that dies.

And those who could still follow sang on with him:

> Cut off from the land that bore us,
>   And betrayed by the land we find,
> All the brightest have gone before us
>   And the dullest are left behind.

Broun paused and his voice was serious. "I will be the next to go. I feel it. Make this one for me."

> Stand, stand to your glasses steady
>   And drink to your comrade's eyes.
> Here's a toast to the dead already
>   And a cup to the next man that dies.

The day was cold and wet. Broun caught cold and the next day he remained in bed. Theoretically, at least. He was up pacing the floor, restless. On the second day he telephoned to Yudain and asked him to bring some copy. Yudain knew what the order was. Broun was cutting his drinking but now and then he employed ruses to prevent Connie, who was serving as his conscience, from knowing how much he was actually consuming. Yudain brought a bottle and a copy of the *World-Telegram*. Broun glanced at the headlines, noting the progress being made by the Russians in their attack on Finland.

"Read Peg's column," Yudain said.

Broun shifted the paper until the second section was before

him. "What's Peg up to?" They had by now a sort of working agreement not to speak to each other. Sometimes it broke down. Once Woodie had met Pegler in the aisle on a train from Saratoga and they had avoided each other's eyes. And then a little later Woodie had found Pegler and his father in the club car having a high time. Broun still made excuses for Pegler in private conversation.

"Just read it," Yudain said.

"Peg wouldn't hit me while I'm down," Broun said.

In his column Pegler leveled the charge that Broun was in sympathy with the Soviet press censorship. "Such being the case," he continued, "the declaration of purpose in the first article of the Guild constitution, in favor of honest journalism and high ethics, need be mentioned only as an example of droll cynicism. I discuss Broun impersonally as a union official committed by certain declarations which have been supported to his official conduct. I have seen recent superficial expressions of disappointment in Moscow, but never an outright recantation, and even if I saw one I would have to treat it the same as I treat changes of front by Stalin, Hitler and Earl Browder."

Broun reread the column. He said incredulously, "Peg calls me a liar! Why does he do that? Peg knows I'm not a liar."

"With you moving to another paper," Yudain said, "most people would have put it, 'Good luck, Heywood.' "

Broun uncapped the bottle. "I've been honest, Harold." He took a drink. "No one ever tried to take that away from me. Not before Peg. I've been wrong. I've eaten words and whole columns. But I never wrote anything that I didn't believe when I wrote it."

Broun lay sick for two more days. The doctors would not allow him to see anyone for more than a few moments, and a group of cartoonists that John Groth brought to visit were permitted only to wave through the window.

The blows had been heavy, and Broun did not find it easy to remain quiet.

Late Sunday afternoon he called Connie in. "Close the house," he said. "We'll go into New York and stay until we go South." They planned to visit at the Harry Guggenheims' in South Carolina before going on to Florida.

Connie protested that he was not well enough to travel, but Broun was insistent. He was tired of the blows that had been raining down. If he were on the floor, then it was time to pick himself up. He would go into the big town and start the circle again. For had he not said that at fifty-one he was a better fighter than at twenty-one?

The local doctor gave permission for the trip in to New York on condition that the car was kept hot and Broun went to bed directly after arrival. They bundled him up. Harold Yudain went to the home of Max Spelke, Broun's attorney at Stamford, and borrowed a rubber cushion.

"He's white and sweating," Yudain said. "Heywood's pretty sick."

In New York, Broun and Connie went to the Chatham Hotel, where they usually stayed, and Broun kept his promise to go to bed.

In the morning he was no better. He called Dr. Alvan L. Barach, for many years one of his doctors and a friend. Dr. Barach, when he came, prescribed rest and quiet. The cold, while heavy, seemed to be no worse than many suffered by Broun before.

Tragic little blows continued to pile up. A photographer from the *Post* came to make pictures for promotion. There still remained the formality of signing a contract. It happened that the photographer had noticed Alicia Patterson

305

Guggenheim in the hotel lobby with Connie—they had been to lunch—and leaped to the conclusion that Broun was dickering with the *Daily News*. The photographer was, as it happened, one of the few New York newspapermen who disliked Broun.

He came in as Connie was painting around Broun's swollen eyes with a purple solution. He accused Broun of double-crossing the *Post*. Taken with Pegler's charge of dishonesty—and Broun's hypersensitive feeling that newspapermen had rejected him—this charge was cruel enough. But then the photographer, hard-boiled, turned to the state of Broun's purple-painted eyes.

"Got drunk last night and beat up, eh? Let's have the story!"

Connie told him to beat it.

"Aw, come on, Connie," the photographer said, and his tone was insulting, "we're all in this racket together. I never liked the guy anyhow. Give me the story."

Broun's code of chivalry demanded that he act. He began slowly to rise from his bed. Connie pushed him back and chased the cameraman out.

There were brighter moments. John Groth brought a small radio and Broun listened happily while the British trapped the *Graf Spee* and it was scuttled by its crew. Friends overran the place. He made plans for the trip South, and he sat up in bed and whipped out his first column for the *Post*— a demand that President Roosevelt be drafted for a third term.

But Dr. Barach was concerned by his lack of proper response to treatment. "You're all right," he told Broun, "but you need more rest. Here the telephone rings too much, people run in and out. Why not go to a hospital?" He was more worried than he cared to say.

Broun agreed. To run the circle again he needed his health. On Thursday he was taken to the Harkness Pavilion of Columbia Presbyterian Medical Center. That afternoon the *World-Telegram* carried the last column it would have from his typewriter.

"And so," he had written, "after 12 years of columning in the same spot, *It Seems to Me* moves on. There were fights, frenzies, some praise and a lot of dough and a good deal of fun in my relationship with Roy. As far as the editor goes I have no squawk coming, and he tells me that he feels the same."

Howard appended a note, "Despite the uninformed and unimportant busybodies who have long whispered and rumored of a feud which never existed . . ."

On December 15 Broun's column on Roosevelt appeared in the *Post*. It was the last column Broun ever wrote, for pneumonia struck suddenly. Dr. Barach hinted to Connie that it was serious but she had faith in Broun's recuperative powers. Then Irving came suddenly to the hospital during business hours. That was disturbing.

Broun was in a coma with a high fever. And now at last his heart, which had so long refused to follow his own analysis, was weak. For a while he was in a pressure hood and later he was placed under an oxygen tent. Death was imminent.

On Saturday morning Monsignor Sheen called at the hospital with the Sacraments of the Catholic Church. The next morning he returned and gave Broun the Papal blessing which Pope Pius XII had granted for the moment of death.

During the day Broun rallied. Connie was allowed to go into the room. "I've been pretty sick, Connie," he said, smiling. "But now I'm going to be all right."

His fever went down. Dr. Barach offered to bet Woodie 8 to 5 that his father would get well. And that evening the waiting room and the corridors were filled with Broun's friends. They stood silent, or talked softly in little groups. It was as if by an army gathered they hoped to help.

Broun continued to gain slightly. And then in the early morning hours of December 18 his fever began to mount. The nurses watched helplessly, as it swept upward—102, 104, 105, 107.2.

In the playlet, "Death Says It Isn't So," Broun had written:

The light softens a little. The room is almost rose color now. The Fat Man gently pushes the head of the Sick Man back on the pillow. Leaning over, he whispers in his ear briefly and the Sick Man roars with laughter. As his laughter slackens a little the Fat Man says, "I'll meet you in the press box," and then before you know it he's gone. The Sick Man is still laughing, but less loudly. People who did not know might think it was gasping. The nurse opens the door and is frightened. She loudly calls, "Doctor! Doctor!" and runs down the corridor. The Sick Man gives one more chuckle and is silent.

At 9:50 Heywood Broun died.

Index

Index

Index

311

Index

Index

Index

Moscow-Berlin Pact, 298
Mouquin's Restaurant, 65-66
Munich Pact, 282
Munsey, Frank A., 128
Murphy, George, 231
Murray, Philip, 292
Mussolini, 6
Mutual Broadcasting Company, 289

NAST, CONDÉ, 130
Nation, 117, 182, 184, 188-190, 295
National Association of Book Publishers, 117
National League, 67
National Recovery Administration, 242
Nazism, 282-283, 298
Ness, Fred, 43
Neufchatel, 84
Newcomes, The, 15
New Canaan, Conn., 278
New Mexico, 25
New Republic, 106, 116, 140, 295
News, New York, 232, 247, 306
Nicaragua, 163, 186
Nick's Bar, 247
Nini's Restaurant, 14, 105
Nogales, Mexico, 253
Norris, George W., 221
North Carolina, 12
Norton, Beatrice, 226
"No Sirree," 136-137
Nutmeg, Connecticut, 278-285, 294
Nutmeg, Broun's, 294-295, 301-302

OAKLEY, MRS. GRACE C., 106
O'Doul, Lefty, 257
O'Hara, John, 203
O'Keefe, Walter, 5
Olson, Floyd B., 221
O'Malley, Frank Ward, 53-54, 132
O'Neill, Eugene, 95-96, 100, 115, 145, 220
Opposite Editorial, 9
Orsatti, Ernie, 236
"Over There," 83
PALACE THEATRE, 227
Palmer, A. Mitchell, 101
Palmer, Frederick, 88, 90
Paris, 82
Park Row, 46, 111, 222-223
Parker, Dorothy, 97, 128, 130, 136-137, 149-151, 182, 227
Parrott, Ursula, 213, 250, 269, 278-281
Patterson, Alicia, 268
Patterson, Capt. Joe, 268
Pegler, Jack, 278-280, 283
Pegler, Julie, 269

Pegler, Westbrook, 249-250, 269-271, 278, 283, 297, 303-304
Peking, 41
Pemberton, Brock, 50, 96, 137, 213
Pemberton, Murdock, 50, 92-98, 137, 153, 171-172
Pen and Pencil Club, 247
Pennock, Herb, 3
Pennsylvania Hotel, 105
Pershing, John J., 77, 85-86, 89-90
Pickering, Mary, 106
Pickford, Mary, 68
"Pie in the Sky," 231
Pieces of Hate, 126
Pilate, 176, 276
Pinchot, Amos, 213
Pitney, Fred, 41
Plank, Eddie, 49
Poland, 298
Polo Grounds, 45-46, 51
Pope Pius XII, 307
Post, Boston, 176
Post, New York, 231, 247, 301-302, 305-307
Powers, Jake, 42
Pratt, Mrs. Ruth, 207-208, 217, 221-222
Presbyterian Church, 57
Princess Mauvhinneyokalai, 40
Prohibition, 97, 113, 186-187
Providence Hotel, 84
Provincetown Playhouse, 145
Pulitzer, Joseph, 110-111
Pulitzer, Ralph, 110, 147, 173-178, 180-181, 190, 193
Puritanism, 50, 69, 108, 152
Putnam, George, 127, 144

"RABBITT THAT BIT THE BULLDOG, THE," 183-184
Racquet & Tennis Club, 2, 57, 146, 204-206, 214, 225
Raison, Milton, 227-228
Randau, Carl, 245, 248, 259, 275-276, 295
Rappe, Virginia, 113
Rascoe, Burton, 132
Raymond, Allen, 245
Reader's Digest, 269
Reconstruction Finance Corporation, 239
Red Sox, Boston, 32
Reed, Jim, 4
Reed, John, 25, 51, 113-114
Reid, Ogden, 42, 53
Reid, Whitelaw, 41, 97
Reid, Mrs. Whitelaw, 97-98
Religion, 22-23, 120, 184-185, 276
Renan's Life of Christ, 165
Restell, Madame, 167

Index

Index